Courageously Alive

–

A Walk Through Military Loss

by

Linda K. Ambard

Kendra,

Keep the faith.
You were called for
such a time as
this.

L.

ISBN-13: 978-1493713035
ISBN-10: 1493713035

ABOUT THE AUTHOR

Linda Ambard grew up in Boise, Idaho never dreaming that she would have the opportunities to get on an airplane, let alone travel the world. She met Phil at 27 when she worked at Mountain Home Air Force Base (AFB) in Idaho while she was working at the swimming pool. A young soldier came in. Linda was not impressed until he asked her out 20 times. When they finally went on a date, they eloped four months later and thus began a love story that spanned 23 years, five children, one naughty dog, and countless military moves. In January 2011, Phil deployed to Afghanistan for a year to train and advise the Afghan military. On April 27, 2011, an Afghan high ranking military person assassinated Phil along with eight other American soldiers. The script Linda saw her life following through old age effectively ended that day. Her adult life had been following Phil, being a mom to children who grew up to join the military, and establishing the sense of home with a person. This story follows the rocky journey of loss when a person is taken far too soon.

Linda is a mom, grandma, runner, teacher and most of all, a woman of faith.

DEDICATION

While I have had a dream of writing a book for many years, the reality is that I never would have written anything meaningful. I would have procrastinated and been stuck on what to write. When the bottom of my life fell out on 27 April 2011, I had nothing except for my faith to fall into. I began to write to deal with the pain so deep that it physically hurt. I used writing to deal with my questions, my loneliness, and my fear. I chose to share my thoughts because I truly felt a nudge from the Holy Spirit. For a quiet and reticent girl, this was quite difficult, gut by sharing my journey, many people chose to walk with me and they still carry me at times.

For the KAIA family, you lived the horrible reality of your comrades being assassinated by someone they trusted. You lived in fear, yet you continued to work to train the Afghanis and to create a better world for the women and children that live in oppression. You choose to continue to stand up to the bullies of this world. I did not know any of you before my Phil was gunned down, but you are my heart.

For my military family far and near, you get it. Every loss diminishes us. Regardless of rank or position, we are grieving as a whole. We have given up families and the place to call home because we believe in what we are doing. So many of you have found me. From the early days of Phil being an airman basic at Mountain Home Air Force Base to the 11 years at the United States Air Force Academy, you are my brothers and sisters. We stand arm in arm, heart to heart, together as one in times of loss.

For my Colorado Springs people, you barely knew me, but you wrapped your arms around me and loved me when I had nothing left to give. Even when I moved far away, you found ways to reach me.

For the many people who have found me and loved me, listened to me talk about my Phil, and who have prayed for me, you have made a difference.

For Brian Christiansen, you are the best friend a girl could have. You have saved me on more than one occasion and your belief in me has made a difference.

For my sisters who I never knew prior to 27 April 2011, if I had to walk this terrible journey, it is easier with you. I bleed for all of us.

For my five children, Patrick, Josh, Emily, Alex, and Tiger, I see your father's legacy in you. You are what he did the very best. I am proud of each and every one of you. Remember the family motto: Don't quit. Don't fail, and don't get anyone pregnant (or don't get pregnant).

For baby Philip Tristan, you have brought this family home. You carry your grandfather's name. He would have loved you so much. Karla, thank you for loving my son enough to be parents together.

Phil Ambard, you loved me well. 23 years was not nearly long enough. I loved you then. I love you now. I will love you more tomorrow.

Finally, I praise the Lord, my God, who gave me Phil and the life I always wanted. I can honestly say that it is well with my soul.

Table of Contents

Relationships, Family, Friends, and Others

Death, the Aftermath and Practicalities

These Hard Times

The Next Chapter and the Changing of Linda

1

Introduction

Three days before I got the news that would forever change my life; my blog on running was published on the Runner's World Website. I ran then to deal with the normal stress of being a military wife and mother. I run now because in the quiet miles, I am discovering who I am without my Phil. I am running from the prying eyes and people who think that I should be grieving in a certain manner. I can cry with the tears of my heart and I can leap to a future that does not include my Phil. While this is a life that I never imagined would happen to me, I find like the miles, time is racing by. More than a year after Phil's assassination, I become breathless realizing that I have made a year of milestones and that I am still alive, finding happiness, and finding a whole new Linda. It is deeply conflicting to consider that my life did not end with Phil's life, but rather in some ways, my life started in a whole new way. I did not choose this life and I would give anything to go back to the girl I once was, but the choice is gone. I step forward. My story is the story of a girl walking through unexpected violence at the hands of a trusted colleague that took the man loved by many…the man who loved me well for 23 years.

The Blog that started things:

I Run On—Part 1

Thirty five years of running has seen me through my youth and well into middle age. Running has opened doors for me by presenting scholarship opportunities through Title IX and travel. Running has also been the friend that I have turned to during the normal stress of life. As a child of an alcoholic, I ran away. I ran from my own demons as a teen dealing with an eating disorder and as an adult coping with a failed marriage. At the age of 37, I developed medical issues that led to doctors telling me not to run (which by me ignoring this advice has led to medical research for other runners with adrenal issues), but this year, running has become my companion as I navigate my daughter and husband being deployed to Afghanistan.

When I married Phil 23 years ago, I brought a bonus three children. Their other father was not in the picture. At the time, my husband was a young airman who wanted nothing more than to get out of the military. After marrying me and taking on the responsibilities of an instant family, Phil committed to a long military career which has taken us all over the world. Somewhere along the way, four of our five children have opted to join the family business.

As a young mom with five children under the age of ten, the best gift that my husband gave me was that as soon as he walked in the door, I ran out the door to freedom. As a stay at home mom, I valued the quiet and the freedom of not having to tend to anyone's needs but my own. When we were stationed in Europe, and my husband was often deployed, I would push the two youngest in a double stroller. There I was pushing two little boys up the hills huffing and puffing all the way. One of them kept asking questions. I was out of breath, but running gave me a sense of comfort and that all was well in my world. Running felt like a decadent treat that I gave myself because it was a selfish investment of time and resources into a hobby that only benefitted me.

As they grew, I was often the only parent at home. I dealt with the terrible twos and the cranky self-absorbed teens. I was the positive spin master each and every time we had to move. I could be dying inside as I left another job or place that I loved living, but I had to be the adventurous fun parent who made each move fun. My family did not see the tears or the disappointments because it wouldn't have done any good. My feet pounded the pavement as I cried over the injustice and fear of the unknown. My shoes carried me during the good times, too. I was there for it all, while my husband who desperately wanted to be there for every family event, missed graduations, award ceremonies, major sporting events, hospitalizations, and the birth of our first child together.

In the past few years, my family has gone to places like Haiti, Iraq, and Afghanistan. The one constant through the turmoil has been my running. I have pounded through the miles of missed phone calls, anniversaries, birthdays, and holidays. Without running, some of these losses would be almost unbearable. Running gives me a sense of security and normalcy when I have fears of my family's safety. By having a lofty goal, I am able to count down the days and months of a deployment by looking ahead to the next race (and by looking at the medals from completed races). I began a journey of trying to complete a marathon in all fifty states. This year I aspire to finish 18 marathons in 12 months in 17 states. Since January 11th, I have completed 6 races.

I am always asked how I can push through the pain and the mental battle with this many races. The simple answer is that this is how I get through the pain of separation and the mental battle of loneliness. A military wife/mom must stand strong at home while her loved ones are away. Some military dependents have a strong network of close friends or family to buoy them through the rough times. Running is that companion for me. Every spouse of a military member who is deployed is in a fearful holding pattern. Our lives are at a standstill while we await our loved one's return. Once our soldier returns, there is an adjustment time for both of us as we face another move, a new job (or lack of available jobs for me), and more change. I find comfort in the sun, wind, rain, snow, or whatever I encounter as I trod along day after day. If I can find normalcy in running, then I am sure to find it in my day to day life.

At the age of 37, while stationed overseas in Germany, and far from my family, I was running the Frankfurt Marathon. At the 15 mile mark, the cameras captured me smiling and waving. At 15.5 miles, I developed major issues. By the end of the race, I couldn't remember my last name, where I lived, nor did I care about the open bay co-ed showers. Over the course of the next year, my health was fragile at best. Between my husband being deployed for six months at a time, having five children ages 5-15, and feeling like I was dying, running was the only constant. If I could get out of bed and run for a few miles through the forest of Landstuhl, I could get through another minute, another hour, another day.

After a year of struggling to discover why I was losing so much weight and why I was sick all of the time, it was discovered that I had an adrenal insufficiency. At the time, I was advised not to push my body like I had been. My thought? What is my life if I have to quit doing everything that mattered to me? To quit running was to give up. I began to fight a little harder. This battle was complicated by having to follow a not so friendly medical system to dependents of military men and women. Appointments are secondary to the non-military. Children are not allowed at appointments, and my husband was gone half a year at a time. We could not afford the day care fees, so it took a long time to earn back my running, but earn it back, I did. One step at a time, one mile at a time, I ran. I ran to feel better about myself, about the loneliness, and about the grief over my lost health. Where many people would turn to a friend or to family, I have never been able to rely fully on having a friend or even my husband around to lean on. Running is that constant. When I lace on a pair of shoes, and I head for the door, I know that I will feel better.

Running has given me something besides mental health. It has given me back my health. Although I must take many nasty medications, the doctor's have used me for research in the 13 years I have had adrenal issues. Where once I was told that my body would not nor should not handle the extreme rigors of marathoning, the doctors that have seen me all agree that running has kept me much healthier than most. Instead of needing antidepressants or gaining a lot of weight due to the long time steroid use, running has kept me feeling good about myself. Additionally, there are about a handful of adrenal patients that can push themselves like I am able to push myself. If I hadn't been so committed to running, I believe that many doctors would still be telling adrenal patients to avoid rigorous sport activity.

Some races are easier than other races, just like some days are better than others. When issues in my life come up, I can't call my husband. I can't call children. I send out the lifeline through a run and the quiet prayers of my heart. I find comfort in the miles as they race past no matter how slowly or how quickly they pass. I find the hope of a race/workout enjoyed and pain free to mirror the life that I wait for. I am waiting for my best friends to come home while embracing the one constant friend that is with me through thick and thin. I will run on.

I Run On—Part 2

On April 27, my life imploded in a blink of an eye. I was at the end of my teaching day and I was thinking ahead to the Louisville, KY Marathon which I was to run that weekend when my principal and school counselor entered my gym. I kept teaching for a few minutes. Thinking that they needed help finding a student, I asked them if they needed my help. When my principal said that he needed for me to come with him, I thought I was losing my job because 143 teachers in my small school district lost their jobs that day due to a severe financial crisis. Oh, how I wish that was the news I received that day.

Instead, my life forever changed when I entered his office. There stood three uniformed military people who began to read, "We regret to inform you..." the words droned on as I dropped to my knees and started to keen. My husband, Major Phil Ambard was killed in action in Kabul, Afghanistan. The life we had planned and lived ceased to be.

When I first heard the news, all I wanted to do was to hide. I laced up my running shoes and I disappeared. Running gave me an escape from the reality of my crushing loss. The nicest gift I received at Dover (where the families fly to receive the body of the fallen soldier back into the United States) is that the casualty officer working with our family came to pick me up at our hotel. She drove me to the running trail on Dover and asked me when she should be back to get me. I could barely stand up at that point, but through my running, I felt a sense of a little control over my world that had quickly spun out of control. I ran even though I felt no joy with my running. I ran and I allowed myself to cry freely.

Through the days that followed, I continued to run on. Though running was difficult and I experienced little joy with the miles I put in, there came a day recently when I began to feel again. I began to feel the happiness of the miles put in. I began to look forward to running, racing, and life again. It is almost scary to think about living and liking my life, but through running I am beginning that process of stepping forward.

Although I am not a fearful person, I have been paralyzed with indecisive terror since I lost my husband. For 23 years, I followed him throughout the world. I have known who I am with him, but I don't know who I am without him. I do know this. I was a runner before I met Phil and I am still a runner. The fear is still there, but running balances me and gives me a way to get a grip when I am drowning in the darkness. Running lets me process and think through the many decisions I am being forced to make. As I plod along, I am able to decide about where to live, where to work, and what to do.

Running has been a major part of who I am for over 30 years. Never more so now. I run on because if I can run even one step, I know that I can make it through the pain so crushing that I can barely breathe. One of my earliest Facebook posts after Phil was killed was: "In a dark spot. I am going running so that I can find my way back to my feeble faith and work through my silent tears. Pray. I will be fine. I just need a little space to work through my broken heart. People deal with grief in different manners. Some self medicate. Others eat. Still others sleep or fail to function. I hide my tears. I slip into a quiet placid façade that I hide behind. Running is the only place where I allow myself to feel. As I run on with the whispered prayers of my plodding feet and broken heart, I feel the tears and the pain. I feel a sense of hope even when I can't see any light. I can feel a sense of happiness and self.

This week, I had to hear the details of what happened to my husband the day he was killed. It was truly my worst nightmare comes true, but through the miles put in the past few days, I have been able to erect some walls and to trust in my faith. While I still would give anything for the events of that April day not to have happened, they did. It is through running that I am able to find solid ground to stand on. I am able to utter the silent prayers hidden in my heart. I am able to weep the unshed tears I clutch to myself. I am able to see the promises of my faith and as I run on, I am able to say, it is well with my soul. I am able to feel small rays of hope as I begin a new unimagined journey.

Phil's Remarkable Journey

Would I be Out of Line if I Said I Miss You?

It crushes me to realize that it has been four weeks since I last talked to my Phil (and over 4 months since we were together). If only for another day, I wish that I hadn't taken for granted our friendship and love. It is strange to be turning 50 really soon and to be alone (for the first time in over 23 years) with a looming endless future. Trying to make pragmatic decisions not based on fear or grief is difficult at best.

I can't even remember the dreams I had prior to Phil. The dreams we had together hold no appeal any more. How can I build the "old folks retirement house" in Port Angeles, WA when the mere idea brings me to my knees? How can I stay here when I can't face the many places we knew as a couple? Church, sports, scouts, apartment, the Y, school. . .we did it all together. If it were possible, I would like to bury my heart. It would be easier.

Fear is a constant. It is amazing to realize just how interdependent Phil and I were. I followed him around the world and gave up many jobs I liked (and the promises of moving up in those jobs) to be the wife and mom I wanted to be. I have never been able to put my needs first in terms of where I wanted to live, work, engagements (calendar), but I didn't mind. I am now trying to navigate a military system that is unforgiving as far as the time constraints (picking where I want to live and moving within one year of Phil's death) and rules. It scares me. To be 50 (almost) and making these decisions makes me want to hide under the covers until I don't have to make any more decisions.

Today, Amazon sent me a notice telling me that Phil's movie had been shipped to Afghanistan. He had been on a kick to read all of the classics that he had never read in high school (for someone who barely graduated high school, he went pretty far--laugh). I read many of these books with him (I am a recovering English teacher). We had finished *The Hunger Games, To Kill a Mockingbird, and Wuthering Heights.* Next up was *Sense and Sensibility.* How I razzed my Phil for that because it was his idea to read Jane Austen next.

If I had one more day with my Phil, it would not be filled with the daily activities that always seemed to compel us at a frantic pace. Rather, I would sit and enjoy the quiet companionship that fills my heart with longing and crushing loss now.

Happy Father's to the Best Father

Dear Phils, you are always on my heart missed by me. Happy Father's Day to the best father. Our children were blessed. Your abilities as a dad are the reason I fell in love with you way back when. I loved you then. I love you now. I will love you forever. L

Running is going well, or well enough right now, but I am struggling. Not so much for me, but for my children. I have five truly amazing (plus one bonus daughter-in-law) adult children. I know that they are hurting. I can't fix their pain this time. The pain slashes through my heart as I watch them struggle with the events that took their father.

Phil was a wonderful father. I loved that facet of his personality. 24 years ago I met this man and I told him no 20 times before I said yes when he asked me out. I thought that he was flirting with all of my friends. I was the swimming pool manager at Mountain Home Air Force Base. I had three children ages 3, 4, and 5. I had just gotten out of a really bad marriage. The last thing I wanted was some young good looking man who was full of himself. At a certain point, he would ask me out a few times a day and I would diligently say no. It became a game that changed when he volunteered to help me coach the Special Olympics.

Side by side we worked. Phil was never comfortable, but our swimmers always loved him best. He made them laugh and feel good about themselves. My only role was to teach them to swim well—we made a great team. We became friends that began to work out together. 4 months later, he asked me out. The twenty first time was a resounding yes.

We never had a normal courtship. Most of our dates were with children seeing rate G movies, skating, playing at parks, laughing. When we eloped four months later to Reno, NV people said that we wouldn't last. 23 years later, some folks are still waiting...

Phil became an instant father to my children. Their father had opted out of their lives. Phil never referred to my three children as step any things. Patrick, Josh, and Emily were his kids. He was dad through it all. There was never a doubt who dad was. As good of a husband as Phil was, he was an even better father. This facet of his personality was not shaped by good parenting when he was young. Quite the opposite. He should have been removed from his home numerous times. Phil was barely 21 when he married me and became dad. Together we were strong. Together we made a parenting team that was hard to beat.

On Father's Day, I am reminded of how much was lost when Phil died. Our future grandchildren will never experience the love, humor, and mentoring of a man who excelled at being a father. Our grandchildren will never experience the total chaos and fun that Phil brought to the holidays. . .to anything really. Phil invested time and unconditional love into each of his five children. No matter how tired he was, he would play with the children and go with them any where they wanted him to go.

How Proud You Were To Fight For Freedom

As I ran yesterday morning, as song that I often affiliated with my Phil began to waft through my head phones. "I could see it in your eyes how proud you were to fight for freedom in our land." Phil never took for granted the freedoms afforded to him by the citizenship he received to our country a week shy of his 18th birthday. He felt civic duty to serve and to vote. While he was not a combatant in any sense of the word, he proudly donned the United States Air Force uniform every day of his working adult life (he enlisted when he was 18).

As a nation, we have grown complacent in our freedoms and the responsibilities we carry to maintain those freedoms. We fail to feel a sense of compassion, empathy, or responsibility to our fellow world travelers. We look only to our needs. We forget the oppressed or the people who can't give us something in return for our actions. Would we even recognize the hurting person standing next to us? The want or need of another human. Sometimes that need is to be touched. To be talked to. To be heard.

When I hear our countries national anthem, I picture a dirty and spent Francis Scott Key sitting in a boat buffeted by the crashing waves. I hear the loud canons and the pops of guns around him. I smell the acrid gunpowder as in lingers in the fray of the midnight sky. I see men in tattered rags holding weapons and pressing on for the freedoms that they believed in. A society they coveted.

While the war raged on and the skies filled with the smoke of the fight, Francis could not see who was winning, but he believed. He believed and had faith that all would be for what was good, true, and right. All he could do in the moment was to have faith and to pen his thoughts. I understand this total sense of lack of control and of not being able to see ahead. I understand being buffeted by the tumultuous waves as I sit in my boat. I cling to the desperation of hope and I have faith that my Phil's death mattered to others besides myself.

While this war was not on our American soil, and my Phil was in Afghanistan as a teacher...a trainer...my Phil stood for what he believed was honorable. He stood for our battered flag being raised in the sky. He stood for the piece of cloth still waving after the attacks on the World Towers on 9/11. He stood for people who had no skills or abilities to change their own infrastructure. He chose to volunteer to go to Afghanistan for a year to effect the change that he felt would bring that oppressed region hope for a better future without the violence it knows now. He stood as a man of faith willing to commit to actions.

On the fourth of July, I remember the patriots that have gone with my Phil and I am humbled by their sacrifice. What sacrifice am I able to give to change the world for others? What am I willing to give up or to do for our country in gratitude for the freedoms and opportunities that I have every day? While I do not carry a gun or go to Afghanistan, I can reach out to people here. I can see people. I can hear people. I can finally feel the pain of others. I can stand for something other than my own wants and needs. I can choose today to honor Phil's memory with my actions and my service.

The 23 Year Love Story

23 years ago, I said yes the twentieth time Phil asked me out. I was not keeping track, but he was. He said to me, "This is number 20. If you say no today, then I will never ask you out again." At the time, Phil was a young enlisted man who would strut around the Mountain Home Air Force Base swimming pool in a little blue Speedo swimming suits (for the record, no man looks good in one of these types of suits). He flirted with every lifeguard working. I had just gotten out of a toxic almost six years of marriage to another military man. The last thing I needed or wanted was another young military man.

Phil was persistent, if nothing else. He always said that no meant that he wasn't trying hard enough. The more I said no and directed him to young available girls, the more he pursued me. As a mom of three young children, I was scared to trust someone with my children and with my heart. I was broken and I didn't see my worth. When I got divorced, the church that was my life shunned me. My own family cut me out of their lives. I was adrift and trying to get a commission so that I could support my children. I didn't need or want another person in my life—especially a 21 year old in a blue Speedo!

Phil began to ask me out. After awhile, it became a game until the twentieth time he asked me out. Along the way, we had become friends. I needed him as a friend more than I needed a relationship. We hung out together, laughed together, and shared sad stories of woe. He even sidled over and volunteered to help with the Special Olympic group I worked with twice a week. Twenty three years ago, something sparked in my heart.

Even though my words were still flat refusal, my heart was falling in love with an improbable man. I am a pretty old fashioned girl. I really didn't think he would ask me out again, but on a fiery July afternoon, he asked me to go to the movies with him in Boise. This time, I said yes. During our drive to Boise, I discovered someone I could not only laugh with, but someone who didn't need to fill every minute with conversation. I discovered a kindred spirit. While we had been friends before that, we were inseparable after that date.

It took Phil forever to kiss me or to touch me. He kept waiting for me to make the first move! As if! Did I say that I am an old fashioned girl? Once we began dating in earnest the end of July, the fires burned so hot that we eloped November 27th to Reno, NV.

Phil gave up a lot when he married me. His family (and I do not mean to hurt his sister) basically asked him to choose between me and them. He chose me. Even now, his family has shut him out. In death, they could not get past their old feelings of betrayal that he chose me. It took him much longer to get his degree because he became an insta-dad to my three children who he has raised as his own since they were 3, 4, and 5. He has always been dad and they have always been his kids—no clarification ever. The word step never left his lips unless he was challenged on the last name discrepancy. Even then, he always said that Patrick, Josh, and Emily were his kids.

We struggled a lot financially when we first married because we made the decision for me to stay at home with our children. Phil was an airmen first class with three children and a staff sergeant selectee with five children. He did not believe in handouts so we lived on his salary. We ate so many potatoes and rice and beans that many of our children can't even lift a fork with those things on it. Even though we lacked material things at the time, as a family we thrived. We went to the park all the time, played games at home, and we went to the swimming pool (where I managed the pool in the summer). Those days are precious to me because our world revolved around our nuclear unit.

People could never understand why Phil and I were so close and why we really never needed outside people or activities (well, I ran—wink!). We had forged an unbreakable bond over the course of our friendship and with carrying each other's hurts. We had each other's back. I was Phil's wingman as he was mine. I would have gladly given my life for him and I know that he would gladly have given his for me. I am thankful that 23 years ago Phil would not take no for an answer and that we had every day of those 23 years. I wish that it had been more.

27 Memories That Linger On Bringing Joy to My Life

1. Eloping to Reno, NV on 27 November 1988, three days after Thanksgiving. Phil was upset that Thanksgiving because of how my father was treating me (I was the first person EVER to get divorced in our family—total ostracizing. He didn't care how people treated him, but it bothered him if people messed with me. As we drove back to MHAFB from Boise, Phil said, "We should get married." We had already covered that ground...my answer was always yes. This time, he added, "as soon as possible." He picked me up from work (I worked all night long at the gas station) and he thought that we would drive to Jackpot. Getting married wasn't that easy. Apparently one needs a wedding license from Wells, NV. We arrived at the courthouse 15 minutes late. We drove on to Reno. Did I mention that there was a raging snow storm and that we arrived back in Mountain Home Air Force Base (MHAFB) one hour before Phil was supposed to start the (noncommissioned officer school) NCO prep school?
2. The total shock that people expressed and still show over the two of us eloping='s priceless. For two super traditional reliable people, we did it right.
3. Lagoon- Our first real date. Phil was a chicken to touch me. He kept waiting for me to make the first move—as if! I am very old fashioned. After sitting close to each other on all of the rides, he finally kissed me—Fireworks.
4. The first time we ran together was the last time we ran together for 22 years. It crushed Phil's ego that he couldn't outdo me here. Laugh.

5. Working to have Alex and Tiger. The prayer was for two children, but the chances were 5% for one child in the first year after having major surgery to have them.

6. Finally getting orders to leave MHAFB and the gossip mill. We were so excited to be going anywhere—even Holloman AFB!

7. The day that we were all a family-Patrick, Josh, Alex, and Emily (before Tiger came along).

8. Driving across the country to move to Germany the first time. We never had money for a vacation. We made it into such an adventure. Gerbert music played non-stop in the car.

9. Arriving in DC on the above trip and having everyone get really sick. Tiger threw up in front of the White House.

10. Living in billeting for three months until we got our apartment in Landstuhl and then Phil deploying for six months right afterwards. I was living the dream in terms of being close enough to travel to so many countries. Our children toured Europe by scouting, sports, school trips (Paris for a week in the 6th grade, Amsterdam for a week in the 7th, London for a week in the 8th grade...), and Club Beyond.

11. The Landstuhl Allwetterbad. Phil used to bring the boys every night after work. I worked there part time. He would come to all of the baby classes and we would use the boys to demonstrate the skills. Emily was on swim team. WE bonded over smelling like chlorine.

12. Reading to the children. We would lay on the king sized bed where I would read for 2 hours every night. Phil would come in and sit or lie next to us and just listen. He always said that he liked the voices I made as I read the different characters.

13. Meeting Phil in Southern France where he was temporary duty yonder (TDY) as an interpreter. WE put the kids in sleeping bags and we toured all of southern France as a family. To this day, none of us can eat chocolate croissants!

14. Coaching soccer. Phil and I coached together.

15. The day Phil found out that he was selected for OTS. He wanted his commission so badly. He was tired of living in poverty. He was so proud. . .we were so proud.

16. Two months after Phil found out about OTS and we found out that our oldest had an AFA appointment. Phil finally felt like people wouldn't see us as trailer court trash

17. Finding our family dog in Bitburg. Tiger had been praying for a dog. We felt that we didn't need a dog on top of five children at home. I was running in the farm fields of Germany in the pouring rain just

after the bases closed to anyone but authorized personnel. I see this dog standing in a cage barking. I ran by wondering about it. A half a mile later, I turned around and picked up the cage. She had been abandoned 8 miles out. I thought I would drag her to the base and give her to the vet clinic. By the time I got back to the base, I had her named. She was my dog. remember calling Phil from the Youth Center and asking him to pick up some dog food. He said to me, "Linda, what have you done?" He showed up to get me from work and the dog ran right over to him wagging her tail—smart dog!

18. Mallorca after Phil's OTS and before his school. He had 9 days off. He flew in and we flew out within hours. Reconnecting on the beach was wonderful.

19. Ireland-going to Ireland with the youngest three. Even Phil wanted to be Irish when we were done. Emily was cranky because she only saw old people on the trip. We were on a bus tour and we were the only Americans. We had so much fun time together.

20. Our first cruise. Phil loved that he could eat as much as he wanted at every meal. What most people didn't know is that he always overate on cruises and gained 10-15 pounds, but then he would work out like a fiend to lose the weight.

21. Phil was on a classic reading phase when he died. Phil was never much of a reader, but he made it through Wuthering Heights, To Kill a Mockingbird, the Hunger Game Series, and he was starting Sense and Sensibility (his choice).

22. The day that we went to Parent Weekend for Patrick and someone called to ask if Phil could come and talk to the department chair. Next thing we knew, Phil was selected for an AFIT sponsored master's degree. Eventually he got an AFIT sponsored PhD. I am so thankful for that extra time that he had with us and that we were in Colorado Springs for 9 years.

23. Buying our first house-Phil felt like we had finally made it when we got our first house and we moved off base. We had the house in the right neighborhood and it was big. Phil was so proud. He wanted this house. I caved in even though it wasn't my dream house.

24. Phil's one and only marathon. I goaded him into running the Mesa Falls Marathon. He swore he would never again run another unless it was the Paris Marathon. I guess he will always have Mesa Falls.

25. Family Holiday Meals-Phil loved the traditional family meals and rituals. He would never stop eating or talking about them (maybe because once I started back to work this didn't happen every night?)

26. Planning for the Venice Cruise-We had never been away from our children since day 1. When Phil got to Afghanistan, he wanted that romantic trip. He wanted to talk about this trip every phone call.
27. The white hankie-Phil made me laugh a lot. When he would mess up, and he would say that it was often (not really), Phil would wave a white hankie, Kleenex, tee shirt, etc. or he would tie it to the antenna of the car. It worked each and every time. I laughed and all was forgiven.

Dear Phils,

As I get ready to embark on our dream vacation, I wanted to tell you that you are never forgotten. You are always, always loved. With every breath that I take and with every life's aspirations and dreams, you are there. I am the woman I am today because you believed in me and gave me wings to fly.

When you met me, I was so broken. I had been abandoned by my church, by my family,. . .by my job, and by my friends. In the name of religion they shunned me because they saw only my divorce. You saw so much more than I even saw in myself at the time. You loved me in spite of myself. In doing so for over 23 years, you gave me confidence.

Together we were unstoppable. We were a force that very few dared to mess with. Even if they did, they messed with us once. You deserved this vacation. . .this time with just the two of us. I am so sorry you didn't get that vacation and that time with me. Just know, I carry you in my heart on this trip. Remember my one request? I always told you, "Do what you need to do. Stay safe. Come home to me." Now, you are my home that I will run to one day.

As I move into thinking about dating again, just know that I am not looking to replace you. You are a force that can't be reckoned with. You can't be replaced, but as you told me the day before you left, hours before you left, there would be room in my heart for another person in a different way. Phil, I never thought that you would die first. You were so full of life. Your star shone so brightly.

I am terrified, but I do know that you would want me to be happy. My moral compass has not changed. My needs are simple. I will honor your memory and the love and belief you had for me by not selling myself short. I do not know if and when I will fall in love again, but I do know this.

You believe in me. You want what is best for me. You propel me forward. I love you always.

I loved you then. I love you now. I will love you more tomorrow.

Lessons Learned From Being Loved By Phil

Looking at the lessons I learned from my marriage to Phil, I need to add a few more tenets etched on to my heart. I learned that humor makes a difference during strife, selfless love, the power of touch, and that an incredible worth ethic combined with loyalty is a combination that is hard to beat. When I married Phil, much of me was a cowering girl who had no confidence in herself or her abilities. Phil, however, never doubted me. He supported me even when I couldn't support myself.

Phil was not perfect. He would react and then he would feel really bad. Early on, he learned that if he could make me laugh, all was forgiven. I would be so upset over his inconsiderate comments and there would be Phil driving up waving a white flag, opening the door and waving a white rag, sending me an e-mail, and on it went. Phil could say things that really hurt, but he knew that humor and a heartfelt apology fixed many a hurt.

Phil would have given anything or any amount to see his children be successful. He fought so hard to leave what he called our trailer park trash or ghetto days behind. He wanted better for our children. From the day he married me until the day he became commissioned, he would study every night for four hours. There he would sit with his PFE's and his yellow highlighter. He made rank the first time he tested every time. He gave up television, working out at times, and hobbies to make sure he provided for us. When he decided that he wanted to try for a commission, he clepped (tested out) out of over 200 credit hours (he still holds the record for the most clepped classes successfully for the AF).

He set an example for his children, but when they started school, Phil showed up whenever they had homework. He would look over the homework, guide them in the process, check grades every day, and he was an active presence in the school. Not only that, Phil would show up to athletic practices and events. He was a Boy Scout leader so that he could be involved. While he felt badly that he didn't always do those things with our older children due to how many children we had, he still took an active interest in all that they did. He would tell the children how proud he was of them.

More than that, Phil knew how to have fun with the children. I am sorely lacking in this area. He would send me away on trips after he returned from deployments so that he could rebond with the children. This meant breaking all of "mom's rules." He would buy lots of pizza and soda. The kids and he would watch movies, many of them movies I wouldn't let the children watch. They lived like slobs until an hour or two before I came home. They would begin a frenzied cleaning process. Phil looked for ways to have fun with the children whether it is a Burger King run after swim team, a movie, throwing the football, or going to the zoo, Phil was the dad anyone would be lucky to have.

Phil was a toucher. He was always touching and kissing on our babies when they were little. No matter where I was, when Phil showed up, it was like he needed to touch me somewhere. Often, it was just a brush, but often it was Phil grabbing my hand to kiss the back of it. While we rarely were demonstrative in public, Phil taught me the need of the human touch. Not so much in the intimacy, but in the daily small connections.

Phil was not a romantic guy, but he did lots of kind things for me. He would bring me coffee and the newspaper in bed every morning that he was home. He was not a morning man, but he became one because I am a morning girl. He would sense that I had a bad day and he would stop to get me a Whole Food's tort and sandwich. He always took me to the restaurants of my choosing. Those small kindnesses equaled a grand slam homerun. I learned to give small kindnesses along the way to people because it made such a difference to me.

While Phil is gone, he will not be forgotten. He lives on in his legacy through his five children. He lives on in me as I step forward and start an unwanted life without me. He has made me a stronger, more resilient, and a more loving person for when, if it is when, I might remarry. He has made me believe in myself and he has taught me love though what he did and didn't do. He made me a better person through his positive attributes and his shortfalls of which there were few. I was blessed to have him in my life for 23 years. I press on with the belief he always had in me.

Honoring a Promise

Today was probably one of the hardest tours for me because we went to Biblical Ephesus and saw where St. Paul and St. John preached and lived. We also saw the Virgin Mary's final home as well as her Assumption area. What was difficult is that this is the tour Phil wanted to participate in. Walking and listening to men and women of faith, however, I am struck by one common thread. These men and women all answered the call of the Lord. They did not stop to ask why not somebody else. They did not bow or break.

While I have often felt broken and bowed since April, I have loudly heard the nudgings of the Holy Spirit. I have at times cowered in the corner trembling and afraid. My heart has often felt crushed under the weight of my loss and pain, but I have felt called since the very moment I found out about Phil to step up to the plate. I may not be the best person to talk about military loss, but for some reason God has chosen me on some level to speak through my written words and actions. I don't feel worthy, but my prayer every day for over five years was for God to help me to live a life of purpose and to live beyond myself. Selfishly, I would have given my own life for Phil's life, but God has something else for me to do. I answer that call when I share my deepest feelings through my written words.

I fail so often, but God has carried me. When I can't see anything to cling to as I am being torn asunder, people, many people, carry me. They stand with me and love me in spite of myself. I am just a simple, quiet girl from Idaho, yet God can use a simple, quiet girl from Idaho. I will not pretend to be anywhere near the caliber of faith of St. Paul, St. John, or the Virgin Mary, but I can choose to step out with what little faith I have.

Praying about where to live this summer was step one. I do not know why I am in Ansbach, Germany yet, but I know, and, oh, how I know, that I am supposed to be there. I was shoved through the door in such a mighty way that who am I to say, "But, God, are you sure this is the answer?" I could go on. My prayers are often not for me, but even then God knows the desires of my heart and my doubt. He carries me with mercy and grace, none of which I remotely deserve. He has provided friends as well as a glimmer of hope in a future without Phil. Granted, I am still lonely, but God is good.

Phil will never be gone from my heart. He is the biggest reason that I am as strong as I am today. He once believed in me when nobody, not even me, believed in Linda. He loved me with all that he had and with all that he was. Whatever my future holds, I will always love that man and value the gift of love that he gave me. Today was about honoring the promise I made to him on his deployment. I promised him that I would go on this trip with our daughter should something happen to him. When I blithely responded to his prodding, little did I know that I would have to take leaps of faith when I wanted to do nothing more than cower and hide.

I am stronger and more resilient than I gave myself credit for, but even strong people of faith need companionship and support. Today, as I toured the Biblical sites, I noticed that the homes of Sts. Paul and John and the Virgin Mary were surrounded by homes of other people of faith. Perhaps that is the key to my healing and resilience. I have surrounded myself with men and women of faith in my dark hours. Even before I cried out, people stood with me. These people standing with me gave me the strength to answer the nudgings of the Holy Spirit. The strength from their love has compelled me to write and speak on my darkest hours. Faith and love have given me a lifeline that is pulling me from the dark roiling waters. I am not worthy and I do not understand, but I am choosing to answer. "Lord, I am not worthy to receive you, but only say the word and I shall be healed."

My Leap of Faith on My 23rd Anniversary

In the early morning hours, I find a peace in the quietness of the dawning sun. While others slumber on, I lace up the running shoes and set out on journey that includes more than the miles of my pounding feet. My soul finds comfort and joy even when there is none to be had. Like my mending broken heart, the sun flits through the dark tree branches. Those rays of sunlight pierce the morning sky. The shattered pieces of my heart are haphazardly pieced together, but the light of day is shining through. I am racing towards a tomorrow I never wanted or saw and in the process I am discovering new joys and hopes.

Today is a marker of sorts. The 27th of November marks not only another month that Phil has been gone, but it marks the years that we were married. Today would have been my twenty third anniversary. Today is also the first Sunday of Advent. Advent marks the start of a season of waiting. Four weeks of preparation for the birth of a baby. Not any baby, mind you, but the son of God. Hoping and preparing ...and finally a birthday celebration where we celebrate the baby Jesus' birth and we celebrate the role of others in our lives, we celebrate. Today, I celebrate the man Phil was...the husband, father, and friend he was to me. I celebrate by being the woman I am because of Phil's love for me.

I have changed since Phil died. I am not sure that he would recognize me. I didn't realize that I had the strength and resilience I do have. I have never seen the girl that others see, but in my weakness, I am discovering that I am capable of so much more than I ever thought. Making that first leap of faith meant taking the job in Germany and leaving not only a job I loved, but the people who carried me through my darkest hours. Those women still mean all to me, but we are separated by an ocean.

I was so scared an unsure. I was so broken that in June, I couldn't see a reason to live. I couldn't see any hope. I prayed to die. Instead, a picture flashed across my heart and mind of me standing with a man at an altar. Peace filled my heart, but to say that I was open and ready for that plan would be the biggest myth of all. I loved Phil and I still love Phil. That is never going to change. At the time, I thought that it was an either or proposition, but as I have changed, my needs and voids in my heart are much different from what I needed and wanted with Phil. I am capable of giving more than I thought and I am more receptive to giving back in a fuller manner. I have learned from the many ways people carried me and loved me. My capacity for loving has grown.

While I know that Phil would be so happy that I am taking risks in driving, moving, and with letting people into my life, I am not sure that he would understand all of the changes in me. Many of these changes were born of necessity and a broken heart. Walking the broken road of loneliness, is a loneliness that only the broken can understand. When all hope is gone and each day is a day filled with loneliness and pain, it is hard to get up and carry on. I have been blessed with friends that continue to carry me and lighten my crushing weight of defeat. Because these friends carried me, and because they still carry me, I have been able to consider a future without Phil.

While some people look to replace the spouse that has been lost, I have discovered that there is a very real possibility that two people could be equally loved in two very different ways. I am not looking to replace or even embrace a future without Phil, but in the small steps that I have taken, I have found that I still need and want lasting companionship. I have discovered the need to share my life again. In these discoveries comes fear and anticipation. There is, of course, some second guessing of myself. If Phil and I hadn't had the "what if" conversation a mere two hours (and not even two hours) before he left, I may not have been able to take the first step of letting the sun shine through the cracks of my heart. With each step, more sunlight blazes and etches light into the dawning day.

I honor Phil today and I honor the life we had together. If Phil had not loved me well, and I had not loved him equally well, I could not open my heart to the possibility of letting another man into my life. I could not love again because loving means risking all. When we eloped after four months of dating, people did not give our marriage a lot of credence. Phil's family estranged themselves thinking that we would divorce before long and that they would get their son back. Twenty three years later, they were still waiting and they missed their son as an adult and as a father. They missed out on being grandparents. They missed the celebration of his life when it ended much too soon.

I am certainly not eloping after four months of knowing anybody, but I embrace the risk of loving and of letting someone else into my life. My heart is healing and in the process of healing is becoming stronger and more resilient than even Phil knew and saw. I celebrate the 23 years I shared with Phil and I am thankful for the life we shared. I will always be thankful and I will always carry Phil in the part of my heart that only he held. I am humbled that he knew and could articulate that I would be able to love another person equally and in a different way that I loved him. Phil had my youth and parenting years. Someone else, God willing, will have the journey into old age. I gird my heart and I fall into the arms of Jesus. When the time is right, I will greet the blazing sun that arises from the ashes and darkness of the tree of life. I will honor Phil's love for me by loving well and staying the course.

Phil's Happy Reunion—Pink Polka Dots and All

On Christ the solid rock I stand. While I will never understand why Phil was taken versus me, I have come to see my own strength and resilience. Tomorrow was his absolute last day to make it home. If the events that took his life in April hadn't happened, my life would look much different tonight. I would be settling in and preparing for a military move. I would be preparing to give Phil a joyous reunion at the airport, and I would be waiting. Instead, the tenth is here, and I have had to make decisions about where to live and what to do with my life. I do not have a happy reunion on earth to look forward to, and though I am crushed this week that we will never have another day together, I am so very thankful for the 23 years we did have together. Many people never experience a love story like we had.

If I could go back through our time together (and I think it is normal when someone is ripped from a loved one's life unexpectedly to ponder the what ifs), I am struck with only one regret. . .the regret of not making each other more of a priority. When Phil married me when I had three children by a previous marriage aged 3, 4, and 5 in the house. We eloped after four months and he was never anything but dad. Patrick, Josh, and Emily did not have any other father from that moment on because their birth father opted out of their lives. While he never showed up, Phil did. We had two more children together. We made quite the team, but all of our time and energy went into being parents and workers. We always thought that one day we would have the time together alone. We could have made the time in the last two years, but something was always more important and pressing. We loved each other more than any written words can convey, however it wasn't until Phil deployed to Afghanistan that he wanted a trip with just me (we never even had a honeymoon). Sadly, that part of our relationship was never recognized.

My life was all I ever could have dreamt of, but I think that we missed out on a richness that would have blessed us further if we could have spent time together on short trips. I am sorry that the happy reunion did not happen because I am sorry that we never got to go through a reunited honeymoon phase of getting to know each other again. I am sorry that I didn't push harder for that time together, but I know that if Phil were here and weighing in, he would say the same. I loved that man well and I still love that man well. In my heart, I am going to give him his happy reunion tomorrow--pink polka dots and all.

One Last Memory that Propels Me Forward One Step at a Time

Phil should have had his happy reunion at our small Colorado Springs airport yesterday. One year ago today Phil deployed to Afghanistan for a year. I will never forget him taking his bags to the taxi and then when he saw me standing on the balcony, running back up the stairs to kiss me yet again. More than that, he gave me a gift that propels me forward now. He gave me the gift of words to move on. Strangely, I am able to take small steps forward because of the actions and words he spoke and did shortly before he deployed.

On the morning of his deployment, he was unable to sleep. He got up and showered. He crawled back into bed with me while he was still wet. He curled into me, not in a sexual manner, but in a manner borne from 23 years of knowing someone well. We talked about the what-ifs. We had never talked with details or depth like we did that morning. I am not sure if Phil had any inkling or subconscious knowledge of his impending death, and I think not, however he was deploying for his longest deployment in the most unstable place he had ever deployed to.

I had completed my on-line application for teaching in Dodds in preparation for our move when he returned from Afghanistan. He told me to put in for worldwide teaching assignments should something happen to him and should I want to leave Colorado Springs. On the day of his funeral, I did exactly that. While I thought the teaching assignment would come a year later than it was offered, it turns out that moving away from where Phil was so well known was the best thing I did for me. While in Colorado, two things happened. First, people we knew very well and for a very long time, were unable or unwilling to reach out when Phil died. Maybe the loss was too much for them or the loss reminded them of their own military risk. Second, I ended up feeling like the wrong person died because Phil was elevated in death to a status that was almost hero worship. Yes, Phil was a hero; however, I couldn't get space from everyone else's grief. Leaving Colorado was very hard because I left a job I loved and I left a strong network of girlfriends, but it was truly the right thing for me to do.

The other issue we talked about that short time in bed was dating. I didn't want to hear it or think about someone other than my Phil. In all earnestness, Phil told me that he wouldn't want me to be lonely and that I had so much more to offer to someone. I felt like he was giving me away. He told me that he wanted me to be happy. I laughed and told him that he would have to push someone into my arms and make it abundantly clear that I should date that person because why would I want to be married again. I made light of it while Phil was serious. With Phil's death I realized what he was saying. I would want Phil to be happy because I loved him that much. I would want him to find the fairy tale again. He wanted that for me and by talking about it, he gave me wings to move forward as hard as it is.

I am thankful, so very thankful for the 23 years we shared. Phil will always be loved and carried in my heart no matter where I go or who I am with, but I learned from the love we shared. I live with confidence because of a conversation that we had two hours before that cab pulled up to take him from me for the last time. I will never forget and I will always be thankful that he had the foresight to talk to me about the what-ifs. I honor his life, his love, and his dreams for me by moving forward one small step at a time.

I Always Thought Phil Was Safe as an Air Force Officer...How Wrong I was

Here it is. Initially everything was hush hush and Prince William's wedding overshadowed something that most people do not want to think about or deal with. This is my reality. I now have a family that I never thought I would have that walks with me. I am the first to say that I NEVER thought the unthinkable would happen to my Air Force husband in what I teased him about--a desk job. I NEVER thought officers were at risk. When Phil was an enlisted man, I worried so much more when he was fighting the drug wars. Guess what? The inherent risk of any military member no matter what their rank is that their life may be asked of them even if their job is communications and linguistic support. The combat boots are the badge of honor for men and women willing to serve. I will always stand with you and I will always understand just how much it might cost.

When Phil deployed, I believed that he would be well and protected as an officer establishing communication with other advisors. In my provincial head, I believed that he would be working in a guarded building with other professionals. He wasn't out on Humvee missions. He wasn't an infantry man on the front lines or in the most dangerous of places. He was a professor at USAFA. He finally had made it into the land of desk jobs, the safest jobs of all. In fact, USAFA hadn't had a killed in action death since the Vietnam War. No professor EVER had been killed. Phil was not a pilot. He wanted to live. In fact, he methodically researched jobs and sites before volunteering for Afghanistan. He never drove across the compound because he wanted to come home. He did not respond to our daughter by e-mail because for the first month he was in Afghanistan, he was afraid she would find a way to travel to come to see him. He never thought he was in danger, or if he did, he never voiced fear.

The hardest aspect of his death for me is that he died at the hands of someone he trusted. He had time to realize what was happening and he was shot enough that though death was quick, it wasn't immediate. Yes, people flip out here in our country, but again the trust that was irrevocably broken also involved trusting the safety of my four military children, brother, and friends stationed throughout the world. I trusted that Phil would be in a guarded environment. I trusted that his weapon would be ready to use. I trusted that Phil would come back to me in 365 days and at the very worst, we would have a period of awkwardness as we readjusted to being together again. I believed that our life would go on with just the inconvenience of him being gone. I never once thought or considered that he would die at barely 44 with a newly minted PhD in hand.

I have seen and I have had my blinders ripped off. Whether a doctor or a teacher, a chaplain or an infantry man, our military family not only deals with prolonged separations, living far from family and friends, but they deal with the unknown enemy lurking amongst the people we help. . .people that are trusted. I no longer believe that there are safe jobs in the military...some are safer than others, but not one job, even a pediatrician, is without additional risks that the general public would never have to think about and if the general public had the unthinkable happen, it wouldn't be in a land far away. There would be something left that smells like their loved one and there would be a more current memory. Yes, the Band-Aids are on and I am finding sunlight again, but joy and hope will never replace the trust and belief that our military is safe no matter where they are or what they do or what rank they are. I am forever changed and my youthful naivety is forever gone as of 27 April 2011.

Through Phil's Eyes, I Can Love My Country

Many people try to pull me into the political fray of debating the cost of war and politicians not understanding that even with Phil paying the ultimate price for our country on 27 April, I stand up. My heart bleeds red, white, and blue because I am the flag. I stand loyal, true, and committed to our country and whoever the Commander in Chief is. If I disagree with world events, I have a vote. It is my civic duty to cast that vote, but it is not my civic duty to undermine people currently in office or people who choose differently than I choose. To be any different would mean that I am diminishing the life that Phil lived.

As a naturalized citizen who spent many years living in corruption and a society of two classes--the wealthy and the very poor, Phil never had a sense of entitlement that many Americans have. He saw beyond the borders of his adopted country and he sought to make a difference by training, teaching, and serving. Phil was never much of a gunman. He carried a gun only when it was required. We used to laugh about his lack of interest in this area considering that he served in the military for 26 years, but this man encouraged our children to seek jobs in which they could make a difference. His life was an exemplary example of service before self. Phil was involved on so many levels. He was a Boy Scout leader, coach, Red Cross volunteer, mentor, substitute teacher, friend, church man, father, and husband. He was a raging burning fire that burned so hot that many people were intimidated and in awe of his stamina and his lifesong. Could it be that Phil's fire burned so brightly for 44 years in order that he could make the difference he wanted to make in the short life he had?

While many people are complacent to work and do only what is asked of them, Phil sought to outperform and outshine everybody. He was always afraid of losing the life he had when he became an American citizen at 18. He recognized even as a young airman that the only way out of poverty and ignorance was through education. Phil drove himself harder than anyone I ever knew. He wanted to be a better father than he had. He wanted the family he didn't grow up with. He wanted stability, security, and love. He was willing to do the menial jobs such as delivering the newspaper for extra money, and he was willing to study four hours a day to make rank the first time he tested every time (line number for senior master sergeant when he got his commission), but he also took time out always to talk to other people struggling. He spoke of the benefits of the military lifestyle and to mentor many cadets and enlisted corp people as future officers. He spoke of his commitment and loyalty to the country who had afforded him so many opportunities. It was through the light in his eyes, his unwavering faith in our country, and finally, through his death serving our country that I fell in love with my country all over again.

I am thankful that people are willing to stand up to the bullies that seek to destroy the very freedoms that define us as a nation. I am thankful for the men and women in uniform that are willing to stand up so other people can escape oppression and senseless violence, many of who are women and children. I may never understand the political ramifications of our troops being somewhere, but if I was a woman living in a country that beat me because I wore the wrong clothes, said the wrong thing, cooked the wrong thing, or drove a car, I would be deeply thankful for someone, anyone, speaking and acting for me. Phil was in Afghanistan to do just that. He was setting up communication components for the Afghanis to stand independently. He went to schools and took gifts. He befriended the Afghan military members. . .one of who took his life. Phil never wavered in his loyalty, commitment, and love for the stars and stripes. Through his eyes, I have fallen in love with my country and my faith in her stands and burns as strong as can be. Even in the maelstrom of the aftermath of Phil's death and wondering what went wrong (and knowing that things could have and should have been done to ensure our troops safety--no, I won't talk about it), I wave my flag because I am the flag.

Let's Celebrate Life on 4 April

Birthdays are a special day where once a year a person is celebrated. I grew up with birthday parties, and as each of my children can attest, I threw birthday parties and celebrated each and every child on their special day. Phil did not grow up with birthday parties celebrating his life. He truly ceased feeling like he was anyone special the day after he turned six. When he married me, he begged me not to go overboard on his birthday, thus both of our birthdays got lost in the shuffle of a lot of children and very little money for many years in our marriage. I had always planned to throw him a big birthday bash for his 50th birthday. Sadly that day will never come.

Instead, I want to throw Phil a big celebration of life party on 4 April. I am taking the day off of work. I want to ask all of his friends and colleagues to do something to celebrate Phil in their life. I want you to post what you think you might do so that others can get ideas. In our family, we were creative because we didn't have a lot of money. We played a lot of games, read out loud two hours every night, and we had backwards meals in which dessert was the main course. We often ate under a blanket draped dining room table with flashlights. I haven't decided if I can face rice and beans because we ate that five days a week for years.

A person never knows the sum of his or her days. I wish that I could have given him a party with blazing candles and the childhood games that he only got to experience through our children. I wish that he could have had a birthday party in a room crammed full by all of the people who loved Phil and who valued the presence of Phil in their lives. Let us do 4 April well. Let us laugh, love, and live because that is what Phil would have wanted for all of us.

I Weep For What the World Lost

My heart is really bleeding this weekend. I just can't wrap my arms around all that is lost to the world with the loss of Phil. Sadly, even he didn't live long enough to see his value and worth outside of being a father and a person who could outwork anyone else. He prided himself in never showing weakness outside of our house, but Phil was broken. As a young child he felt largely abandoned, unloved, and like he was nuisance. As a non-native speaking English speaker, Phil never felt smart enough or worthy enough for the commission he received after 16 years as an enlisted man. He always felt that someone was going to realize that he was a fraud and take it all away. He would lie awake nights and worry. He was so wrong.

Phil was always one of the smartest and one of the hardest working people I knew. He was a stubborn as a bull dog when it came to the kids and I. He fought to ensure that our children could break out of the bonds of poverty that we had lived in for so long, but long before we were married, I watched a man ask me out time and time again even though I kept rejecting him. I saw a man who fought to overcome his poor writing skills and to rid himself of his accent. I saw a man who fought for me and believed in me when nobody else did. I saw a man who had vision.

It took awhile, a long while, but Phil created the life he wanted even as a child. He was the father he always wanted and he told me that one of the reasons he loved me so much was that I had the qualities he wanted his mother to have--I am/was deeply committed to my faith, the children, and him. I am nonconfrontational and flexible which meant that we did not argue and fight very often. It worked for us for 23 years and it would be working still. We were not perfect, but we brought out the best in each other because we complimented each other so well. Phil was not into grand slam romantic gestures, but he did something every day that I miss terribly. He would get up before me to bring me coffee and the paper in bed. He was not a morning person when I married him ,but he did this for me. When the children were little, he would walk in the door after a long day, and then he would send me on my way out the door to run for a few hours. He never complained--ever.

Phil's insecurity about his role as a husband and father came with providing for us. He pushed himself harder than anyone I have ever known. He wanted better for us. He always asked me if he was enough and if I had enough. Yes, we struggled mightily for many years, but we had such a tight knot family. As my daughter says, we put the fun back into dysfunctional. We liked each other and wanted to be together. Phil strove for achievement, and accomplished so much more than people thought he was capable of, to provide security for us. I didn't always appreciate it. I certainly didn't react well when he told me that he volunteered for Afghanistan because he felt like he needed to go for military advancement and security. He hurt my feelings when he told me that I liked to spend money. I never spent it when we didn't have any money to spend, but that wasn't what Phil meant. He meant that he was afraid of being 55 an retired and me having medical issues and not enough income to cover the care I might need. He wanted to give me and the kids the world.

Phil's research is being published in a national journal this summer. I wept today. I rarely, rarely cry, but I wept because he never knew how much he had to offer. He had finished a second master's degree and a PhD five days prior to his deployment. All of us teased him about PhD standing for phony doctorate. He would be embarrassed, but secretly proud, that a boy from Venezuela could accomplish the American dream. He had so much more he wanted to do and I wept because his light blazed. I stood in his shadow in awe because he had accomplished so much in 23 years of our marriage, but he never once stopped thanking God or me for believing in him when nobody else did.

It has been interesting, also. The people that knew Phil when he was a nobody autotrack radar person have found me and have genuinely reached out to me. We had longer term friends, but those friends largely abandoned us when Phil's star began to shine and when he died. It hurt an already hurting heart, but the people that knew us when Phil was in Mountain Home, ID and when I was the swimming pool manager there, have found me and have given me back a piece of my Phil. They have but band aids on a broken shard of my heart. They have given me laughter as I remember Phil doing a boys weekend at Lagoon, nacho night, running victories and practice, a rolled government vehicle (bet a person would never guess, but the cow lived) and so much more. Could it be that his success as a family man and as an educator could only be appreciated by those who knew just how far my Phil had to go to achieve that success? Could it be that he needed people to love him unconditionally and to believe in him without reservation? Phil Ambard will forever be young, successful, and terribly handsome, but my Phil was successful long before the world recognized it. He was successful because he recognized what he had and he put all into that relationship. Though we had our cracks like any other couple, Phil was loved well and will be loved until my dying breath. He would have done the same for me.

25 Things that I Love About Phil on his 44th Birthday Plus Twenty More To Celebrate his 45th Birthday Wednesday—Memories are written for each year. I added 20 more this year.

1. He was loyal, so loyal. He chose me over his family who 23 years ago were sure that I was marrying him for his money (for the record, he was an A1C making $485.00 a pay check)
2. He was a great father. He never treated any of our children differently. He raised the three older children with the same love he gave to the younger two. He was dad from the day he married me at barely 21.
3. He put his needs last. Phil always invested in my running (time and resources) and in the children's activities. Even when he wanted something, he deprived himself so that everyone else had what they wanted or needed.
4. We eloped to Reno, NV on 27 November 1988. For two super responsible people, this was a pretty shocking event--laugh.
5. He was good to older people. He used to flirt outrageously with my grandma--even in front of my grandpa. He talked soap operas with her because when Phil was in high school, he watched soap operas to work on his English. I never have watched them. It was so funny hearing the two of them talk about the people and what was going on in the soap opera.
6. He was game for almost any activity that I throw at him.
7. He was the fun parent.
8. Phil still made my heart go pitter patter. Yes, really.
9. Phil was very funny, but few people know it. I loved his chollolo boy act.
10. He still made me coffee and brought me the paper in bed.
11. I was and am proud of his chosen profession. As a military man, I am proud that he was willing to stand up to the injustices of the world.
12. He was a slob, but he was my slob. He packed by throwing the whole drawer in the suitcase. He washed laundry by throwing way too much into the washer without sorting any of it. He liked living out of a pile of clean laundry.
13. He was a softie. He acted like he didn't care, but he did. . .
14. Phil was a Christian. He stood for what is right and true.
15. He was the only guy who looked cute driving a beat up blue minivan.
16. We never had a honeymoon. Phil came up with the idea of meeting somewhere in October. After 23 years, we are meeting in Venice and

taking a 10 day Mediterranean cruise. This singular event is something I wish he could have had (well, that and commissioning his son).

17. Phil smelled good--a combination of Old Spice and soap-MMM!
18. He stood behind all of our children even when they make choices that were not our decisions.
19. He snuck the two of us in to Doolie Day In to see Tiger during the height of the Swine Flu epidemic at USAFA. We were kicked out twice before we left.
20. He would go out in the middle of the night if I want ice cream or chocolate (even if I was not pregnant--laugh)
21. I loved the way his eyes change colors. . .
22. I also liked his musician's fingers.
23. He would chauffer me almost anywhere.
24. He was generous beyond belief not only to his family, but to others that need something.
25. He spoiled the dog rotten and acted like he was being wrongly accused!
26. He was righteously indignant when Emily called him boring--or he thought she was calling him boring when he talked about boys yet again as he took her to and from Baumholder to Ramstein for swimming practice. He was so upset that Emily did not get Burger King that day and he was still talking about it 13 years later.
27. He had the talk with any boy that picked Emily up for a date or showed interest in her at USAFA--you know, the one that told boys that if they were looking for a good time to go elsewhere.
28. He once told an operator that Emily might be getting taken advantage of because the phone at the boy's house she was at was busy for an hour. He convinced the operator to break in on the phone call so he could check on Emily.
29. He would wait outside with the dog (after driving to check on Emily) for Emily to return from her dates.
30. He loved watching Patrick and Josh wrestle. Josh had given him so many fits that Phil never stopped talking about Josh instilling fear in his opponents. One of the last things he shared with Patrick before he went to OTS was Europeans.
31. Phil got his commission two months after Patrick started USAFA. He was terrified that his kids would think he was stupid. He had completed his PhD and a second master's degree five days before he deployed to Afghanistan. He won the highest honors. He is getting published in a national journal.

32. Phil cried more than I cry. He cried the day I agreed to marry him, at our wedding, at the birth of our children, when Josh's knee was destroyed, when Alex had a tumor in his arm, when I was pregnant with Tiger and the doctor thought that he would have Down's Syndrome or spina bifida.

33. Phil tried to send me flowers once on his last Valentine's Day. The stupid flower company never delivered the flowers. Three days later, I cancelled the order.

34. Phil was not romantic in terms of grand slams. He did one thing that was such a grand slam that I still stand in awe. He submitted an essay for me to carry the Olympic torch in UT. When I was selected, I was so shocked,. He was so proud.

35. He must have gained twenty pounds on our first cruise. I never saw anything like that. He was at the buffet line all of the time and he had multiple entrees every night. None of his clothes fit when we left. It took almost six months for him to lose all of that weight.

36. Phil ran a half marathon right before he was killed. There weren't enough medals for every finisher, so he gave his medal to a man that had never run a half marathon. He wanted to run one more marathon--the Paris Marathon this year. I am running it for his 45th birthday.

37. Phil was all about his kids. He drove them really hard in school, but at home, he was fun. He played WII games, watched stupid movies, and threw balls with the kids. He was invested.

38. He loved Christmas. Phil didn't grow up getting Christmas or birthdays, thus he loved the mass chaos of lots of people and lots of holiday cheer. It made him so happy.

39. Phil had a soft heart for the homeless because we were so close when we were first married. He bought an expensive Marigold's cupcake in NYC for a toothless homeless person and defended the man to the police officer trying to take away the cupcake.

40. Phil talked to everyone. He got to know people's names and soda/food preferences. He talked to the invisible people. He also never stopped talking up the military and being proud of what he did. He was always so loyal to his adopted country. He never stopped being thankful for the opportunities he had been given.He had the what if talk with me before he left and even though I was nasty about it in terms of making jokes and changing the subject, he said some things that have made all of the difference. He told me that he wanted me to be happy. When I made a joke, he said, "Would you

want me to be happy if you died first?" Uh. . .yes. Yes, I would. There is more to this story, but I can't share it until I share it with someone first.

41. He loved going away on boy weekends with his sons. He thrived on being a scout leader, dad, etc.

42. Phil broke rules when he subbed while getting his PhD and master's degree. He was one of the most popular subs in Colorado Springs. Everywhere we went, teens talked to him. They liked him. Grief counselors were needed throughout the city because of the impact he had.

43. He was reading all of the classics when he died. He barely graduated from high school and he blew off most of his classes. He had completed the Hunger Games, To Kill a Mocking Bird, and he was almost finished with Wuthering Heights. We were going to read Sense and Sensibility together--his choice. I teased him about his girlie choice.

44. Our family had fun names for each other. I am Wonder Woman. He loved the shirts, family Bingo, making nachos and fajitas, and being a buffoon at cards.

45. Phil Ambard, happy 45th birthday. You are forever young. I loved you then. I love you now. I will love you forever. Thank you for loving me well and for giving me the words to push me towards loving another. You truly were a man above all.

The Last Time We Talked-Easter Sunday 2011

Oh, glorious day. Today, hope is restored. I may still be like Thomas and doubt the whispers and nudges from the Lord, but I stand confident in what this day means for me. As dark as it has been this April and last April, Easter is the cornerstone of my faith. I truly believe that without the darkness and sacrifice of our Lord, there would be no hope. Death would conqueror. I believe that it is only through an earthly death that we can know the glories of residing with the Lord.

Does that mean that death hurts any less? Heck no. I so wish it had been me in that room on 27 April. I would gladly have traded my breath for Phil's breaths. He mattered to so many people and his footprints are so large. I am just a girl drifting along and who is happy in the shadows supporting others while they shine. I was not given a choice and the suddenness and unfairness so mind boggling and crushing that I often can't allow my mind to go there, but I have the past two weeks.

Many things transpired to bring me to my knees, but ultimately I felt consumed by darkness and the loss of hope. I lay on the floor yesterday and wept. I begged God to take my life, but it isn't my time yet. There must be something left for me to do and there must be something God has planned for me. I may not see the stray whispers of hope, but they waft through the darkness and I can see brief spots of light. I know that another day will dawn and that I will feel joy in all realms. I also know that there will always be gaping holes where Phil once filled my life. I do believe that there is room for another in the gaps between the holes, and I believe that God is still defining my life with a push into a realm that I am not really comfortable with--that of a spokesperson on military loss.

I have learned from Phil's death. I still feel guilty about not having contact with my Phil for three days prior to his death. We last spoke on Easter Sunday. He called and when he found out that I was at a friend's house, he kept the phone call very short. He promised to call the next day or the day after. That phone call never came. I made it easy. I made a conscious decision to play a game, and, oh, how I wish I hadn't. I knew that Phil shut down TDY. I knew was married to that man for 23 years and that was him. It wasn't personal, but I made it personal when I made the conscious decision to play a game. I wish I had a time machine because I would go back in time and I would thank him for 23 years of loving me well. I would make him a priority. The house could have waited. Running could have taken less of my time. He deserved more.

I should have insisted that we take time for each other without the kids. I should have written more in e-mail. Lastly, I should have told him more often how much I loved him and how he mattered to me. I wish I could have been the girl under the desk. I hope he knew how much he was loved and how much his life mattered. As guilty as I feel, I know that Phil would want me to get past this insecurity and reach for the hope of the resurrection. God is here and the light shines brightly even when I can't see it. The light blazes because life really isn't defined by the days we live here on earth for no matter how many days a person lives, life is temporal. If only I can continue to fall to my faith, I will feel the rays of hope sprouting again. I will find joy in the morning and I will see the light of day because the rock is rolled back and the tomb stands empty because he has risen, risen, risen from the dead.

Running the Paris Marathon for my Phil

Phil was a naturalized French citizen. Few realized that had he not served in the USA military, he would have had mandatory military service with the French. This mandatory draft ended awhile ago, but in the mid 80's, he chose. He was thankful every day for the opportunities and freedoms that our country gave him, so in some sick manner, it is only fitting that he gave all to the country that he loved so much. Having said that, Phil never lost the love of France. He always said that he would do one more marathon--the Paris Marathon. I am running the Paris Marathon to celebrate the man Phil was and the life we had together.

While here in Paris, it has been inevitable that my heart has bled. The course finish line is at the Arc de Triomphe. As I walk the streets we once walked together and I see the places we once shared, I am reminded of what Phil wanted for me. He wanted me to be happy again should something happen to him. While I believe that happiness is a choice, I am tend to define my life by what was lost and the dream I had of growing old with Phil. While I believe that falling in love in a new way can happen again, I am no longer thinking that it is a reality. I do think, however, I will come to a point where I am content no matter what my lot in life. If I am lonely, God will provide. If I drop to my knees and break, he will carry me through the reaching hands of my friends. I have seen this very action time and time again since 27 April 2011.

The one thing Phil would not want for me is to settle and I do not want a man that is not the man God wants for me. My moral compass has not changed so loyalty, fidelity (body and mind), and friendship are tantamount to any relationship I might enter. Sometimes I wonder if once was enough. It might be, but I know that Phil meant it when he said to be happy and to find the fairy tale again. It is scary because Phil left such a big yardstick to measure a relationship by. While I do not want a man like Phil, I think it would be too easy to settle. It is hard finding what I am looking for a t 50. I am pickier and I want a comfortable, fun, passionate relationship based in faith. Many men my age see only beauty, easiness, and broken women who faun all over them. I am not that girl. I want more. I just don't know if it is a feasibility, thus I fall to my faith to carry me and give me strength not to take someone with whom I do not have these things with.

It has been interesting to remember conversations and letters where we wrote about the what ifs. I temped so many of these words down. I always thought I would die first. I wanted to die first because I never wanted to find out how empty my life would be without the people I love. That didn't happen. I have discovered I am stronger and more resilient than I ever thought. I feel the nudgings of the Holy Spirit and I feel my Phil here in Paris loving me and pushing me forward. I would like to close my eyes and retreat to the days I cherished so much, but somehow, some day, I see a life of happiness and contentment. I may be alone, but I will be happy and I will be falling into my faith. I cannot see the life God has for me, but it is well, it is well with my soul.

Our First Date and the Next Chapter

I watched a romantic movie based on a true story of a woman who loses her memory and the man who loved her well. It is the first romance I have watched since Phil died. Half way through, I realized that the tears were falling. I hadn't even realized that my heart was weeping. I remembered the young GI who strutted into the Mountain Home AFB swimming pool in an ugly blue hammock swimming suit and who relentlessly pursued me. He wouldn't take no for an answer. . .and even later, he believed that no meant he wasn't trying hard enough.

Our first date was to Lagoon, an amusement park in Utah. I will never forget the car ride--five hours where we talked nonstop. The comfortable companionship set the stage for 24 years (including the courtship). He made me laugh, but more than that, he listened to me and he defended me (us) to the naysayers. I was so uncomfortable with the age difference, the fact that I met him so soon after my divorce, that he was military and in the same squad as my ex-husband, and the fact that I had three children. I felt so broken and so unlovable, but Phil loved me from the start. When he looked at me, I saw the promise and potential of myself. I saw somebody worth loving.

As he sat next to me on a roller coaster, I looked over. He had this look on his face as he looked at me. I could never describe it if I even tried. It was a look of total admiration and awe. Phil was 21, barely 21, yet he knew exactly what he wanted. He was not afraid to tell me or to risk rejection. To be honest, I leapt with faith that day. Our early days were so difficult. So many people did not think that we belonged together or that we would last. Our song was a song my Jefferson Starship, Nothing's Going to Stop Us. There is a line, "some say we're crazy, but what do they know? Baby, put your hand in my hand and don't ever look back." I never did.

As long as we stood together, nothing in life seemed too big. I always knew that he was there. As I watched this movie that touched me because of its basis in reality, I know that my mooring is gone. Maybe that is why I second guess myself so often. It is about more than the loneliness and wishing that he were here. He was me, and I was him. Somewhere we had truly become one and we truly loved each other enough to want the other person happy and well. Even now, the best gift Phil gave me before he deployed was minutes before the cab came to carry him away from my arms for the last time. As he tried to have the what if talk, I made jokes which is what I do when I am stressed out. He was having none of that. He had a plan that I have followed to a tee which is why I am teaching in Germany. He asked me the one question that still stops me in my tracks: "If you died first, would you want me to be happy? That is what I want for you."

Yes, Phil, I wanted you to be happy. Since Lagoon, I lived for the way your eyes lit up, your laughter, and your smile. I honor our love by stepping forward even as I want to cower in the corner. I am afraid and broken, but I believe in the promise that God gave me in those dark hours of June. In the dark hours of June as I totally broke and as I totally hid under the covers of my bed, I cried out to Jesus and begged him to take me home. I had no hope. Not a spark, not a fire. I felt an electric jolt and saw myself standing at an altar with a man in front of a minister. I couldn't see him, but it scared me so much that I leapt out of bed and fell tangled in the blankets. As I lay there doubting what I had seen, it happened again. I was terrified. I looked out of my window and there was the first full double rainbow I have ever seen. I cannot question that this was a promise from God--a holy fire.

I stand and I wait. I am petrified and wary, but someday I will not be alone or afraid. Someday somebody will make me laugh and will love me enough to stand up to the naysayers. I may not be in need of a knight on a white horse to defend me to my father now, but I need a strong man that can live with the legacy that Phil left and my commitment to the military families everywhere. Someday, I will be ready. Until then, I weep unconsciously because I know what agape love is. I know what it is to love someone so much that I would gladly have given my life to him. I know what it is like to be on the roller coaster that flies through life. As long as I was leaning on Phil, I could be brave. I lean right now on the faith he had in me and I believe and wait for God to answer the promise he gave me last June.

Relationships, Family, Friends and Others

The Simple Acts of Kindness that Have Changed Me

Two weeks ago, I totally broke. My heart shattered into a million pieces. I couldn't wrap my arms around the images in the pictures of my husband broken beyond repair. I could not dig myself out of the dark abyss I fell into. Every time I closed my eyes, I saw images that no one should ever have to even imagine for their loved one. I hurt and wished with all of my heart that I could have taken my Phil's place.

I am not sure why Phil was called home at such a young age. The man utilized every God given talent he had. He reached people on a level that I cannot. For an immigrant to the United States, his life was about selfless service and sacrifice in gratitude for the freedoms and the life he was given when he entered the USA. I, as a lifelong citizen, had grown complacent in the privilege of my country. Phil, having come from Venezuela, saw firsthand that in some countries privilege is extended to those with wealth, in a certain position, or to those who believed a certain way. He was proud to be a volunteer to train the Afghanis and to open the doors through education for freedom from oppression.

His death has caused me to reevaluate myself. I stop and stare at the woman in the mirror. I don't exactly like what I see. I see weakness and her broken heart flitting across the planes of her face. I smell her fear that roots her immobile and unable to move. I sense the inertia that has consumed her for years. I have never been comfortable needing people or reaching out, yet I found that simple acts of kindness have carried me through some of my darkest hours.

A lady in Dover picked me up and took me to the running trail to run 10 miles the day my Phil came back to the states. I had Marathon Maniac friends stand with me and run with me during the first two marathons. I have had local girlfriends who keep reaching out to me even at my most unlovable self. I have had FB friends reaching out through encouraging messages. I have had two military friends that have walked with me and cried with me during some very dark moments. I have had people send me pictures and stories of my husband this week.

It has been two months. The military community has largely forgotten and moved on. I suppose that I can't fault them for that, but I cannot forget the man that I loved truly, faithfully, and with my all for 23 years. I need to know that his life mattered. To that extent, I find myself being yanked from my complacency. I have never been comfortable in the limelight or with letting people in too close. I struggle with my own brokenness and humanity right now. I see my past interests and talent playing a role in a future I never asked for or wanted. My running and writing are moving me forward and providing direction.

I will one day take these thoughts and I will put them together. In the meantime, I continue to heal and self evaluate while I run with the whispered prayers of my feet and through the words that pour out of the honest cries of my broken heart. I would not have ever wanted this life, but I pray that I can stand worthy and ready to be the woman that God calls me to be through my pain. I pray that I can be a person to effect change in others and in a system that doesn't always work. I want to like the woman in the mirror staring back at me.

Trust? Is It Possible?

As a military wife of a fallen soldier who believed in what he was doing (training the Afghanis), I am still wondering why people are never more wary and distrustful in warlike situations. While my husband was in Afghanistan as a trainer, a teacher, a mentor, it seems ludicrous to me to trust that all people in a nation filled with Taliban sympathizers. While I understand, and while I still support what we as a nation are doing there, how do the troops go on believing and hoping and trusting when 9 comrades are killed? I am not sure what the answers are. I do know that if I lived in Afghanistan, I would be thankful for the men and women who were willing to help train and educate in order for me to have freedoms. I would embrace the man sitting across from the table from me teaching and guiding me on the path of positive change. Unfortunately, not every man or woman wants that change. To trust fully and unequivocally is to be naive and it sets up a very real possibility of a repeat.

Forgiveness and Apologies

Forgiveness is something that is easier said than done. Though the words "I am sorry" and the words "It is okay" are easy to utter, the heart does not easily forget the wrongs that are perceived or done to us or against us. Is it true forgiveness if a friendship changes or if trust is gone? Recently, I have challenged my own heart in this area.

While it is not secret on this forum that I have felt abandoned by my military family in the days since 27 April, yesterday I had a handful of seemingly genuine apologies as a result of my finally voicing how I feel. Is it up to me to determine the genuineness of the apology when I struggle with forgiveness in terms of trusting and believing in the sincerity? My own human frailty shines through my insecurity. I question other people's motives without seeing my own glaring flaws (of which there are many).

True forgiveness means that I choose to restart, or reset as one will, the relationship. I choose to move forward and to stop visiting the past. I choose to say and feel that the hurts are going to be forgotten even when I may not believe that the hurt can go away. I choose to forgive because life is too short to live in the constant morass of my own faults let alone those of others.

A Heartfelt Note

Recognizing people's efforts on my behalf is just as important as speaking or writing about the injustices. Just now, and when I had my meeting today, I had the opportunity to move away from dwelling on the negatives. I had the opportunity to recognize people who locally have gone the extra mile for me. There have been a few military people who have. I was able to talk about a doctor who came in on his last day of leave to make sure that I got my physical done in time to accept the job offer, a military friend who walked with me non-stop the first six weeks voluntarily, and two higher ranking individuals who didn't have to and could have foisted me off on other people. I am indebted and I do have gratitude for people who have gone to bat for me. It is amazing the level of e-mail and FB support from all over the world. I am thankful for the messages because they keep the loneliness at bay.

Apart from the military people, I have a group of ladies that know that laughter and shared fun times are what the heart needs at this juncture. Early on, many meals and prayers were offered. I had the most wonderful birthday ever in the heart of the grieving times. I came back recharged and ready to face the daily challenges of new information and dealing with my loss. They believe in me and stand with me. I need that.

I have a school that opted to give me a one year leave of absence and to create my replacement position as an INR which means that I can have my exact job back if I so want it in one year. This means so much to me because Stetson gave me my dream job. I have loved working there.

Often, in the heat of the moment, I forget to thank the people that really matter. I concentrate on my needs and wants that weren't met, yet I fail to recognize the helping hand that is being proffered right in front of my face. To those friends that have walked with me, carried me, and loved me from wherever you are or whatever you do, your kindness is not forgotten. You have been the glaring steady beacon of hope showing me the course to chart. Thank you.

The Amazing Gift of Friendship

I had an amazing polka dotted purple party tonight. I will so miss my circle of girlfriends. My peeps have walked with me through the darkest hours. They have taught me so much about the gift of friendship and loving unconditionally. I will not lose the lessons or the connections.

Many people ask if I knew these ladies before Phil died. I had just started going to Bunco. I went to Easter service with another woman who I met the weekend both of our husband's deployed. When Phil died, these ladies took over. They scooped me up and carried me with kind thoughts and actions. Not only were they present in terms of meals and listening when things first happened, they have given me rides to the airport, opened their homes, bought me socks and brought me coffee, thrown me a remarkable unforgettable 50th birthday that made me laugh so hard that I smile still, they prayed and cried with me. Isn't that the true definition of a friend?

They all had their own problems and issues, but they still made a choice to be a friend of mine. Through the gift of their time and compassion, I learned that helping others makes me own burden seem lighter. While it would seem that the opposite might be true and that by reaching out to another person in pain, I might become deeply rooted in darkness that was not the case. I received joy, satisfaction, and for the time I was reaching out, my own demons were allayed and put to rest.

They did not worry about saying or doing the wrong thing. They acted. They encouraged me on Facebook and in person. During dark hours, they found ways to touch my aching heart. I have never had a circle of friends like this. I will miss them so, but I take the lessons and the connections to Germany. Oh, I am a better and more empathetic person for having had their friendships enrich my life. I am standing with them. I will walk with them. I will laugh with them, and I will stay forever loyal to my peeps (people).

Fixing the Hurt in My Children

As a parent, one of the hardest things that I faced lately is seeing the pain in my children at the loss of their father. I want to kiss their boo-boo and make it all better, but there is nothing that can right this foul wrong. Today, I had to go through the details with Alex, my only non-military child. While nothing changes the outcome, there is something so horrible about hearing about one's loved one getting shot in this manner. The details are so unthinkable that the mind cannot wrap itself around the vile reality. Perhaps it is good that mind wants to close in and pretend it is like a movie reel because it is just too much to consider when it is a person that is loved.

I can't fix the pain in my children, nor can I fix the pain I carry. Innocence and unwavering faith that all would be well was lost that day. Trust, a gift I always had, is shattered. It is hard to explain, but I can't even trust myself and my ability to make decisions that are the right choices. I find myself doubting that my life will be safe, secure, and full of blessings. It is a terrible loss for someone that always believed in what is true, right, and just.

As a believer, I have always thought that somehow things would work out okay if I believed enough or had enough faith. There are even faiths that do believe that tenet. A lesson that I have learned? Bad things can and do happen to good people. I will never, ever understand the events that led to 27 April, nor will I ever understand why my Phil, but I believe that somehow something good can arise from the burnt ashes of my life. I may not be able to fix this terrible wrong, and I may not ever be able to be fully happy again, but I so stand on the promises of my faith. I stand with the military men and women still serving because it is only through continued education and training that oppressive societies can change. I wish that it had not been my Phil. I wish so much that I could kiss my children's hurts away, but my reality is that I have to discover away to deal with my own pain, help my children through theirs, and I have to find away to honor Phil's memory in a way that will honor all military people willing to give their lives for the freedoms of people that don't even live in our country. I stand up to be counted as the tears reign in my heart. I grasp at a future where every man, every woman, every child has basic freedoms no matter what their religion, sexual preference, gender, and age. I stand for the people willing to make a difference with the willingness of their very life. I stand today.

Today Was a Difficult Day Made More Difficult by People who Pushed and Pried

Today has been difficult. As I struggle to find a foothold, the day has been made harder by people who poked and pried. One lady kept asking, "Single? No dependents with you?" Like I want that announced to the whole world. She kept looking me up and down until I told her that I had dependents--just not with me. She then proceeded to keep prying about a husband. When I had enough, I finally told her. She didn't miss a beat. She proceeded to comment on my singledom two more times.

I am not single by choice, nor is this a place that is very fun. Today was a day I struggled. I know there will be days like this, maybe even weeks, but words can cut as deeply as a weapon can. Words sluice through my soul and leave me gasping for air. I am not sure how to answer the military dependent question. I feel like the 22 years I was a military wife have slipped into the nether land of being shoved from the arms of the military family. I know I remind people of loss that can happen. I know that I am single without children living with me. I have not forgotten who I am. I am the wife of a military man who gave up his life serving for his adopted country. I am the mother of five children, four of them serving in the United States military. I am a teacher teaching military dependents. I am the flag waving in the wind.

Missing the Connections I Once Had

The singular thing I miss the most about Phil is having that connection. Waking up next to someone and being excited to see what the day might bring. I was the planner in our marriage. Eyes would roll and huffy breaths would be expelled, as mom came up with yet another way to get everyone to exercise and spend time together. Hours later everyone would be laughing and joking over a good meal. Phil was just like one of the children sometimes. He would go along with whatever I came up with, but he would be talking to the kids behind my back.

Being alone without someone to talk about the shared memories with is the worst part of this lonely exile. I am consumed with a sense of drifting alone. Germany is an exciting place that I should be jumping for joy at the opportunity to work here, but it is merely an extension of standing alone. It isn't fun to travel alone, try new things alone, or to spend hours and hours alone. For me, the experience was sharing it with my family. Phil was the fun parent, so it was always an adventure. I would plan; he would make it fun.

I wake up in the morning and I run. After running, my day fades into meaningless tasks and a sense of being different and disconnected from everyone. Other than my birthday weekend, I have not felt joy or laughter in my heart since Christmas. Yes, I know that Phil has only been gone since 27 April, but I was waiting for him to come home since 11 January when he deployed. I have always had an optimistic humor laden life. Not so much now. As each day fades into another day without promise, I shrink from a future that looks pretty bleak.

I miss having children at home because children gave my life purpose and direction. While I know that my job will help, is it wrong to want a connection somewhere else? I miss the small things. I could give up the bells and whistles, but I miss sharing the good times and the bad times with someone. I miss being excited to come home at the end of the day. I surely miss being needed and wanted in someone's life.

I always thought that I would die first. Phil was younger and healthier than I am. When I look at the crushing defeat I feel, however, I am not sure that Phil could have survived. He grew up in a home where connections were not forged. He shut down on deployments and he would have shut down in death. I feel like I am shutting down, but here is the thing. Phil always had confidence in me that I could bounce back and that I would find away to survive should the unthinkable happen.

I may be cowering in the corner and drowning, but I have one finger up. I am barely breathing, but I am not giving up. Until my very last breath, I will fight to find footholds. I may be lonely. I may be alone. I may never feel joy again, but I have this innate sense of fighting for something again. I am not sure what, but I am following the answered prayers and open doors. I have no idea why I am at Ansbach, but I know this is where I am supposed to be. It would be nice to meet some runners and other people to spend time with, but I am going to trust that if God can take care of the sparrows of the field, he can take care of me. I may sink in the buffeting roiling waves, but somewhere God is going to meet me and carry me. I hope that it is today. I am lost and afraid...drowning and adrift...I need his touch today.

My Reset Button Has Been Pushed

To borrow a phrase from my friend, Brian, today I found a reset button. Somewhere in the drizzly rain, I was touched by the kindnesses of others. I received a pair of polka dotted earrings and I heard from a friend that I hadn't heard from in some time. The act of receiving those earrings and the card soothed my heart. In the process of feeling loved and valued, it as if my reset button has been pushed.

In the military system, it almost feels as if the wife and dependents are a liability. When the military member loses his/her purpose within the system due to death or retirement, the spouse is forgotten. For 23 years, I supported every military move and endeavor my husband undertook. I did more than support him. I raised our children with the same sense of civic duty and pride. I was and am proud of being a military wife and mother, but I have no identity. Thus, when someone greets me by first name, it matters to me. It pricks my heart because it makes me feel like I am a person and that I count. When someone goes over and above using my name for me, it is almost too much.

When I feel my most helpless, a friend brings me a cup of coffee because I can't leave my house, buys me socks, mails a package for me, picks me up at the airport, plans a 50th birthday for me, buys me polka dots just because it will make me happy, and so on and so on. I have been drowning without a lifeline here for a few days. Today, a lifeline was thrown to me. My lifeline came in the form of a card and polka dotted earrings. I am treading water while the reset button is pushed.

And, I Wish I Were There

I have felt out of sorts all day. This weekend in Parent's Weekend at USAFA. This is the first time since the year 2000 that I am not there. I still have a cadet son and other cadets I know there, but I am not there. I am sure that if I were in Colorado, this weekend would make my heart bleed a lot.

It was at a Parent's Weekend that Phil was asked to talk to a French class about language opportunities in the military. He was there as a dad in ratty blue jeans. He hated the pomp and self-importance of many ranking parents visiting their children. They walked around all super starched strutting about with their rank on. Phil looked like a duffle bag.

After speaking, he was asked to meet the department chair. At that point, he had a mild fit of panic. There he was unshaven and rumpled. This meeting led to his master's degree and then a second master's degree and a PhD. He loved teaching and mentoring cadets. He was so happy when he had a full house of cadets. The same rang true in Afghanistan. He loved mentoring and compelling people to move forward and to improve their lot in life.

I miss walking with him on the Academy and seeing the light in his eyes as he spoke of his inability to ever believe that he had a place there. He never felt like he could relax. He always felt that he would lose it all somehow. Phil had great value to so many people, yet he could not see it. I am thankful that I got to attach myself to his star before anyone else ever saw it. What a ride it was.

I am thankful that he is buried on the hallowed AFA grounds. I am thankful because Phil never would have recognized how valued he was there. He always said to flush him down the toilet when he was gone. After ten years of being a part of Parent Weekend, I am so glad that he has a front row seat to all of the action. I wish I were there to share the ride. . .and the pride for I am a proud AF wife and mom always.

Home

Home. Home is a feeling that I buried deep inside of a person. Is it strange that I feel like my sense of mooring and warmth in the hearth of home is fleeting now that Phil is gone? I didn't realize that home was about more than a place, memories in that place, or four walls. I know what home is now that I have lost my rudder and my anchor. I bob about the waves, but I can't see the stable ground just beyond my drifting boat.

When Phil was alive, I couldn't wait to go home to share my day with him. I never cried. I never needed to because it always felt like someone else was sharing the onus. Standing as one made everything seem like an adventure and an "us versus them" mentality. My home was rooted in the man and in the family we had together.

While we moved many times in 23 years thanks to a military career, it always felt like home whether we lived in Mississippi, Germany, UT, ID, NM, or CO. I truly detest airports now. All I see are the happy reunions of people coming "home". I wanted Phil's homecoming because he was my home spot. I may be a girl with proud Boise State roots, but I am a nomad with no place to call my own. I do not have a home. . .a mooring. I drift.

Part of the home concept is warmth and a sense of security. Building something together. Four walls can keep many a storm out. Being wrapped in Phil's arms sheltered me from the battering rains. If this protective cover was all about a physical connection, then it would be easy to replace. For this girl, my moral compass hasn't changed. A home shelters and protects. A home provides a safe haven. A house is a happy place filled with laughter and shared memories. My home was with Phil wherever he was. As I sit drifting from wave to wave, I long for my home, but all I see are the miles and miles to go before I sleep.

Somebody Said His Name Today

Somebody made my heart fill with tears in a very unexpected way. Many people no longer say Phil's name. I even find myself drawing his name like a tattoo on my heart vs. a spoken bubble. This friend of mine not only spoke his name but gave me the gift of acknowledging not only Phil's heroism, but his life as a wonderful father, husband, and man. Even if I had never married my Phil, I would have wanted him in my life. I am a better person for having known and loved Phil.

God Bless the Broken Road That Led Me Straight To You

While my scars and wounded heart is visible to many people, there are many aching hearts and broken lives. My favorite line in the Catholic mass is "Lord, I am not worthy to receive you, but only say the word and I shall be healed." For many years, I felt that healing meant that the body, soul, and life returned to the state before the affliction, but what then does that mean when a loved one dies or suffers? I won't pretend to know how to repair or allay other people's pain and suffering, but I fall to my faith. I crawl to the cloak of Jesus and I tentatively touch the dusty hem because I know that I am unworthy of being healed, yet the Lord sees what I need, and I am being carried and met on that broken road.

Healing isn't always in the way that I envision healing. In my darkest hour, I cowered under the covers of my bed. I wept from my soul. I was beaten and I was in a dark, dark place. I cried out to the Lord in my despair. I felt so very alone. I am not sure where it came from, but I had a vision of me standing in a church with someone tall. Now I am not saying that Phil is replaceable or that was what I was looking for. Oh, how it was not, but peace flooded my heart. Somehow, some way I knew that my life was not over…that I was destined to continue on. I can't even say that I felt no darkness since then, but I began to honor what I would have wanted for Phil if the unthinkable had happened to me versus him. I would have wanted him to be happy. I know that Phil wanted that for me because he told me so just before he deployed. Healing came in the form of a glimpsed promise.

Healing has also come through the kindness of many, many people. Even if I wanted to, I would not know or remember all of the wonderful things done on behalf of me and my family. I am deeply humbled. I have learned to be a better friend and to reach out because the very act of just standing with someone is all it takes sometimes to help the heart to mend. Sometimes a quick e-mail, card, small token, or just a touch brings joy to my heart. I had become pretty insular prior to Phil's death. I had raised five children. Whatever they didn't take, I gave to Phil. When he deployed, I put my life on hold. This works until the soldier does not come home. People found me and chose me. They chose to be a friend to me when I had nothing, nothing to give. I healed through the love, compassion, and service of others.

Lastly, I have healed through the promises of my faith. In my provincial view, I see only the life I have on earth. I forget that there is life beyond today and tomorrow here. I believe in the ultimate healing of bodies and lives upon communion with the Lord. I do believe even when it hurts so much that I want to die (and there were days) that God's plan for me is much bigger than the plan I have for myself. His vision for me is much broader than I would ever embrace. He is walking with me and he feels the touch to his dusty hem. He reaches down and grabs my hand. He is healing me on the broken road and reminding me that there is so much more…

I Was Wrong. People Can Say the Wrong Thing.

I once wrote that it is better to say the wrong thing than to say nothing at all. Today, I learned that I was dead wrong about that statement. Prying people with no sense of boundaries that do not know me shouldn't be asking for the most intimate details of what happened to my Phil or my experiences IF I am not talking about it. I think a person in authority over me did a mental health screening on me today--very badly. I was the flight chief and the director of both the child development center (CDC) and the Youth Programs. Every year, I got the e-mails about being vigilant for employees under a lot of stress during the holidays. Today, my a person in my chain of command who I have never met or e-mailed except once to tell him I liked my job and to thank him for taking a chance on me, e-mailed me an overly friendly e-mail. He wanted to meet with me, be my friend. Mind you, I have not met him. Mind you that I have been a part of this community since early August when I could have used a friendly face. Mind you that I am on time every day to work, I am good with the kids, I do not cry or talk about my life to students or parents in a detailed manner, I go to church, I run, I do not drink or self medicate, or sleep around, etc.

He's in a position of authority over me. I had plans for running with a marathoning friend after school. She was ready for me, but I can't really say no to this person. He tells me that he wants to spend a few minutes "getting to know me" Instead of talking in the office, he takes me to a small, small office. Remember, he doesn't know me. The first thing he starts asking me is how I found out about Phil. How he was killed. Where. Blah, blah, blah. I don't even talk about those details with my closest friends. I have kept certain details from my children. My own family does not know the details because there is no sense of giving people more details than they can handle. Two people. Two people know all of the details outside of the briefing walls. Those two people were in Afghanistan and we shared details. I do talk about Phil's assassination, but generally. This man kept delving. I tried to change the subject. I change the subject to my classes, running, my children, church. . .nada. I didn't cry. I did have my voice waiver, but the only thing I thought about while I ran is that if he knew me at all, and if this was a poor mental health screening, he would know to be worried if I withdraw. If I stop writing or talking, people should be worried. I don't cry (well, not in 42 years before this). I finally stood up and told him that I was sorry but I had someone to run with me. I told him we could do it again another time. No. . .sorry.

If he decides that mental health evaluation is what I need, I am going to be livid. I mean, who does what he did? No small talk. He doesn't know me. So, I am not crying? Not falling apart? So, I am serving GIs on Thanksgiving and not celebrating the holidays. He doesn't know that I am listening to Christmas music, going to Christmas markets here in Germany, sending Christmas boxes to someone, and I am getting excited to see my kids. He doesn't know one thing about me. Nice.

By the way, he didn't let on that is what he was doing, but what 42 year old says, "I want to be your friend," when he doesn't know me at all?

I'll Be Home for Christmas

Home is a feeling that is buried deep in my heart. As a military wife, we never stayed rooted for very long. We lived all over the world, but all of us knew that no matter where we went we had each other. We knew that home was buried deep within us. Something broke with my family on that dark, dark day in April.

Before Phil's death, we were a close family. Perfect? Heaven's no! Our family always circled the wagons and drew near during hard times. We looked to one another for advice and to share life events. Most of all, we laughed and played together. Phil was the consummate Disneyland parent. He was often gone for months on end which meant that my role was one of consistency, rule enforcement and routine. Phil was the one that brought pizza, laughter, bad movies, paintball wars, the buffoon when we played games, and the one to whom the children ran to in efforts to commiserate against my rigid rules. Someone had to be the voice of reason. Sigh. That was me.

It wasn't as if my children didn't like me. They love me, but could it be that my pain, or their pain, has put a canyon between us? Could it be that we stand on distant shores calling and appearing strong for the other so as not to maim anymore? Phil and I trained our children to be strong and resilient, independent and unemotional. Maybe the pain of the loss of the fun parent is better masked from a distance that includes emotional distance?

I am not sure, but it is strange, ever so strange. Close family members and close friends have maybe minimally contacted me since Phil's funeral. This abandonment surprised me so much at first. I couldn't understand why I was no longer worthy of friendships or family relationships after Phil's death, but is it possible that they didn't know what to say, thus they said nothing. Now that I am working on eight months with Phil gone, I have established and forged deep friendships with people I barely knew or did not know at all when Phil was killed. Often these friends just told me that they were praying, but many times they listened and made me laugh. They did not expect me to be a bundle of laughs, and they forgave me for by broken selfishness as all I could do was take and take some more.

I am hoping that this trip to Hawaii helps this family forge new ties and that it helps us move on. Traditions will be different. The holidays will always feel like somebody is missing because how my Phil loved

Christmas. He didn't grow up celebrating Christmas. Phil was like a little boy (and just as noisy and out of control) Christmas week. I don't know what the Ambard/Short family will fall into as far as the holidays go, but I hope, how I hope, that we can find solid ground to stand on. I hope we can find our way back to being a family. I will be home for Christmas because I will be with my five children, one bonus daughter-in-law, and the hope of this family's future--a grandbaby.

Today Fox News Got It Wrong

Thanks to Fox News, I am feeling really weak and vulnerable today. Nine months gone, but never forgotten, always loved. April 27, 2011 is a day that makes for a sensational media story even when the media only knows part of the story, but for the nine of us that lost our loved ones, this is our reality and our lives. The bleeding hearts are the other consideration in responsible reporting. My Phil's life is not a political agenda or a interesting story to titillate. Fox News really did the story of that day wrong in order to titillate the public. The reporter went looking for sources willing to talk. She found one source, one source. That one source was not intimately involved in the shooting. The people that were there and living through the hell of either losing their lives or being a comrade who saw more loss in one day than ever seen since the Kobart Towers, are not talking about what they saw.

Want to know why? Our reality is much worse than spouting downright lies about a man not worthy of our time. To insinuate that every person felt that he was a walking time bomb and that he had a mission to kill Americans is not only erroneous, but irresponsible. The man could speak enough English. He and my husband (who was a gifted linguist) spoke often. By saying that every soldier saw the signs makes this girl really cranky. Doesn't a person think that if even a few people felt that way that someone wouldn't have said something? Let's be real. If the soldiers felt that way, they certainly wouldn't have been in Code Amber (medium safety measures). Their guns would have been clipped and ready to shoot. There would have been awareness and a sense of hyper vigilance in an area that this man had his office. This assassin was trusted. He had rank and he had a reason to be in the building. Maybe there was collusion. Maybe there is a tie to the Taliban, but neither of those events can be proven and maybe even if they were, we would never know. Politics seem to be the nature of the game.

This shoddy reporter sought to gain interest, but if she had any source that had been closely involved, the facts and the aftermath would have been so horrific that I hope even she would have had some decency. This haphazard approach did aim an arrow straight at the hearts of the people involved. I had purposefully withheld information from family members knowing that the truth was too much. I am now in the terrible position of juggling the lies with the truth as I have been told. Family members may not want to hear the truth and they may need to compartmentalize and move on. This nitwit has reopened many wounds and created a division. I can't fix the pain she inflicted on people close to me. The other issue I have is that Fox News did interview my children and I just after Phil was killed. We were willing to talk. I would have been willing to talk yet again if given the chance. I wouldn't have been talking fairy tales or politics, however. I would have spoken of my military family.

I suppose that my feelings about the military family that has carried me through these nine months is not an interest grabbing story, but it is the story of military families everywhere. We come together in times of loss and hurt. We pull together and bond in a manner that brings us in tighter than the families that we are born into. We understand all too well that being in the military means missed family events, long periods of separation, multiple moves, and it means that we, or someone close to us, might be touched by the realities of war whether it be death at the hands of a vile monster, a loss of a comrade, PTSD, a failed relationship due to the rigors of long separations and emotional weariness from having seen too much, or the loss of limb(s). We have seen too much. I would have talked about that. Sadly, this so called reporter missed a much better story—a true story, not a fairy tale.

"Let us therefore come boldly to the throne of grace, that we may obtain mercy and find grace to help in time of need." (Heb 4: 16).

Forgiveness and the Unexpected Gift

As I walk this Lenten season and finish my blogging journey, I am working on forgiveness. I never once imagined that in forgiving and reaching out, I would receive the best gift of all. I received the gift of a friendship restored. Forgiveness sometimes illuminates a misunderstanding or a notion that is so wrong that a person is left gasping at the time lost. Today, I see the hand of God working to restore a relationship that was never truly broken.

My friend withdrew because she didn't know what to say. She is Muslim. She thought that I would hate her because a Muslim killed my Phil. I was stunned. How could that be so? I love my friend. I never once stopped loving her. I look at her and li see only her goodness and her soft heart. She is a woman who would give to a person so that they might not have need. She is a person who will cry and rail against the injustices in my life, yet not her own. In short, she was often a better friend to me than I was to her. She made me a better person because she was my friend. I never thought that her pain and anger at the assassin would lead her to withdraw from our friendship. I never thought that she would withdraw to save me more pain.

While I do struggle with the most extreme Muslims, I have friends that are Muslim. They love me. I love them and I see them as people. I don't see them as terrorists. They eat with me, know my family, and they are good people. I am better because they are in my life. I would be remiss; however, if I didn't acknowledge that I do feel fear and trepidatation in certain countries and situations. I feel anger at a society that can call for violence and death because their holy book was burned. While I would not like my Bible being burned, I would not see to exact revenge through death and violence. I cannot understand the extremism and fanaticism that compels a person to do unthinkable acts in the name of God.

Jesus did not call us to violence. He called us to love. He showed us love by forgiving and healing the most corrupt, the most depraved, and the most unworthy. He forgave me all of those things. He was willing to die for me. He suffered a brutal death for me. He forgave his killers even then. Maybe in forgiveness, my faith can shine the beacon of light and hope. Maybe in forgiveness, extremism and fanaticism can be negated. I know that in forgiving and reaching out, I found a friendship that lay dormant because of misunderstanding. I have been blessed with a remarkable person in my life that I am proud to call friend.

Karzai Should Have What he Wants

I promise. . .this girl is going to shut up today, but Karzai saying that no way it was one man? Really? Can I start hysterically laughing? This is rich from a corrupt man. There is no way one person could have perpetuated the crimes against our nine in a building with many rooms and in a room that had more Afghans than Americans. It is amazing that none of the Afghans were really injured other than by ricochet bullets and that they all got out alive. MSN prints this about Karzai. WE apologize as a nation, yet where is the apology for my husband and the other soldiers killed on a routine basis over there? Where is our truth? Where is our apology for the corruption and the integrity to be straight with us? That is just this girl's opinion. I still want to know where the one, the ONE Afghan was that was willing to stand up for any of our men and women that day. ONE! My soldier would have stood up for any of their Afghan comrades, and so would any of the other eight massacred in that room. It is time to do what Karzai is asking for. Let us get the hell out and take every one of our resources with us. Let us stop catering and placating to corrupt people who do not value the lives of the American soldier.

I Cannot Rejoice in Retaliation Killings

I have been working on forgiveness in my life this Lenten season. It is easier to say the words than it is to practice in reality. Some of my attempts have been rebuffed and mocked, but some of my attempts have led to a relationship restoration. The hardest part of this process is letting go of my anger at the Afghan military, Phil's assassin, and in some ways, our own government. I do not believe in exacting vengeance or the eye for an eye mentality. I just don't. Violence begets violence. When is it going to end?

Today, I read about how the Afghan president was calling one of our American's an assassin and saying that it was unforgiveable. I thought to me, "That's rich. Coming from a man who knows about the corruption and who is probably corrupt him. Rich in that we have lost more soldiers to their assassins than they have to ours." I caught myself while I was running. What separates me from the terrorists if I keep wanting a violent retribution? What makes me stand apart as a woman of faith if I want annihilation? I struggle with the concept of forgiveness.

Phil was in Afghanistan as a trainer and an advisor. He told many people how much he believed in what he was doing. He trusted his assassin, ate with his assassin, and had a friendly allegiance with his assassin. When an American betrays the trust and confidence of an already distrustful nation by killing innocent people, that American is no matter than the assassin who killed my Phil. Killing innocent people is wrong. It will always be wrong. I need to stop making it about Americans versus the Afghanis. I need to keep my eyes focused on a life that transcends the one that I have here and let God do the judging. I am not so good at that.

I want to see vengeance. I want to see hurt. I want to see someone hurting as much as I hurt, yet as a Christian, I should want people to see my light of faith shining through the maelstrom of a loss so great that words cannot describe the brokenness and devastation of 27 April. I should embrace the opportunity for people to come to a personal relationship with the Lord as they watch me fall to my faith. Sadly, I fall short so often. I struggle. I want to be better and I want my forgiveness to be more than words. The killing fields need to end somewhere. An eye for an eye is not going to change the violence or trust on any level—American or Afghan. I may not ever get to full forgiveness in this life, but I am going to practice it and work towards it because then maybe Phil's death will not have been in vain.

When Did I Become That Girl?

When did I become that girl? Could it be that I have always been that girl and I never knew it? Even with an ocean, a military branch difference, and a situational shift, somebody recognized me today. I was in charge of the shot-put. I wore wearing six layers of clothes and I looked like a roly poly. I was checking people in and I was too busy to notice the adults hovering in the shadows, but at some point, I realized that one couple kept walking by me and whispering. Still, I didn't get it until I heard, "I think that is her." I made eye contact and the man apologized and said, "You look so familiar. Were you stationed in Colorado?' That question was followed up by, "Were you on TV?"

Without identification of any kind (words, pictures, etc), these two who had just glimpsed a small snapshot of me in my most broken state remembered the girl hugging the casket totally broken. They did not know me, but one year later, they remember the indelible pictures. For them, they remember how the story consumed Colorado news. For me, I remember nothing of how I reacted other than falling to my knees and keening when I saw the military team. I would wake up crying and not know what triggered the visceral reaction. I never once thought that my pain was so deep that people would remember that girl. I still don't know what pictures were published and what the televisions played. I just attempted to walk with grace, dignity, and faith.

I don't know if I was successful at letting my light shine. I am not perfect--far from it, but I chose in the first minute that my faith was going to be front row and center even if I got angry or if I totally lost everything. Phil's and my marriage wasn't perfect, but it was a good partnership and coupling because we like each other more with each passing year and we were deeply loyal and committed to the other person. We rarely fought and we enjoyed the other's company to the point that we shut people out. My grief and loss is playing out in the most public manner possible, but here is the truth. I truly am not putting on a facade or faking the faith I fall to. Sometimes, that faith is all I have--the confidence in things unseen.

I ran away to Germany to get away from the spotlight of Phil's beacon. While people know my story, and while I talk about my story, and while I write about my story, it is different. People know me as Linda--not as Linda, a part of a team. They do not refer to me as 'that girl" in terms of pity. They may feel bad for me, but they see my light faintly faltering, but still it is mine. They see my value independent of Phil. While my life will never have the impact or brightness Phil's had, I am content to be the girl rocking pink polka dots. I just need to be more that "that girl". I need to be Sasha. Sasha, the fierce, the girl who is resilient, strong, and the girl who can laugh at her own life. I cannot control the events that took my Phil, but I can embrace the life that I have been given and I can leap with confidence into life.

Or if I totally lost everything. Phil's and my marriage wasn't perfect, but it was a good partnership and coupling because we liked each other more with each passing year and we were deeply loyal and committed to the other person. We rarely fought and we enjoyed the other's company to the point that we shut people out. My grief and loss is playing out in the most public manner possible, but here is the truth. I truly am not putting on a facade or faking the faith I fall to. Sometimes, that faith is all I have--the confidence in things unseen.

Broken Trust

Trust is one of the traits that I value the most in a person. I am, or at least I was, the Pollyanna who tends to believe people at face value. I am a positive person sees potential and promise in every person--or at least I was until Phil was killed. His assassination may have irrevocably changed me, but it was the first person I took baby steps forward with who obliterated the way I feel about trusting someone in a relationship. Both issues of trust are closely twined.

If Phil could have thought that his assassin was trustworthy enough to practice his language skills with, share food with, and talk about his family with, then how could I be confident in my ability to read people? The assassin knew Phil, yet he looked at him and shot him so many times that there is no doubt that sheer hatred and lack of a human heart compelled him. My Phil not only had time to realize who his assassin was, but he had time to feel fear and pain. That is the singular facet that haunts me more than any other part of this unthinkable atrocity.

I didn't think that I could trust a person implicitly again because I have problems not second guessing myself or my perceptions now, but I had become friends with this guy and then started to step forward with really small steps. We were in a distance relationship that did not include any physical touch at this point, but I realized that I fully trusted him around Valentine's Day. I believed the words he uttered and wrote just like Phil believed his assassin. Without getting too specific, fidelity is both physical and mental. While I was not assassinated, my bleeding heart had its scars laid bare.

Are my trust issues a forever problem? I do not know. Between Phil's death, losing family and friend relationships because people could not handle the death, and this guy deeply wounding me with his sins of omission, my trust meter is pegged, battered, and broken. I would give so much to have the girl I once knew back. I liked her rosy outlook in life. I liked her quiet confidence and faith in people. Can I have a do-over and have her back?

I Need My Grandma Today

My Grandma Rocky (Vavrosky) has been gone for many years, but today I missed her. I missed sitting down, playing cards, eating cookies, drinking coffee, and visiting with her. Grandma taught me by the way she lived her life. She was strong, filled with faith, and she always took time to talk to me. Today, I needed her advice and encouragement as I step forward. With my grandma, I always felt that she had my best interests in her heart and that her faith would give her insights that I need. I need her now...today. I need her to be my mooring as I step into the light of day while I yet battle the raging seas around me.

When Phil and I met, he was barely 21. I was about to turn 27. I had three young children ages 3, 4, and 5. My family had a hard time with my divorce because I was the first one to get a divorce. I started dating Phil the weekend my divorce was final. I cringed every time I thought about the timing. When I introduced Phil to my grandmother about one and a half months into dating, my grandma was charmed. Phil flirted outrageously with her, talked soap operas with her, played the buffoon when he played cards, and he answered all of her deep probing questions. I had no idea where my relationship was going, but the two of them hashed it out while I was out running. When I got back from running, Phil left with my grandfather. My grandmother sat down with me and told me what a special young man "that" Phil was. She also said something that stuck with me. She told me that while the timing may not seem right, God knew what he was doing.

I need my grandma today. I need her wisdom and her encouragement. I am starting to slowly take some steps forward. I just feel too broken at times to have much to give. I second guess myself. As I have grown older, I have become even more cautious. I talk myself out of feelings and actions because of fear. My Grandma Rocky was strong. She married later in life and had children at what was considered an old age. She was a teacher that continued to teach after marriage for a number of years. When she left teaching, she and my grandfather ran a grocery store. She lived her faith. While she would not always agree with my actions or words, she loved me enough to forgive me, offer advice, and to walk with me in the hard times. I need the cards, the coffee, the cookies, and her.

I need for her to tell me that God's timing is not our own. I need for her to pray with me as I step forward. I need her to check out the man that I am taking small steps forward with (there is an ocean between us). Mostly, I need her to be my prayer warrior. I need to be able to talk to her about my life and my loss. My doubts and insecurities. My failings. I need her to pray with me and to ease my fear. I need her steady love and gentle spirit to walk with me through the dark days and the days of hope. These days seem so enmeshed right now. I have never missed my grandmother more than I do today. I have never needed her more than I do now. I hope that she, my grandfather, Phil, our dog Bailey, and our unborn baby are sitting in rocking chairs in heaven looking down and sprinkling blessings on me today. I hope that I do not disappoint the people who loved me most of all.

What I Want My Children to Know

I have been a mother since I was 21. I fell into that role naturally and I was proud of being a mom to Patrick, Josh, Emily, Alex, and Tiger. I was a bit of a tiger mom in that my life revolved around my children and their activities. On the day that we decided to elope, I gave Phil and option that few know about. I offered to let him get out of the military to go to school while I went into the military and attended medical school (I was hours away from signing my papers), but he was old fashioned. I never regretted it. . .still don't. My children grew up with a mom who pushed them and who rarely showed any type of weakness or emotional bleeding (tears, yelling, etc). It wasn't that I was perfect, but I had this thought of how I wanted my kids to look at me--strong, unbreakable, competent, and loving. When the bottom fell out of my life on 27 April 2011, my children saw a very different mom--a broken and scared mom. A lost mom and a mom facing things I never thought I would be facing at my age.

My children saw me too broken to remember anything when Phil died. My daughter stepped up and handled all of the many logistics of the funeral. I sobbed noisily and publicly on an airplane which still embarrasses me. They saw me speak to the media which for a very private family, this was a lot to handle for some of them. They have watched me write and fall into my faith, but they are also watching me begin to date. None of this is easy or wanted on any level, but if I had some wishes for what my adult children could learn from my walk of faith this year, it would be that faith matters. Love is second, and that life is short so pursue what matters.

Faith is what has sustained me in my darkest hours. If I didn't have faith of a life beyond this life, I would have quit living in April. I do not know how to be anyone except Phil Ambard's wife and mom to my five children. Faith to me isn't just words. It is a commitment to things unseen even when I do not understand and even when I will never understand why my Phil. It is a commitment to keep picking myself up no matter how broken my life seems. It is a quiet confidence that somehow all these events are working together somehow and that my God hears my broken plea.

I had two choices that day as I heard the words that forever altered my life--to fall into my faith or to fall out of my faith. I decided within the first minute to fall into my faith and to trust in God's mercies and grace. While my walk has not been easy and while my heart has been broken, I believe and I reach to my faith. It has made all of the difference in the world.

The second lesson I wish I could impart to my children is that love is worth taking a chance on even if on paper that love does not make sense. Phil and I did not make sense on paper. I was five years, nine months older than he was. I had three children by a previous marriage. I was college educated and working towards going to medical school. He was an airman first class who did not have faith. He had barely graduated from high school, but underneath it all there was a steely will. I saw that. I saw his need and he saw my brokenness. We both valued family and he quickly adopted the role of dad--and within a short time became the only dad any of our children had. He found faith and he was deeply committed to me, the children, to his career, and to God. We both created the family we wish we had and it worked. He showed up and was not only a father I stand in awe of (even if he was a Disneyland parent), but he was a husband who put his needs last to make sure that the rest of us got what we needed. I respected Phil. I respected that he always stood up for us and that he was willing to give up anything to keep us. He gave up his parents and he stood up to my family for me. He put his needs and wants last always because he was deeply committed to all of us.

Our children didn't see the tears we wept for them. They never realized the normal hurts inflicted from child to parent wounded us. They never saw the unified front that Phil and I presented behind their backs to advocate for the good of them. As a family, we did all that we could together. We liked spending time together. Phil and I stood together even when we didn't agree. We made a team and that team was built on love, respect, and flexibility.

As I began to step forward by letting another man in, this man deeply hurt me on Phil's birthday by unexpectedly dumping me to return to an old girlfriend. I am trying to walk this path of dating with grace. My children have never seen their mom as a single person. Here is what they are going to see. My moral compass hasn't changed. I am still not settling. If I never find the fairy tale again, my children are going to see a mom that makes good choices and who respects herself enough to pick up the pieces. My children are going to see that their dad will always matter to me and that if I do find love again, it will be between the holes of my heart. They will see me having faith in my relationships. God has to be a part of any relationship because times do get tough, but faith is an unbreakable tie. Am I sorry that I took a chance? No, my children will see that I was willing to take a risk and to put myself out there which is harder to do at 50 than it was at 17.

I would also tell my children that life is too short to dwell on past mistakes or what ifs. I can only walk the path that God has put in front of me. Do I sometimes feel regret? Yes, but I do know that the life I lived with Phil was worth every day of those 23 years. I wish it had been longer, but now, I am looking to see where God wants me now. I am going to go back to school and shift into the realm of family counseling and grief management. While I still may teach, I see where the Holy Spirit is leading me. I will take the leap of faith and I will keep my eyes focused forward. While I am still uncomfortable in the limelight, I see a bigger purpose outside of me. I may put a face on military loss, but the picture is everyone walking this walk. We all are living a life that few can understand. By speaking, people are seeing. . .

My children are seeing a human mom. . .a mom who cries and a mom who is lonely. My children are seeing a stronger more independent mom-- a mom that can move half way across the world. They are seeing a much more public mom and a mom with a very active social network. It is not new to them, but it is new to me. My children have become adults and they have become peers in many ways. Yes, I am still the tiger mom, but I see their strength and goodness, too. I am blessed and learning from Patrick, Josh, Emily, Alex, and Tim through our walk.

Being a Mom Is All I Ever Aspired to Be

There is something so special and sublime about a mother's relationship with her children when they are young. Even as the children are beating on the bathroom door and there is nowhere to hide, children innately reach out for their mothers. They run to them when they have a skinned knee or a hurt heart. A kiss to make the boo boo better is the standard. As children grow, they race home to talk to mom about friendship issues, opposite sex questions, and to share the joys and disappointments they contain far from their peers eyes. Having a team with a spouse that feels the same way I did, made a huge difference.

Phil did not grow up with the kind of mother he loved that I was. I think that he feel in love with me the first time he watched three wet bathing suit clad children curled up next to me or in my lap as I read to them. Arms were flung around my neck or my arm was clutched. He would sit or lie next to us and just soak it all in. He loved nothing better than those hours and moments. Even after we had five children, Phil would lie next to us so that he wouldn't miss out.

Because Phil valued the mother that I was/am, he supported me no matter what I did. We opted for me to stay at home when the children were under six. Eating rice and beans almost every day was revolting, but we had each other. It was always the Ambard/Short family against everyone else. We knew we were a force to be reckoned with. We knew that we were better as a united team. Our team stood so strong and so successful that many people stood in awe. While I have always said that good families can have children that make bad mistakes, our five children stood together as a pillar of a family united by faith. When it felt like the whole world thought of us as trailer court trash, our five children had two parents investing everything they had into the lives of their children. We were the coaches, the scout leaders, the room leaders, the ones outside playing with our children, the church going family, and we were the mean parents. WE were parents when it wasn't easy and when it wasn't fun.

I once had a relative ask me why my routine for bedtime couldn't change while we were visiting. I couldn't change the routine because there were so many of them. Five children is a lot. Early on, I was often a single parent as Phil deployed time and time again first for the drug wars and then to southern France. All five children would be up before six no matter what time I put them to bed, so I discovered that reading to them for 1.5 or more hours every night not only gave us "lovie time" where we cuddled, laughed, and just enjoyed each other, it gave me at least a few minutes that were just mine. Any parent with children understands just how precious that time can be.

Phil was the parent that when he was home, he would walk in the door as I literally ran out the door. He never complained that he worked all day and then came home to showers, homework if it wasn't done, dinner. He never complained when our scant resources funded my running shoes--a very expensive proposition indeed. He encouraged me to run and he supported my dream when the children had all left the house. It was he who suggested that I run a marathon in all fifty states as a way to save my desire to run across the country (my version of running far, far away). It was he who suggested that I continue on should something happened to him. Because of this support from day one, running was a gift that I felt he kept giving me. By giving me running, I was a better mother--a more patient mother.

Neither of us believed in physical punishment. Were we perfect parents? Heavens, no, but together our team was so strong that people constantly expressed awe. I didn't see that in myself. I beat myself up every night over the small things I had done wrong. With so many children, I did always let someone down, but I loved those babies more than life itself. I became a mom at 21. I was a collegiate runner in a bad marriage who was on the pill. When I found out that I was pregnant, it was only my faith beliefs that kept me from hurting my baby. When Patrick was born and I looked at that remarkable boy that was mine, I knew that I finally found my calling--that of being a mother. I am proudest of that role. It defines me and it is a role that I embrace at school. I am not the students' mom, but I nurture and look for ways to let the students know that I believe in them. I do not want one of them to feel like nobody cares--I do.

I was a strict parent asking my children to try their best to be the people God was calling them to be. I pushed my children and submitted them to multiple activities in which they could find a niche or a sense of belonging. I was never tolerant of missed assignments, disrespect, bullying, lack of effort, or poor attitudes. I demanded that they behaved a certain way, so then what did Phil and I use for punishment? First we were consistent. Although our children would tell you that dad was the Disneyland dad, he was the chauffer, the fun parent, and he was the slave driver in school. Discipline changed with the age of our children.

Tiger, the youngest, was a little human fireball. He couldn't wait to outdo his siblings, thus he potty trained himself at 18 months to get his brother's Barney underwear. He learned to read and ride a bike by the age of 3 and 4 respectfully so that he could beat his brother, yet he was a pincher. He would look at Alex with this huge grin on his face and pinch Alex's face as hard as he could. Alex would be screaming, "No, baby, NO!" but Tiger would grin away and pinch some more. I would send Tiger to his room for the requisite three minute time out (one minute per year) and when he would come out of the bedroom, he would scream, "Sorry. I said, Sorry!" He would then pinch again immediately. Did he mean his apology? No, thus I began to require something to show the apology--a picture, doing his brother's job, giving a compliment. Often times the time out was bigger than the minutes, but the action helped mend the fixes. That was my parenting style and the parenting style that Phil fell into when he married me. We kept this style until the day the children left home. As they aged, the actions became deeper--quitting the swim team after misbehaving, writing to the base commander, talking to a teacher, etc. Every one of my five children knows how to apologize in a meaningful manner.

I also restricted my children TV, computers, Facebook, roaming, etc. Phil and I set standards in terms of how much TV or computer time they could have per day. It amounted to something like 45 minutes a day when they were preschoolers and then 30 minutes per day when they were school age. Weekends and holidays they could watch a movie. Phil and I took the kids on picnics, walks, to the park, and we played games with them. WE tried to make everything an adventure that we did together. I read the Little House on the Prairie series when the youngest two were in second grade. On our way across the country when we moved from Germany, we traveled to De Smet, SD to see the homestead. I read the Diary of Anne Frank to all of my children and then I took them to Anne Frank's house in Amsterdam. That is what kind of parents Phil and I were. We invested in our children, not the new cars, expensive jewelry, eating out, etc. We wanted to spend time with our children and each other. It made a difference when times were tough with any of them.

They weren't always easy children. Sometimes I thought I would go crazy, but then the little arm would grab me and say, "I love you, mama." Sigh. Josh gave me more gray hair than anyone. I grounded him to his room until he had an attitude adjustment. He was so angry because he had nothing but a bed in his room. I served him a peanut butter and jelly sandwich, an apple, and a box of milk for dinner. He screamed at me that it was child abuse. I picked up the phone and dialed child protective services and made him ask if it was abuse. When they got done laughing, he never did that again. Josh was also my boy that told me every night until he left home how much he loved me.

As the children grew, Phil always felt like they didn't need him as a father. Quite the opposite. Parents have less control of the choices their children make when they leave home. He worried so much for all of them. He mentored them and was so much fun when they came home. He genuinely liked them as adults. Since he didn't experience this with his parents, he thought that it meant that our children were tied to the apron strings, yet that is what he wanted. He was as bad as the kids were at Christmas. He loved it and was the nosiest most obnoxious one of them all. He dreamt of the day that he would commission our youngest (May 2013) and the day he walked our daughter down the aisle. He loved how I was as a mother so much that he reminded the children all of the time to remember mother's day and to treat me well. I miss that. I miss knowing that Sunday would be a day where he honored me just as much as the children honored me. In fact, when his things came back, the mother's day card that he never got to send was in there. I still haven't read it. . .maybe this week.

I loved being a part of the parenting team. I miss the family we had. I am hoping that all of us can get some of the closeness back when my grandbaby is born any time now. I am thankful for a man that let me use my education, passion, and heart for children to lead him. Phil Ambard became better than the teacher. He was a wonderful parent, friend, and spouse. He will forever leave holes in my life as a parent, grandparent, and woman.

A Grandson Who Came at Just the Right Time

Dear precious baby Philip Tristan,

Welcome to our world, my precious grandson. You do not know it yet, but you have brought so much happiness and hope to our family. It is interesting that your birth coincides with a holiday that will be forever linked to a hero, a grandfather you will never know except through the stories we will share with you. You share his name, and, oh, how proud he would have been to hold you in his arms. Make no mistake, you will not be inundated with spoken memories and shrines, rather, you will know your grandfather in the way your father raises you. You will know whispers of your grandfather in the ways your grandma and aunts and uncles love you.

You see, Philip Tristan, I have a feeling that you will hear the family motto over and over again. Your dad coined it and used it since Uncle Patrick was almost six: "Don't quit. Don't fail. Don't get anyone pregnant." I know. What five year old needs to know those words, but it worked. Many times your dad wanted to give up, but Philip, your grandpa pushed him. He wanted him to be the man God was calling him to be. He wanted your dad to find love before he gave love, and he didn't want your dad to struggle the way we did early on in our marriage. If you try your hardest and if you don't quit on people or pursuits, you will be successful and you will know happiness.

You see, Philip, your dad was taught that One must never take for granted the freedoms and opportunities given to him by virtue of being an American citizen or through family circumstance. Your father was raised to work hard. He could get a b only if he had no missing assignments and if he had gone in for help. If he missed the bus, why, he better start running because there were no rides because one was too lazy to get out of bed on time. I have a feeling that your dad will adopt the AIS rule. You will have to ask him about that rules as you watch the family car drive off as you run down the street carrying your shoes.

Your father was raised by a man who noticed the invisible people. Your grandfather had a knack not only for foreign languages, but for making connections to people that other people did not notice. Your grandfather could speak ten languages fluently--English was his third language and he spoke it flawlessly. He spoke to others struggling with language or intellectual or status deficiencies. He knew people's names and what kind of food they liked. He spoke to them all of the time and made them feel important and like they mattered. He mentored so many people on the freedoms and opportunities he received when he joined the Air Force for American citizenship. He would be passing that torch on to you, but he would tell you that if the military wasn't for you, to find another way to give back. Your grandpa was a coach, a Red Cross volunteer, a Boy Scout leader, a homeless shelter volunteer, and a church volunteer.

As far as love goes, Baby Philip, your grandpa would make jokes about running away from love, but do you know what that man did? Do not throw up, it is pretty amazing. Your grandpa met your grandma at the Mountain Home AFB swimming pool. Your grandma wanted nothing to do with the young airmen who came in to the pool in a yucky blue hammock swimming suit (ask your dad about that). Your grandma thought he was flirting with all of the women at the pool, so I said no to every offer of a date more than 20 times. Your grandpa, a man who was barely 21, persisted. He volunteered to help coach Special Olympics with grandma. Before four months had past, my answer became yes to the date. Four months later, he asked me to elope to Nevada

With him. We had no money and your grandpa lost his relationship with his parents over us eloping, but he chose me and your dad, Uncle Patrick, and Aunt Emily. He pairs everything into his family-time, money, talent, and his youth. He was a wonderful father and he would have been a wonderful grandpa. He always said that he chose well and that he would want you to do the same.

He had faith, Philip. He would have told you about his faith, but more than that, you would have seen it when you spend time with him. You would have known that you mattered to your grandpa. Your grandpa would have spoiled you rotten, made you laugh, but he would have shown you a steely resolve about the things that matter in life: God, family, country. . .He would have kissed on you until you smelled like spit. He would have bought ice cream for you minutes before lunch. He probably would have broken a few of your mom's and dad's rules, but make no mistake, that family motto encompasses it all and you would have heard it from him, your grandma, your aunt and uncles, and even the media.

Philip, be your own person, but know that you will be that person because of the wonderful grandpa that loved your dad well. Remember, the big blue van will leave you if you are not in the car on time. Remember, too, don't quit, don't fail, and, don't get anyone pregnant. Look for the invisible people and remember that someone always has it worse than you. Honor the freedoms given to you by either serving your country or volunteering. Vote. It is your civic duty. Lastly, on your birthday, a day that will fall on Memorial Day on in awhile, to remember the grandpa who was willing to stand up to world bullies, who was willing to give up all for love, and a fun grandpa who would have broken rules about the small things, but who would have showed you faith. Remember, grandpa put his love for family, God, and country before himself. He knew what was important.

You are important and you will know your grandpa through the people in your life. Your grandpa left big footprints all over the world, but Philip, the biggest footprint of all is that he loved your dad, me, your aunt and uncles, your mom, and he loved you. He knew that you would come. Grandma Sasha's arms are waiting.

Death, the Aftermath and Practicalities

How it all started:

My heart is broken. I lost my best friend and husband of over 23 years today. He paid the ultimate cost so that all might live free.

The Theories Run Rampant

With military death, and in the situation of how Phil was assassinated, there are no Americans alive that can tell the events as they unfolded that day. Though the Afghans outnumbered the Americans in that room, no Afghans in that room were killed and their injuries were very minor. Their injuries consisted of ricochet wounds and one broken leg, yet none of them choose to speak of that day and the events that unfolded. Rather they all fled. I have heard so many theories and stories about the events of that day that I have begun to call them versions of a fairy tale. If I hear the term "speculation" one more time, I may physical react. THAT IS NOT HELPFUL.

Asking for Help Is Not Easy For this Girl

I have never been good at asking for help. It is a character flaw that I have long held. As a lone ranger, I have often been in a position where I have so many balls up in the air, the people stand agape at what I am able to do. It isn't that I ever want recognition or that I do not trust people, I can't even explain it other than to say that I feel like a failure or that I have failed in something if I ask for help. It is not a healthy way to be. I know that I derive pleasure from helping people, so why is it that I have such a hard time letting people help me? Speaking up and letting people know what I need? That I see asking for help as weakness in myself, yet when others ask, I am so thankful and I feel so good that they trusted me enough to ask me for assistance?

Recently, I have had to ask for help to make this move to Germany happen in record time. It is humbling to see people who are in positions that I stand in awe of stepping up to help me. It is daunting to have my new boss in Germany make a simple statement, "As you can imagine your move has the attention of some higher ranking officials." As a military spouse for 23 years, I would never, ever considered asking people in a position of power for help. Things are just not done this way, but in my time of loss, I am truly appreciative for the help and support that I am receiving from these levels. It calls me to continue on this journey of standing with grace, humility, and military decorum. It calls me to remember that we all need help. We all need to ask for help at times. We all need to recognize the efforts that people make on our behalf.

So many people have helped me and stood with me through my darkest hours. Many people have done what they could. I have had people bring me meals, who have sat with me, made ribbons for the funeral, got me appointments that I couldn't get myself, given me rides, and the list goes on and on. It does not take rank to step to the plate. It takes action and a willing heart to see what a person might need even if they are like me and they are not asking. I have discovered that it really doesn't matter what a person's rank or job is, it is the willingness to step up and help that matters. While I will never abuse the help of my friends, I am thankful that they are offering it willingly now.

I hope that I can continue to be the person I need to be. One of the aspects about being on everyone's radar, is that I want to be the girl that I am called to be. I want people to look at me and see my life defined by how I carry myself and who I am when nobody is watching. I want to live out loud and to make a splash in the lives of others. I do not have many talents, but it is interesting to see my passions and talents colliding in the way of writing and running. While I never would have chosen to live so publicly, I am standing in awe of how God is working through the ashes of my life to reach others and to help me. I am standing as an active spectator in a life I never imagined. It is a wild ride, but I stand poised to answer the call and to walk with the people who are walking with me. I will reach my hand out to my brother walking with me, but I will also take the hand of help and love that is carrying me now. Thank you for walking with me...for carrying me...for believing in me.

Lessons Learned Along the Way

The Music by Casting Crowns (Always) today spoke to me today. I may be broken, but through my faith I have hope and faith in a future where there will be something more than the broken girl who stares back in the mirror. I already see glimmers of promise arising from the ashes. My life is marching on at the speed of light and the lessons that I am learning on being a better friend, asking for help, faith in the hard times, and relying on my own judgment have been invaluable.

Prior to the events that took my Phil on 27 April, I was pretty insular. I prided myself (without thinking about it) on being a lone ranger and in being content with myself. While those tenets will always be a part of my personality, I have come to realize how much I missed through fifty years of not reaching out. I could render help, but by not opening myself up, I was not a friend that people turned to. I perfected a facade that didn't show weakness or need. Because I hid behind that mask, I lived a pretty lonely life in terms of being enriched by friendships.

Through my need and through my darkness, I have realized two things. First, many people have reached out to me even though I am not the friend or person that I should be. I often fall short, but I have had people do simple and elaborate acts of kindness for my family. I had people bring toilet paper and tissues for the initial onslaught of visitors. I had people make phone calls and return Phil's things on my behalf. I have had people call and battle the airlines for me. People have run errands, and they have brought me meals or taken me out for meals. I have had people take Phil's clothing to make it into memory blankets and I have had people stay up with me all night on line during some of my darkest moment.

Many people could have, or perhaps should have, showed up and helped, but people that I didn't know well or at all, stood up and acted. Those actions have meant all. Those actions have deeply humbled and touched this broken girl. Other people who we knew well and for lengthy amounts of time haven't shown up or called or e-mailed. Perhaps they are afraid of saying or doing the wrong thing. In situations like this, there is no wrong thing. The effort and reaching out is tantamount to a lifeline. Many nights I have been drowning, but a kind message has pulled me from the crashing waves that are threatening to consume me. A simple message, a card, a phone call, a lunch, or even a touch on the arm went a long way. It gave me a connection when all felt lost.

The second aspect of people reaching out is that it taught me to see the pain in others and to reach out to their pain. By being a lifeline and seeing the pain of others, I am healing. My biggest surprise was in discovering that when I was able to stand strong for another person, I was healing and becoming stronger. I felt better when I wasn't in my own black pit. I may not have the capacity for large magnanimous acts of kindness yet, but I can listen and walk with another person. I can be a friend and I choose to be a friend.

I have been blessed by the burgeoning friendships that mean all to me now. Some of these friendships have emerged from relationships with people I didn't even know prior to Phil's death. I had a group of women who have adopted me and made me feel loved and cared about through all of this. They threw me a wonderful 50th birthday party and they have run so many errands for me that the words thank you are simply not enough. I have learned that deep committed friendships are not necessarily the people that have been in my life the longest. Some of those people have chosen to leave me life. Perhaps my loss makes loss to real for them. Maybe they are afraid of loss in their own lives. By withdrawing, I don't think that these people realize it is yet another loss for me. Selfishly, I have realized that I need the reaching hand of friendship as much as I need to give my hand.

I have learned to ask for help. While I am still not very good at it, I have learned that there are times I need help. I can't always fix the hurts in my own life and I can't always do all of the things that are being heaped on me. It has been eye opening and wonderful to lean on others for awhile. I couldn't have done it without the help of others and that hand that reached for me has made all of the difference in the glimmers of hope that I am starting to see and feel now.

Faith has been strengthened and forged through the shattered pieces of my life. While many people might turn from their faith or question God, I have chosen to rely on my faith to get me through the dark times. While I will never understand what led to the events of 27 April, I do know this. God is still working. I have always been on the quiet and shy side. While that is still my make up, I am learning to open up and to be the mouth piece for military loss. I didn't ask for that role initially, but I stand as part of a global military family. One loss is a loss for my entire military family. I have adapted and learned to stand up, make eye contact, and to speak up. I have chosen to put a face on the names that flash across the TV screens. I have continued to write and speak even as I would rather hide because I know that I am not the only one walking through this dark valley.

I get through the crushing pain by knowing that there is something beyond this life. I get through this time by knowing that while I will never understand what happened that there are some good things emerging from my loss. I would never have wanted this life, but I do see the hand of God working through the debris to bless and enrich my life. I have learned so many things and been forced to make decisions on my won for the first time since college. It hasn't been easy but I am getting stronger. While I still may doubt myself and see a scared girl staring back at me in the mirror, I see the strength and resilience that is starting to emerge. As I continue on this journey of self discovery and healing, I am utilizing the lessons I have learned with the talents that I have always had to be a lifeline to someone else. I reach my hand and I give my heart because by sharing the burden I am strengthened and blessed. I press on.

Taxes, W4's, and Financial Concerns

Every time I think that nothing more could possibly throw me for a loop, I get hammered with a curve ball. I have to fill out my w4 form so that I can get paid and get the army post access card so that I can be on base, get housing, etc. I don't know what I am doing. I think I can claim Phil for this year. I think that the money he made in Afghanistan is tax free. I don't know anything on taxes on life insurance. This SUCKS. It is crushing and it is frustrating not to know this and to have the need to know this yesterday, I suppose.

It seems to me that this should be a part of a checklist that is handed over to the surviving widow (or to the estate person). I am now overseas without an answer that I needed yesterday. It is not helpful to be told to ask questions if one does not know what questions to ask and the person to whom I am supposed to ask, never picks up his phone. There is not a message system which further complicates the situation. I am frustrated and feeling the pinch of loss right this minute. It is hard to have the tough questions come up on and off.

These types of things are useful to know immediately. Another issue that needs to be addressed is access points and bank accounts. Phil and I were married a really long time. When we went to online banking, we had one access point and one password that we both used. This is great until the person who set up the online banking dies. At that point, until one goes in to fix this in person, the bank account is frozen. We had joint banking accounts, but we never considered the one access/one password scenario.

Another area for consideration is that Phil rented a storage unit. We never even thought about the fact that my name was not on the unit. When I went to move, even with a will and certificate of death, it created problems. Two groups' legal departments had to get involved. Because of this, I ended up having to put the entire storage stuff into long term storage for as long as I am in Europe teaching. All of the family photos, Christmas materials, and my cold weather running gear is now effectively out of my reach for a minimum of two years.

I hated talking about the financial aspects with Phil because it reminded me of how volatile his job was. What I failed to realize is that if the unthinkable happened--and it did happen to me and my family)--then what? I think that every soldier needs to have a briefing about these issues because God forbid if their wives or husbands ever put them into the same situation as I am in.

Airports Hurt the Most

Will there ever be a day when I am excited again to go to the airport? Since 27 April the airport has been the place I cry the most. It hurts the most. Everyone else is having their happy reunions or flying to one. My reunion will never come. I feel my loss in the airport hustle every time. Flying into Colorado Springs crushed my heart every time because my mind and my heart expected Phil to be there. I don't have that thought in Germany, but it is difficult. I know that this bleeding heart will get enough band aids on it that I will camouflage the pain that wants to escape, but right now the planes of my face show every broken facet of my beating heart.

Today I Heard the Muslim Call to Prayer and I Did Not Cower in Fear

As the Muslim call to prayer blasted in Bodrum, Turkey and I saw many Muslim's in prayer, I was forced to confront my own humanity in terms of my xenophobia. Before April, I believed, really believed that people were innately good. I trusted pretty much everyone. After April, that trust and sense of wellness went away with my Phil. Today, hearing the music made me pause. It wasn't as if I was afraid, but rather, I had forgotten to be afraid for just a moment.

In the forgetting of my fear, and in the laughter of my day, I sense that the healing process is about a whole lot more than just beginning to date again. The journey is about trust. Trusting and having confidence in all people. I am certainly not there yet. I still am afraid of the Afghanis and their allies, but today showed me that one moment at a time will help me to move beyond that provincial viewpoint. I am not sure if I will ever fully believe and trust again because I no longer trust my own abilities to judge people, but I do believe that I will get to a place where I will not look for sinister motives and vile evilness in every Muslim.

The process isn't easy because Phil was killed by someone he trusted and called a friend. How could this man shoot my husband so many times when he had eaten with Phil so many times and he knew about the children and me? How could this assassin look at my husband who trusted him and shoot him so many times as he crouched under a desk with two other people? I don't understand evil. I don't understand evil intentions and motives, let alone actions of any one person or persons to include all no matter what race or religion. I just don't.

I choose to press on to believe in humanity. I choose to continue my journey of forgiveness which means not only forgiving and forgetting, but it means trusting. I choose to take each day one step at a time, one minute at a time. I will hope that education and working together will bring a renewed sense of all getting along no matter what religion or nationality. Today, I heard the Muslim call to duty. I did not fall to my knees and cry nor did I look frantically around for a sinister lurking individual. I chose to trust that all was well. I chose to take the first step in forgiveness.

Dealing with My Xenophobia

Today, in Ephesus, I had a Muslim tour guide. She did not wear a head covering. Apparently, it is against the law in Turkey. She talked about the commonalities of her faith and Christianity all day long. She attended church and respected the Christian holy places. What struck me was that her message was simple. Love and respect for all religions.

At lunch, she sat across from me. She and Emily and I were chit chatting. She asked me if I was divorced. When I said that my husband passed away in April, she asked if it was an auto accident or cancer. When I told her, she began to cry. She apologized for the sins of the people in her faith that went to extremes. She continued throughout the rest of the day to seek me out to ask me about my faith and to tell me how sorry she was. She did not choose to assassinate my Phil, but she was trying to bear the sins of the man who acted in vile evil intent. It made me realize that no matter what religion or belief system a person claims, people choose to interpret the religious words the way they choose when they want to succumb to depravity. I realized that this woman, a Muslim, wanted what I want. . .peace, tolerance, and forgiveness. I am not there totally, but I am taking steps towards moving beyond my xenophobia. Trust has started with step one. I am leaning towards walking forwards one baby step at a time.

The Spirit of Christmas in October

Today I heard my favorite Christmas song on my I Pod. Christmas Vacation, the song from Chevy Chases' movie, embodies my family to a tee. We are big and loud, but we stand united. We have a lot of fun, but we it is chaos and family drama at times. Until this cruise, I dreaded the idea of Christmas this year. It was crushing to consider a celebration that has meant so much to me and to consider that Phil should be anticipating his return in early January. I had already told my children that I couldn't do Christmas this year, but my heart is shifting. I have found hope and a knowledge that my future is going to be okay, happy even.

It is so foreign to be creating memories and a future without Phil. For over 23 years, my every consideration and plan revolved around the two of us and our family. I knew Phil almost as well as I knew myself. I didn't have to ask what foods he liked, what movies he wanted to see, what he needed, what he wanted, or any other question about his desires. There is comfort, ease, and security in finding the warmth of a long term love. I wanted that for all of the days of my life. I imagined growing old with Phil, sharing grandchildren with Phil, and eventually dying as an old woman. I never wanted for more.

Losing Phil was the most difficult thing I have ever experienced. The pain was so deep that it was physical. My heart literally felt like it was being crushed. Imagining Christmas vacation brought me to total inertia and pain. Christmas, however, is about hope, a hope born of a Messiah's promised birth. In the Christmas season (and I mean that globally since it is nowhere near the Christmas season), I am awakening in another area also. While I will not play this area out in my blogging journey other than in non-specifics, I have discovered feelings for another person are possible. With those feelings is a possibility...a renewed sense of hope.

While I stand rooted by my fear, I am awed by the very thought that my heart is capable of feeling. I am in awe of the fact that I feel hope in this area. No, I have not dated him yet, but I those feelings that I had forgotten are springing up. It is really difficult to be single at 50 and to be single after having a long and successful marriage, but I am walking forward one step at a time. It helps that I have time and distance to navigate the fresh waters. I am in need of that slow entry and in need of a safe zone, but I am moving through my dark tunnel towards the light of day. I step in hope towards the promises of my faith.

I feel a sense of excitement and quiet longing that brings me to my knees. I am navigating turbulent waters that I forged last 23 years ago. I am not the same girl I was in my 20's. My needs are simpler and more defined. My children are grown. I need someone who wants to journey with me, that understands that I can love two people with all of my heart in different ways, and a person who needs me as much as I need him. I am not sure what the future holds with anyone, but I was caught unaware. Unaware and surprised is part of the appeal of the Christmas season. I will stand and sate my heart in the joy of the season of awakening knowing that my heart is not crushed beyond repair. I will embrace the chaos and the drama that brought me to that sense of belonging and comfort. I carry the spirit of Christmas promises in my heart today.

How Can I Rejoice?

One of the most surprising and disturbing questions asked of me just after Phil's death when Osama Bin Laden had been killed was if Osama's death in some part avenged Phil's assassination. How can anyone's death replace or atone for a massacre of a loved one? On national television, I was forced (and I chose to let Emily answer this question for me because she articulated it best) to give my opinion. My thoughts, such as they are these. While Osama's death and that of Gadhafi yesterday may be a moral victory to the people living in oppression and terror within their own country, no death can atone or avenge my Phil's (or any other innocent bystanders) life.

When did it become about a life for a life? Would I feel the same if the man who assassinated the nine people (to include Phil) on 27 April had lived? What would be a reasonable punishment? For me, that judgment comes at death. In life, no amount of punishment can make someone pay. Innocent other people are then caught in the snare of violence and loss. What then is the answer? I don't know, I just know that I am not going to stand and rejoice that someone, even if he has the face of evil, has been killed.

Make no mistake. I am so pro-military and American that my heart beats red, white, and blue. I stand for what is noble and true. I stand for those who cannot stand for themselves. I am deeply disturbed by injustices to any people no matter what they look like or where they live. I am committed to educating and helping people change a country from within. I also am committed to seeing the bullies stopped. As a woman and as a mother, I am forever grateful for the people who stood up so that I have freedoms and rights so that I can vote, speak my mind, get an education, drive a car, and most of all, have an opinion. For these reasons, I am the most committed loyal pro-USA and military supporter. I just can't be joyful in the eye for an eye mentality. I just can't.

I do not strive to make a political statement or to disparage those men and women serving who do have to make decisions about a person's life; I am just stating where I am on this issue. I am thankful that I do not have to decide or to look into the eyes of the evil monsters, but evil monsters are lurking everywhere. For every death, more evil is created as hatred, misunderstanding, and retaliation create more death and more vile acts. What then do we do with the monsters?

The First Signs of Christmas Put Me on My Knees Today

I hadn't stopped to consider Christmas and the holidays recently until I hit the airports today. It is as if since Halloween is over and the calendar shows November that the commercialism of Christmas is free to emerge. I saw the trees and the other decorations and my heart literally felt crushed. I am and always have been quite the holiday girl. I love the decorations, the smells, the hustle bustle, but most of all, I love the family togetherness. I love the chaos, in my case, the utter chaos, of my family and the holidays.

I started decorating and baking in early November to jump into the fracas of the fun. My tree went up before Thanksgiving. The socks were hung; the lights were strung. Baking cookies filled the house with a scent that promised happy memories. I was always done buying and wrapping my gifts long before Thanksgiving. This year, however, I feel stuck. What is going to happen to those traditions? Who is going to want to share the enthusiasm of children tearing into the gifts? Who is going to want to be excited with me for the promise of the holiday?

I spent time with many of the widows from April this weekend. I also spent time with someone who was stationed with our husbands. All of the women were saying that they feel like people are telling them to move on and to get their act together because after all, it has been over six months. It is interesting, however, the holidays and the days that have special meaning (anniversaries, homecoming due dates, birthdays) bring memories crashing into where ever we are in the grief spectrum. People do not ask other people to get over being excited and happy, but it seems that people have a calendar for what is acceptable for grief. It is almost as if with the impending holidays, people do not want to be reminded of sadness and loss so deep that it is felt and that loss is so visible that it reminds them of their own mortality.

I have one friend that I love dearly. She is struggling a lot. She cries a lot. She has the softest and most gentle heart I have ever seen. That heart is what her husband loved. Yes, her pain is palpable. Yes, she wears her emotions on her sleeve, but she is the most loving woman I know. Her husband loved that in her. How can people put a moratorium on her tears?

I struggle with the loss of tradition and the rituals that Phil and I developed over 23 years of marriage. Our anniversary is Thanksgiving weekend. His homecoming was due 11 January. The calendars, the season, the decorations all remind me of what is gone. My heart bleeds. While I am beginning to slowly move forward, I am terrified of losing my entire past. I am fearful of losing the holidays and the celebrations that matter to me. I am not even celebrating the holidays this year. I am meeting the children in Hawaii because I just can't do what is the normal holiday. As my world spins, and as my children come together for the first time since 2004 to share Christmas, I feel guilty that I can't do what I always do. I feel a sense of loss anew. I feel like I lost my military family, my culture, my adult life as I knew it, my traditions, etc.

I am not sure how to navigate the waters of the holidays. I am afraid of losing the family jokes and the family traditions born of so many shared Christmas seasons. 23 years meant that we established Christmas customs, inside jokes, and memories-Secret Santas and family bingo for small gift cards- Christmas dinner and Christmas cookies-the ornaments. I stand adrift and alone. I am so unsure if I will ever feel excitement at the holiday again. I struggle with the loss of a whole lot more than Phil. With each and every lit Christmas tree, I feel a prick that makes the salty tears in my heart bleed. Survival. . .band aids. . .a swim suit. . .running and water. Hawaii is not the Christmas my children know or want, but it is all I have to give this year.

Phil's Assassin Will Not Win

I have always trusted and believed the best in people. It isn't something I think about, I just want to believe in redemption and the basic goodness in each individual. I approach adults the same way I see my students. My students trust me. They basically want to be liked by me. I see my students as blank slates that absorb life lessons in addition to the academic lessons taught, however, these students grow up. They change. I have changed since April 27th.

I am not sure if I like the changes I see in me. Where once I never questioned other people's motives and goodness, I am wary. If Phil could trust the gunman as much as he did, then how could I trust and believe in my own powers of discernment between good and evil people. In the past day, I opted to trust someone's motives. I was feeling a sense of the old Linda returning until two people that I care about cautioned me on this other person's motives. I stand paralyzed once again.

Why is it that my judgments are so off? Why is it that I want to trust the wrong people? Why is it that I no longer allow myself to reach beyond the confines of my close knit of friends? I am being briefed by the military again Monday. I have always trusted and believed the military. I wear my military badge proudly as I stand as a mother, wife, sister, and an American, but now, I am stepping back. I do not know why the military would lie (or omit) information. I do not know why the military has been so hush hush on the united 9's deaths. I do not understand why we continue to support a country that is capable of so much destruction. It is a killing field. A red field that has heard the cries of far too many.

While I live on, I am damaged. I lack fundamental abilities to recognize malice and ill-will. I lack fundamental trust in myself let alone others outside of my circle. For the first time, I question the decisions being made to place our military people in harm's way without the ability to properly defend themselves or their colleagues. I worry that the killing field is hungry again. That mass destruction of so many lives is going to feed that desolate land. The beast is never sated, however. He rises time and time again. We, as a people, need to say enough is enough. Although I am not a soldier, I am tired of the many bleeding hearts that equal my own. I cannot let these evil vile people win. I must learn to trust and to step forward or the assassin will have murdered two people that day. I raise my fist. Though I am battered and broken, I will live on and I will learn to trust and believe again.

One More Minute Is All I Need

One of the aftermaths of spouse dying in a far off land after many months apart is the feeling of wondering if he knew I loved him enough. After 23 years, it seemed as if everything else took priority over time together, caring about what I looked like, or even pushing for the time alone together away from our jobs, the children, our daily responsibilities. While I did do many things right, I regret that I did not tell him how much I appreciated his work ethic, his devotion to our children, and the little things he did for me every day. I would give anything for the gift of one minute, one minute. I don't need more than that moment, but I would touch his cheek, or stroke his hand. I would look into his eyes and tell him that he was loved. I would tell him thank you for being the man that he was. I would give him a quick kiss and then I would commit his soul to God. I wonder if because I had no inkling that Phil was going to be taken from me if somehow I failed at loving him enough.

Phil did want what was best for me. He didn't always give me the gift of time either. I remember the last four years in CO and many years along the way. Phil carried the weight of the world on his shoulders in terms of providing for a big family. We chose for me to stay at home except for the summers when I managed swimming pools. He did not believe in handouts, thus we lived on rice and beans. I still to this day cannot eat that combination. He did everything he could think of to make enlisted rank the first time and then to win awards as an officer so that he would not be booted from the military which was his very worst fear.

One year, he worked so many hours and dealt with such emotional battering that he literally withdrew all of the way. He stopped running, stopped eating at times, and he lived at work most of the time (12-16 hour days). When he was at home, he would sit with a glazed vacant look on his face. I never thought that year would end, but Phil kept reminding me that it would and that he would get the PhD that he wanted. The thing is that he went straight from that to subbing full time and pursuing his PhD. Phil was the golden boy no matter where he went. I was content to let him shine because his star did shine so brightly. I just wish that he knew that things didn't matter as much to me as he did. I wish he knew that it would have been okay not to have been so successful. I would have loved him still.

It wasn't until he got to Afghanistan that he began to realize that it was the two of us and that I had been on the back burner for awhile. He began to do things he never did when he was deployed. He finally wanted a trip without the kids. That trip never happened. Again, my culpability is that I never made a big enough deal over my need for us to connect like this again. It is too easy to think that in the tomorrow s there is time, but what happens when there is no more time? When the sands of time cease to fall?

I cannot fix my shortcomings with Phil, but I can learn from his death because had Phil had time, he would be feeling the same way that I do. It isn't rational, but it is still something that I have on my heart as I approach my 23rd anniversary. I have learned to let people know that they matter to me. I have learned to let people help me and I have learned the art of taking gifts. Gifts from the heart, time, and love…things I never could do before. I have learned to speak up and tell people how much they mean to me and I have learned not to wait for what I want. If I could, I would take the minute with Phil, but in the absence of that minute, I have learned and I step forward. I step to the person I should have been all along. I step to making my priorities people. I step….I give…I love…

Will His Life Have Been In Vain?

Many people wonder what led to me breaking and falling to my knees yesterday. A culmination of events and emotions temporarily ripped the scab off of my bleeding heart. While I thought that I had weathered my 23rd anniversary fairly well, all it took was the screaming headlines of the Stars and Stripes Paper of November 30th talking about troop drawdown in 2012 in Afghanistan. Throw in the modified IRS return and the claim for household goods, and I bowed and bent. I withdrew from the people who love me most.

I was deeply wounded by the very thought that the Afghanistan mission is all about politics. So, my Phil died and because it is an election year coming up, people will be removed in droves so that a politician can gain more of the popular vote? I don't see the stability yet in the Afghan people. Do they really want our help? Or do they just want the good and services we provide? If so, then have our soldiers lost value as human beings? The government is willing to throw money at me in terms of tax forgiveness for three years; however, they are unwilling to stay the course?

I am not political. I am the first to say that I am ignorant about military strategy and geopolitics; however, it just seems too convenient that there is simplistic explanation that still does not make sense. People matter. Phil believed in what he was doing in Afghanistan in terms of mentoring and teaching the Afghans. He trusted the people he worked with. One of the trusted people he worked with assassinated nine people on 27 April 2011. Phil, like the other eight, paid the ultimate price for his belief and efforts on behalf of the Afghan people. If we leave in large numbers, will his life have mattered there? Will his belief and efforts be for naught? Will the infrastructure of what has been accomplished fold in upon itself like a deflated dream dying yet again?

Christmas, Why Can't I Find You?

I wish I had the capacity to post a YouTube of the song, Christmas, Why Can't I find You? I have changed. Many of us have. The interesting thing is that the spirit is awakening to the possibility of the promise of the coming Messiah. I reach for the joy in the meaning of the season. While I have become softer in my stance of some Christmas cheer, I won't lie and say that it is easy. I see the lights of the neighbors, the trees going up, and I hear the Christmas music and there is a part of me that drops to my knees. Phil should be coming home by 10 January. I believe, and I really believe, that he is in communion with our Lord, but I hurt for our children and I am at crossroads in terms of what to do with the family ornaments and traditions. I then wonder if I should give all of the Christmas stuff to our children and start over. Somehow it seems like I am losing my past--a past that has meant so much to me- past that made me who I am. Yet, if I cling to my memories and things from the past, will I ever see the light of day in terms of moving on? Where is the balance? For this reason, I take the step back this season. I need to know.

I also wonder how fair it is to cling to traditions I established with someone else if I let someone into my life. Where is that line? The interesting thing is that I established most of these traditions because I am a holiday and family girl. Phil was often deployed and when he was home, he gladly followed my lead with the holiday fun. I am the one that enjoys the smells, the memories, the giving, the joy, and the togetherness of the season, yet I feel like I am stuck in Limbo in terms of what to carry on. Twenty three years of ornaments and memories. I don't know how to sort them through the sieve that filters my heart.

My children have not weighed in on this subject, and they are adults, but Christmas draws them home also. Are they going to want to come home to their momma when dad is never coming home? Will they allow me to maybe have Christmas in a different way one day with someone else, or will they eschew wanting to be with me because Christmas will be different. It is confusing and almost too much to consider. My children mean so much to me, but they are at a juncture where they are establishing roots and a life without me. If my five children were younger, this would be a no brainer, but I feel that I am fighting against myself today. I stand paralyzed at crossroads wondering what to keep and what to let go. Nobody has the answers, but I wish, oh, how I wish, for Christmas past. I wish for the five young children messing with the presents and the crèche. I miss the birthday cake for Jesus and the Secret Santas. I miss letting the children shop at the Dollar Store or Santa's Workshop in school for cheap trinkets. I miss baking for weeks. I miss the holiday music and the naivety that all would be well in my world.

I had that ignorance last year. I had that mistaken feeling that my life was blessed and that the magic of our family would last forever. As we played Bingo for small gift cards with Emily's Flat Stanley because she was deployed to Bagram, Afghanistan, and as we readied for Phil's upcoming deployment just after Christmas, we lost ourselves in one small apartment. There warm and snug, loudness pealed out. Brightly wrapped gifts piled all over and the smell of cookies baking. . .magical and all too short. In my heart, all has changed. Home is gone. Christmas has changed, or is it just me? I can't find my Christmas star, but I know it is here guiding me and leading me to the promise of the Christ child. I follow the breaking rays of light trusting and believing in the hope that is seeping through the cracks of my heart. I continue my journey of self discovery and a life without Phil, but Christmas traditions are shifting and changing.

Who Will Remember? Who?

"A day that will live on in infamy." Seventy years ago, our country was attacked. This unprovoked terroristic attack took countless lives and compelled us into a war that we had not been previously involved in. Even today, people remember and pay homage to the men and women who lost their lives in a senseless attack against humanity. Today, I pay homage to these soldiers because they are never forgotten and they are always loved.

I hope that in seventy years, people will remember my Phil and the other eight who were in a country trying to mentor and train the Afghan people. Sadly, I know that these nine will be forgotten. The story never even came out in the paper. My nine were overshadowed by a royal wedding. As my life was crushed and as I sat hopeless in Dover, every major newspaper and television channel flashed endless hours of the royal wedding. While I have no problem with the media coverage for Prince William, I find it ludicrous that as a society, these nine soldiers didn't merit a news article.

My united nine were there doing nothing except giving and serving. They were not there playing GI Joe, yet one man, a trusted man, had the time and the opportunity to take all nine of them out. The attack took fifteen minutes. Fifteen minutes. Yet, nobody was able to respond. I have a problem with that. It seems to me that we are not learning from people who seek to harm us. It seems to me that as a general, our society is inured to the names that flash across our television screens. In seventy years, who will remember? Who will honor our dead servicemen and women? Who will call their deaths unnecessary and evil? Who? I will be gone, and the history books will turn the Afghan mission into a footnote. That bothers me. Like the men and women of Pearl Harbor, these nine mattered. Their lives were filled with promise. All were successful, but more than that, EVERY ONE of them was loved and waited for.

My Phil was due to deploy 22 December last year to Shindad. Only because of a raging snow storm was he home for the holidays. Only because of a coding error did he end up going to Kabul. So many what ifs, but I do believe that God knows the day and minute that we are going to be escorted into heaven. I believe that Phil and the other eight were carried in the arms of angels to the pearly gates. As I approach my holiday season and the day Phil should be walking into my arms, I can't help but wonder where the politicians are. Where is the outrage? For me, 27 April is a day of infamy. For me, my life as I knew it ended that day. While I am slowly moving on, this is not the life I chose or wanted. I have changed and my faith is stronger, but who wants to find this out about themselves? I have been blessed by so many friends, a good job, and even someone that I have started stepping forwards with, but I still wonder, who will remember? Who will pay tribute in 70 years?

The Unexpected Fear Within

This week, I have seen how I have changed since 27 April. I am not the girl I once was. I am a lot more open about my life and feelings than I ever was in 50 years preceding now. I was always a little afraid of the dark and the unknown things, people, and situations that arise at night. I have always innately turned to the sun and activity as I embrace any light. As today unfolded, I realized that I now have a fear and the illogical reactions that go with terror. I see that there is something so much bigger than my fear of the dark and unknown.

Today was a terrible day for me as a person and as a teacher. Something really awful happened to a student of mine. I reported the situation without a thought. At the end of the day as I am walking out, I see my principal and a man in a suit walking towards me. I greet my principal and ask if he is looking for me. I was told, "Yes, Mrs. Ambard, we need for you to come with us." Something immediately shifted and I stood rooted in stupefied paralysis as my mind raced to my five children. Four of my children are in the military; two of my children are abroad right now.

Logically, I should have known that since three people didn't show up to my school in dress uniforms that all was well, but I am here as a civilian and few know my military connection and that I am still a military dependent. Also, I don't know what the procedure is for injury vs. death. I hope to God that I never find out. My fear must have been evident. I did not speak. I stood rooted with my heart in my throat. I felt the blood draining from my face. My principal immediately put two and two together and told me why the man was here. He was basically a detective investigating the terrible events of the day. I was still reeling at my reaction long after I finished my statement.

Am I ever going to react normally and not automatically and without thought go to the worst possible scenario? I have never been a worrier. I do not dwell on the what ifs. . .or at least I didn't until the unspoken tacit what if became a reality. I hate that I am a fraidy cat and that I can't control the visceral reactions of my psyche. I hate the weakness that has arisen and is now evident in this once strong girl.

I'm Coming Home. I'm Coming Home

Phil should be home or at least he should have started the journey to his happy reunion. I should be waiting for the happy reunion and for our life to begin anew with a base change and a new job. Instead, he came home much too early in a cold wooden box. Instead of a happy reunion, he got a very public viewing of his return. Instead of my warm arms, my cold fingers grasped the foot of his holding box as my body broke and bowed at the thought of the injustice of a life ended much too soon. While Phil never got the happy reunion that he so deserved here on earth, I believe that there will be a reunion one day. I have to believe that.

Coming home, coming home. Home is a place in the heart. It has never been a physical presence for me; rather it has been a silent mooring with the people I love. Bonded by the ties that bind through time and love, my home was wherever my family was. It is discombobulating to have adult children who live all over the world and no other mooring. I am a nomad that yearns for a sense of home, a safe harbor in which to rest.

I have made giant steps forward to finding that I am without my children and without my Phil, but it is all unchartered choppy waters. I am not a good solo sailor in terms of trusting my own decisions and commitments. I doubt myself, but through the past eight plus months, I have found that I am beginning to take my boat further into the undulating waves. I am still finding my home and my port, but I can see that the day is coming when I will feel joy at a different kind of homecoming. The fire for the home I shared with Phil is etched into my heart forever more. No matter where travel, Phil is a part of me. His fire blazes within me. That will never change. My sense of home may shift to include another, but home is a shared space. I gave my youth and middle age to Phil, and God willing, I will give my later years to another person because I do want to love and be loved again. It isn't that I want to replace Phil or pretend that Phil was not a part of my life--this would not be true because his loss was so devastating and life gouging that I forever changed--but I believe that the home I carry in my heart that makes me strong and makes me content will be complete whether I am alone or whether I love another. My fire blazes because I fall into my faith and I believe that I will have a happy homecoming again with Phil and with the baby we lost. I even believe that our little dog Bailey is there in heaven waiting to be the naughty little dog that runs to my feet joyously wagging her tail. I reach to the quiet mooring the beckons me home in the future.

I have recently begun to let someone else into my life, but it is a very slow inching forward. This person lives eight thousand plus miles away from me which has given me the time and space to figure things out. Two steps forward, one step back. I may or may not be alone for the rest of my days, but no matter what, I am moving forward. I have no choice. I will never be the same Linda who loved Phil for 23 years. I will never be the same person Phil knew and loved. The events of 27 April changed me. The change has not been all bad, but it is change nevertheless. I am in no manner trying to replace Phil because it cannot be done. The relationship is different and no less important or wondrous, it is just filling the needs and wants of a very different Linda. I do not know where the relationship is going for I am not on a fast train. I need time to figure out my sense of home and self within. I need to stand alone in the raging waters and discover the strength within. I am on that journey.

I have not felt guilty for letting someone else into my life, but sometimes I feel guilty for finding happiness in the darkest of times. I sometimes feel guilty that I am stronger and more independent than I ever was with Phil. I still feel Phil's loss acutely and I still mourn that his homecoming will be a greeting when my last breath is taken, but I do know that Phil would be happy that I am stepping forward and finding any modicum of happiness and peace. I know this without reservation because that is how much I loved my Phil. I would want him to find a sense of home again. I would want him to feel the warm fires of love that wrap around people when they have that sense of home. I do not think that moving on means that I loved Phil any less because I am the Linda that I am because of how well and how long Phil loved me. That Linda can step into a free falling abyss and know that she will find the fires that will light a new sense of belonging.

As I face a year without seeing my Phil, I am reminded of how happy and proud he was last year this time. While Phil was never one to flaunt his many awards and achievements, he pushed himself harder than anyone I have ever known to win those awards not for recognition as some might assume, but the awards meant job stability and longevity. When I would complain about his hours or work focus, he would remind me of all that the military had given us. Few know exactly how far this family had come.

Phil joined the Air Force at the age of 18 to get his United States citizenship. He was still mastering the language and he had barely graduated from high school. When we met, Phil was barely 21. He was an airmen first class. I was 27 and a mom to three children. I worked at the base pool and at the gas station just off of base. Phil did not believe in welfare or handouts, thus he worked as a newspaper boy before work. He was so motivated that he won many awards with the Idaho Statesman. We lived on rice and beans for years. Fun times were walks, picnics, and the swimming pool because it was free for us, the gym, and board games.

We made our fun when Phil was home which exactly half of the year was. When he wasn't being volunteered for TDYs, he volunteered because the TDY (temporary deployment down yonder) money often carried us. Those TDY times away from home came at a cost, however.

Phil missed so many family events. He missed major surgeries, graduations, births, behavior issues; moves, broken cars and appliances, and he missed the joy of the day to day family time. My job for years was to be that stable secure parent. We chose for me to stay home not because we didn't need the money that a teaching job would have provided for us, but because we knew that we had one chance to get our family right and that there were no do-overs. One of the many sacrifices I gave up was being a single parent half of the time to five children. The other half of the time, Phil was home being a Disneyland parent because he was gone so much. I didn't complain because I knew that my soldier was doing what he felt he needed to do to provide for us, but more than that, he felt a calling to serve his adopted country. It is that calling that I could not fight. I chose to support him and to be the home fires as he laced up his combat boots and strapped on his gun.

One particular time frame was very, very difficult. Our marriage took a beating. While we recovered and rebounded, the commitment and drive Phil had cost us so much in terms of shared family time. While we lived in Bitburg, Germany, Phil became motivated to get his bachelor's degree. Between being deployed six months a year, going to leadership school, clepping(testing for college credit), and taking 21 credit hours at a time, there was nothing left for any of us. Phil still owns the record for number of passed CLEP tests (over 200 credits). He finished a bachelor's degree in 15 months. He then deployed for 15 out of the last 18 months we were in Bitburg. In the meantime, I had three teenagers, two grade school children, and a high pressure job of running the child development center (a very broken center). The cost was tremendous as the missed family events mounted, but still as a family we were committed to serving our country.

While Phil could have left the military, he never once wavered. The more rank he achieved, the more he realized that his work mattered and that he was impacting change. He was so proud of the many people he mentored along the way. Everywhere we went, Phil eschewed the military lifestyle. He loved serving our country. He could have taken the easy road after his PhD and returned to the Air Force Academy, but that was not Phil's style. He felt that if he deployed, one less parent would have to deploy away from their family. He felt that it was his turn and that he had something to give back. He believed in what he was doing which made his death at the hands of someone he trusted even more unthinkable. He taught me so much about commitment and passion for his life's work. While he couldn't effect change as an enlisted airman, he worked, sometimes at the expense of his family and his own personal time, to move into a position where he could effect change. It was only to me that he ever voiced dissent or doubts. To all others, he coined the phrase, "Consider it done." When Phil uttered those words, he found a way to do what he had committed to doing. He would do whatever he had to do to complete the task.

I suppose that I blog and speak as a way to carry on Phil's life song. Phil was extremely quiet about his humble roots, but it is in knowing of a poor immigrant boy's story that people understand the fires that fueled Phil to a commitment and a loyalty to the United States Air Force that spanned 26 years and would have lasted until the Air Force booted him out. His commitment was truly more than the pay check. He was deeply appreciative of the opportunities afforded to him through the military and he had seen corruption in the Venezuelan militaries. He had seen a rampant sense of indifference in the French military. Phil owed service to both countries, but he chose the American military and then he gave so much more than he had to give. Phil did not have a sense of entitlement; he had a spirit of giving. In that spirit of giving, he gave his youth to our country, he gave four of five of our children to the military, he gave countless volunteer hours to mentor and help others, and he gave his life.

Phil would have said that all of the accolades were too much. He never saw his worth, but he deserved everything he has received and so much more. Phil was a man that lived his life to the fullest. I do not think any person has crammed more life into 44 years of living. I can only aspire to leave the same ripples when I am received into the arms of heaven. His death continues to inspire others, and it is in the inspiration that motivates a person into action that deeds and lives are paid forward. I honor Phil and the life he had by speaking and writing about military loss. I know that there are others who are more articulate and more able to be the face of military loss, but I have chosen to step up and embrace the purpose I was given to my own life when Phil was assassinated. I honor Phil and the life we had together by being the woman I am meant to be.

Crushing Guilt

Guilt is such a powerful counterproductive emotion, yet I find myself in the dark morass of its all encompassing weight. One year ago, Phil's deployment was pushed back due to the weather in Europe. As he rejoiced in more time at home with our youngest boy with whom he was close, he urged me to go on ahead to a preplanned running race in Florida. Yes, I begged him to come with me and I offered to stay at home, but it was too easy to let him push me away and to think that in the scope of our life together that there would be more opportunities for us to bond and for us to create memories. One would think that after 23 years, we would have known better, but alas, we often took each other for granted.

In long term relationships, there is a comfort in knowing a person so well that nuances are recognized and needs are met long before they are voiced. There is a confidence that comes with knowing someone almost as well as one knows them, but in that confidence and knowledge often comes a silent complacency. Phil and I were no different. I made it too easy for him to withdraw from me because when he withdrew, I withdrew into my own shell. He withdrew every deployment as a way to get through it. We always found our way back home, but this time there is no fixing the distance. I have forgotten his laughter and the way his eyes lit up when he was messing with me (which was all too often).

The guilt I feel is that I wish that I had stood up and voiced how much I wanted that time with him. I should have insisted. To have had one weekend without our children away from home would have been a sublime memory that I can only crawl to in my crushing pain. I can't fix the choices we made. I can't even get over the guilt of not making him priority one over my running, the kids, work, and whatever else seemed to need more than he needed, but I can change. I am changing. If only Phil could see it.

Part of my blogging journey is me working through the stages of grief. Another part is that I am willing to talk about the insecurities and doubts that come from losing a long time partner. I have to wonder if I will ever be whole again or if I will be forever broken and stooped by my own self doubt. Yes, I wonder who would ever want to love me as I am. I think it would be very difficult to love someone who actually loved someone to the end. I think that it would be hard to compete with 23 years. While I realize that Phil is never coming home and that he would want me to move ahead, I almost feel like the only place I can talk about the life we had together is in writing. It has been a year since I saw him and almost a year since he was assassinated. He is still a part of who I am...he always will be, but I realize that I need to step forward. I am a different woman than the one who shared a life with Phil. I gave Phil my youth and I gave him the family he so desired, but he would he even recognize the girl I am now?

The guilt that descends upon my beating heart is because I see my own shortcomings and failures. I see where I should have been a more giving spouse. I see where I failed in voicing my own needs. I am still so terrible at that. I want to withdraw and hide. If only I could take back that weekend from the darkness in my heart. If only I had insisted that the man learn to Skype (he was a com officer...he could have learned just like I taught him how to text). If only I hadn't made it easy for him to go two to three days without communication. Yes, I was the calming hand and presence in his shadow, but, oh, how I wish for the gift of time passed. I can't fix the past, so I step ahead and with all that I am, I will fight for the people in my life. If I am blessed with love again, I will fight for the relationship and for the moments that so quickly pass in the night.

It Is Just Such a Personal Journey

Grief is such a personal journey. While some people want to pretend that the death never happened or are content never to speak of the unthinkable tragedy in their lives, others need to talk about the dire circumstances and events that led to the crushing loss. While I am not a talker, I am a writer and in writing, I have injured at least one of my children because he is just the opposite of me. Initially I began blogging because it was easier than talking about how I feel and the fact is, I can write about things I could never say out loud. I continued writing and in my faith and in my process of dealing with Phil's death, the compulsion has been unquenchable and the desire burns torridly hot to continue this journey until 27 April 2011.

I have tried to honor Phil's memory and his life song because I truly believe that he led a remarkable life that left such a legacy. His life song is etched on to this girl's heart. I am the woman I am today because he loved me well for 23 years. He believed in me and he supported me no matter what my dream was. We made quite the parenting team. I think that was what we were called to do as a couple because we have five remarkable children etching their own way in life. Do I think that my Phil was perfect? No, but I am not either. He was perfect for me, however. My words will never give Phil the man justice, but my writing is my heart.

Going back to the way people process death, my journey is solely my own. I cannot fault another for anger or for his words disagreeing with the way I am processing Phil's death. I am not sure that there is a right or wrong way or a definitive timeline. Where one day, one week, or even a month slips by and I am feeling like I am gaining control over my feelings and life, the next day, week, or even month can break me anew. Something happens and I am immediately thrown back to the insecurities of walking without my Phil and facing a future without him. I wonder if the 27th of any month will ever pass when I don't think of our anniversary and his death. I wonder if April will ever bring joy. I wonder if I will ever be whole again. Yes, I have found happiness and I am stepping forward, but the journey is so terribly difficult and personal. I do what I do--run, write, and pray, especially, I pray--to process my own emotions.

I am not asking for permission at the age of 50 on how to live my life. I am not asking or seeking validation in my writing because like the child who struggles with my writing, there is a choice. I choose to write and he can choose to read or not to read. My blogs may only be for the friends and family walking this journey with me, or God may use them in a bigger plan as other people walk this same trek, but here is the thing. I am healing through the writing of my thoughts. It is like letting go of a balloon and watching the red lazily disappear into the velvety skies above. I press on because at some point the red balloon will be hidden behind the white billowing clouds. Though ever present, the balloon, or Phil's death, will compel me like an arrow to my own destiny wherever the will of God takes me. I step forward confidently and with a sadness borne of Phil not being able to share this journey knowing that although he was a very private person, he did like knowing that his life mattered, and, oh, how his life mattered to so many.

Military Loss and What Helps

I have been approached by many military people asking about the Survivor Outreach Program (Army) or Family Liaison Officer (FLO/Air Force). I have had two FLOs and I have had a very supportive army community. As this army community prepares to deploy and with the Air Force loss of another four gone too soon, I am writing about what went well, what totally fell down, and I am writing to forgive the initial FLO I had until January. I am so thankful that through him I have been able to see just how strong and resilient I am. I do think he meant well. I still think that, but for a military spouse who is dealing with the death of her husband of 23 years in a land far, far away, the program was grossly broken. I was ignorant, and I am still in the dark about so much, of the military system for survivors. Even if I had been stronger, and even if I had some knowledge, I had no idea what to ask for, what I needed, or what was going to happen. I didn't need information about the notification process. Every one with a television knows that uniformed members come and read that terrible letter, "We regret to inform you. . ." I didn't care what rank those people were and they could have worn polka dotted underwear. I wouldn't have known or cared. I did care about being in a house for two hours alone after finding out that my world had imploded. I did care that my children found out by Facebook, phone calls from friends, etc. I did care that I had been told that they had been notified.

Initially, being a FLO is time consuming. Families need a physical presence. I didn't know I had a FLO, let alone know what a FLO could do to help me. I had my bank accounts frozen, media hounding me, my id card taken due to an AF coding error, black foot lockers delivered without anyone, autopsy pictures/reports given without anyone, etc. All of this except the banking business happened after you left. I didn't know who to call or what to do. Even if I hadn't been in a fog, I wouldn't have known what to do.

My daughter did things as a family member that a FLO could have been helpful with. My girlie did all of the driving, coordinating of base resources for family get togethers, etc? If she hadn't stepped up to do this, and if you hadn't had your military background, it wouldn't have been done. I know we have a large military family, but it all fell on her. It would have been nice for her not to have to do all that you did. You were a daughter before you were an AF officer.

Coordination of the funeral, transportation, airport runs, etc requires a physical presence-a presence that does and listens versus offering advice. A FLO that brought me a cup of coffee would have gone a long way. While Phil's funeral was done so very well, I was by myself afterwards. Nobody from USAFA called or visited. Again, what FLO?

My FLO did not call me until July when I was to get a briefing from the military. This is not okay in any world. After the briefing, he didn't call or e-mail for another month. Again, this isn't okay. I would have resisted daily phone calls and visits, but the bottom line is that most widows need some type of daily communication for the first two to three months. They need physical meetings--not daily, but those meetings establish trust. Another wife's FLO took me on the last two days I was in CO. He brought me coffee, called and showed up when the movers were there, and he let me rail against my FLO.

I ran into snags with the storage unit that Phil and I rented when we sold our house. We never imagined that the unthinkable would happen. I was at the house boxing things up. Phil drove the moving truck with our two youngest sons to the storage unit. It was rented with his signature only. CO is a no probate state, but even with the will and the certificate of death, the storage unit drug their heels. If I had an active FLO, this could have been fixed easily. By the time I knew I had a problem, it was too late. I couldn't go through the things in the storage unit, get the items for Germany, rescue the family pictures, or declare professional weight which will haunt me when I move back to the states. The mover even asked where the person was that was supposed to be with me. I didn't have a clue.

My fiftieth birthday was just after dad died. I didn't hear from most of my family/kids. I know everyone was in pain. My daughter was there. My peeps (people-friends) were there. What if they hadn't been? A lunch or coffee would have maybe helped.

Again, people like me hide behind a mask of stoicism, but it doesn't mean that our hearts aren't bleeding and weeping. I needed a helping hand. I had nearly 30 years of military affiliation if a person counts my first marriage. I still didn't know what to ask for help for. I still didn't know what questions to ask. I still felt like I couldn't ask for help.

I didn't know about the tax forgiveness for three years. I still don't know how long I have to be moved--I heard different things. I still appreciate the occasional e-mail or phone call. I have a FLO here and he has called me and e-mailed me more than the first assigned person did. He calls just to talk about normal things. He asks me about hard things like when the media had their fun lately. That is what makes a difference after the first few months.

I don't have kids at home, but there would be needs there. Maybe taking the kids or setting up family time at a park so that the kids can have "normal" play opportunities.

Errands initially would be helpful, also. An example is dry cleaning or grocery runs in the first month. I couldn't go anywhere without people coming up to me and wanting to talk to me about what happened. It didn't help that dad and I were so visible in the community. I went to the Y to swim one day. I figured nobody would talk to me. There I was dripping wet at 0630 and I had a handful of people trying to hug me and talk to me. It was so hard that I ran away to Germany.

Now, my new FLO lives two hours away from me, but he still makes a huge impact on this girl. My FLO now lives in Ramstein. He has called me, coordinated tax things, and he came to see me once. He e-mails now and he has opened doors both at the AF and Army level for me. I don't know how that would work initially, but even though I had proximity, John sucked as a FLO. He gave me a phone number that one couldn't leave a message at and then he never responded to e-mails. The military person assigned to the family needs to be someone who is emotionally strong (John cried all of the time when he talked to me in July), they need time, and they need to be in secure faithful relationships. In essence, they need to be available and friendly without crossing any lines. There needs to be some type of follow up to ensure that families have someone that is actively acting on their behalf. If the system isn't working, then another person should be assigned.

So what can a civilian do for a friend who suffers death? Be there. Show up. If not in person, e-mail, call, send a card, send a teddy bear, or bring her coffee and socks. Throw her a 50th birthday party and bring back her laughter. Sit with her in church where the songs make the heart bleed. Run with her and let her talk not only about the unthinkable, but about her fears and insecurities as she navigates a world she never quite fit into the first time she was single. Make her laugh or give her a hanky when the tears silently fall because they do fall.

Evil is Evil

Another two advisors gone today. Another two gone far too soon at the hands of someone they trusted. Two more advisors. The issue is the lack of moral courage. Let's call evil evil. Let us hold these assassins responsible. Let us work with people who will actually be PARTNERS. A partnership means that all sides value the life of another. When an Afghan military person will stand up to the life of an American soldier just like my American soldier was willing to stand up for his Afghan comrade then it will be a partnership. Until then, let's get the hell out TODAY!

Why is it that people are so afraid to call evil what it is? How often are we going to enter the snake cage, get bitten, and then return? What exactly is it that we are hoping to accomplish? It just seems to me that people get too inured to the iniquities against our country and our people that the names that flash across the screens of our televisions and flit across the newspapers do not mean anything. We, as a nation, scream about the military misbehaviors, but we never look at how many more atrocities are playing out every day against wonderful human beings whose lives are cut short by evil people. While I think that we do need to hold individuals accountable for bad decisions, crimes, etc., why is it that we apologize publicly for our bad decisions? Where is my apology for the loss of my husband? Where is the genuine sincere embracing of our help? If the Afghan people wanted our people there, and if they wanted something more than our re-sources, then why aren't these people holding their own people accountable and protecting all soldiers?

At what point do we say, enough is enough? I am not a provincial nationalistic person. Phil believed in what he was doing. I believe in education and I believe in standing up for the rights of the oppressed, however, if the very military that we are trying to help implement these changes do not value human life enough to protect the people that are helping, then should we keep risking the lives of our good people? What are we gaining? I realize that it isn't about what we get, but when we are losing so much, then maybe it is time for us to look at what we are doing. Again, the argument comes down to how is it that the Afghan army that is supposed to be our friend, fails time and time again to stand up to the violence against our men and women who would be willing to stand and take a bullet for them? Where is the ONE Afghan that was willing to risk ANYTHING for my husband or for any of the soldiers who were killed yesterday?

As a nation, we sugar coat and call it "mental illness". Mental illness? It comes down to value of life. If a nation does not value life and if they look at us like we are infidels, they will look at our resources as theirs. Like a two year old, they will demand what they think is due to them, and then they will use violence to get what they want. When are we going to respond in an appropriate manner? When will we decide to hold the people responsible for their bad actions, choices, and behaviors? Until we do, the violence will continue and escalate. Our nation is willing to apologize, pay restitution, and die for our allies. All I ask is that the nations who claim to be our friends, do the same. Until then, let's call evil evil. Let us flee and let us not lose any more to the monsters who do not value the life of any other person except for people that believe and look like they do.

Homeless

I am homeless. Not in the sense of having a building, but for me, home is a feeling that I carried in my heart. Home was the mooring and anchoring I felt with loving and being loved. I never wanted for more. I knew I had been blessed. There truly wasn't a day that I didn't get happy when Phil walked in the door or when I walked in the door to him. He saw the joys and the crushing disappointments on the planes of my face without me ever saying a word. He knew that when I got really quiet, I was in a dark spot. I knew that when he got quiet or when he reacted out of the ordinary that he was stressed out about something--usually work. I knew without Phil ever voicing a word when he finally had enough of the rejection of his family. Being known this well, and having Phil know me that well, was a gift I never expected when I eloped with him after dating him four months.

This confidence wrapped me in a warm blanket of security and gave me a sense of home whether I lived in the slums of Lanstuhl or the Project Rejects of Bernallilo Court in New Mexico.

I never cared where we lived. Home was our family. It is discombobulating to be fifty and have nowhere to call home. My children are strewn all over the world. We raised them to be confident and independent. We also raised them to find home where ever they were stationed. They, too, found home in the reuniting of family during the holidays. This feeling has shifted and it makes my heart weep. The phone calls, the e-mails, the visits have been reduced because it is as if with Phil gone, all of the fun and sense of family is gone. Since all of my children are independent adults, I think it is easy to think that home is forever gone, which in the way they knew is gone. I think that the distance and daily life make it easy to eschew remembering to call or write the surviving parent. I do not think this is intentional or malicious. They, too, hurt. We are broken. Phil was the parent urging them to do things for me, to call me, and he was the one they went to for military advice. I knew what my kids were doing.

I drift in a raging sea today, because I have no mooring. I have a building to live in, but I have no home. I do not have someone to read me like a book or to know that a Whole Foods Sante Fe sandwich might do just the trick on those do over days. I am losing Phil's laughter, his smell, and the way his eyes lit up when he talked to me, about me, or when he saw me. I want an anchor or a safe haven in which to retreat. I want more than a nice house. I want the eyes that light up and the loyal, true partnership I shared with Phil. I want the knowing of someone so well that I know him almost as well as myself. I want a home-a warm home.

I Am Not Giving Phil's Assassin the Gift of my Anger

Hating Phil's assassin has never crossed my mind. I don't understand how someone could pretend that well. Phil's assassin was on friendly terms with Phil. While Fox News portrayed a man who struggled with English, he certainly had enough English to talk to Phil. Phil had the language skills to communicate with him in his native language. This man chose to look into the eyes of someone who trusted him and to take his life. The assassin did not win that day.

While evil was prevalent and while evil temporarily won, the story is simply not over there. I miss Phil and I would gladly have given my life so that his star could have sparkled longer, but for some reason God is not finished with me. My journey isn't over. I am not sure what there is to do or to experience, but someone somewhere needs me or God wants to use me to bring awareness to military loss and painful loss being walked with faith—the only thing that has brought me peace and comfort. If I believed that the gunman had won that day, I would not be able to crawl out of bed and to go on. I believe, and, oh, how I believe that Phil resides with the Lord. The gunman? Unless he had a very quick conversion, he resides elsewhere. Guess what? It just doesn't matter to this girl. The gunman robbed me of the life I had and the dream I had of growing old with Phil. I choose not to be angry because anger isn't going to change the horrible events of 27 April.

Having said that, and even as I find answers in my faith and in my reliance on that faith, I am warier now. I second guess myself, so how can I trust my perceptions when Phil's were wrong? How do I become the girl who believed in the good of every person she met? How do I become the girl I once was, the girl who believed that world peace was possible through training and compassion? Phil believed in this ideal, lived this ideal, and ultimately gave his life to the very people he was invited to help? In one sense, the gunman killed a very vital component of me. Yes, he took my best friend, but he took the sense that all is well in my world. I can't stop to give the assassin anger. He already has taken far too much from me. I am not going to give him, or any other violence prone militant, the satisfaction of seeing my anger because I will let my God mete out the justice. I am going to fall into my faith and continue a journey that I gladly would have given to Phil.

Practical Things I Should Have Known Prior to Phil's Death

I have considered not writing about the practical matters that people should consider before deployment primarily because most people do not want to think about the unthinkable loss of a spouse gone far too soon. I didn't. I made jokes and tried to change the subject when Phil tried to talk with me about things. He left an extensive file with important information, but there was so much more that I should have listened to and that we should have considered. While many of my friends here in Germany are facing deployment in the next month, and while I understand that thinking about death of a military spouse is beyond comprehension and by not thinking about the unthinkable, we can wrap our arms around our spouses going to war stricken areas, I am still going to write about what I should have done or known.

I was a military spouse for 23 years—almost thirty years if you consider my first marriage. For years, Phil deployed to countries where many things could have happened. It was only with this deployment that he took out extra life insurance. I begged him not to and I made jokes about the policy. He insisted. When he was killed, my father, like many others voiced that now I would be set for life. People do not realize that if Phil had lived, within eight years, he would have out earned both policies. Eight years even if he never got another raise or promotion. My survivor benefit is less than his retirement, about half, if he could have retired versus dying.

When a spouse is killed in action, the pay check is frozen. Phil was killed on the 27th of April. I was told by the casualty affairs officer on my first day back from Dover not to touch the pay because it would be pulled back as part of the estate. I was fine because I had a job and we had a cushion. I never felt this, but had we been enlisted with five children at home and me not working, this would have been a big deal for about two weeks.

I found out about Phil dying late on the 27th. I was set to fly to KY first thing in the morning for a marathon. I had forty dollars total in my purse. When I was notified about Phil, nobody told me how Dover worked, how it was paid for, or how the flights worked. I knew that Phil had a life insurance policy due on the 27th. I couldn't find a payment to USAA, so I called them on the 27th. When the plane landed in TX, I had a message. Every USAA account and credit card had been frozen because we did all of our banking online through a central access point that Phil had set up with one password. There I was, half way to Delaware with forty dollars and no credit cards. Total panic set in. This was not something that could be fixed on the phone.

While the hotel and flights to Dover were covered for all of us, it wouldn't have been the case if four of my children hadn't been military. Each family is allotted two people to accompany the spouse. A voucher goes in after the fact for per diem, but a spouse needs a credit card or cash to pay for the meals and incidentals up front. I was fortunate that three of my children were in a position to pay for the meals and incidentals.

A power of attorney becomes null and void immediately upon death of a spouse. It takes much longer to get a military equivalent of a certified death copy. Many organizations don't understand it. I should have looked at our storage rental agreement. We had sold our house just before Phil's deployment knowing that we would be moving when he returned. While I packed and unpacked boxes, Phil and the boys dropped off the boxes that didn't fit into our apartment at a storage unit. When I showed up with a copy of the will (CO is a no probate state), the agreement, and the certified death copy, I was not allowed to access the unit. Public Storage drug their heels and went through their legal team because my name was not on the agreement. Yes, the unit was released, but it was released far too late for me to go through the unit before I moved, to declare professional weight, or to get things out of it that I needed for my move to Germany. I will feel the repercussions of this oversight for a long time because I will have to rip off band aids to go through Phil's stuff and I will bust my weight coming back from Germany which means that I incur a financial penalty.

I should have had all of the important papers in one place. When Phil died, I wasn't thinking straight. I couldn't find his will. Base legal did not keep a copy on file. While Phil had the normal military paperwork filled out showing the distribution, I spent one solid week trying to locate it. In the move, I lost track of my tax paperwork from 2010. I had paperwork dating back to 2000, but I couldn't find what I needed for tax forgiveness. Yes, another thing that the Air Force didn't tell me was that I get tax forgiveness for three years on Phil's income—the year before he deployed, the year of his deployment, and next year. The caveat? All of that paperwork I couldn't find. While I eventually either got another copy or found it, I should have put it all in a binder or a brief case before Phil left.

My ID card to base was frozen, also. Out of error, the Air Force coded Phil's status wrong. Instead of saying deceased, when I tried to get on USAFA, my card said that he was separated from the Air Force. My card was taken temporarily at the gate. I didn't know who to call because I did not know who my FLO was or what he was supposed to be able to help me with. There has to be a connection with someone for those days when a person is walking around in a fog of pain. I couldn't remember anything. I was lost. After my daughter went home, I would lose hours and days and never realize it. I needed help, yet I did not know who to ask for help.

When Phil's stuff came back, I did not know that it would fall on me to help carry the 14 black foot lockers up the stairs. I did not know that his wedding ring wouldn't be on his hand when he came home. I did know military forms or resources because Phil's world was that—mine was being a wife and a mom. I could have done anything with school records, medical records, etc, and while I knew the jargon, I am still adrift on where I stand with the military. I am still a dependent I think. A dependent wife of who, though? Retiree? Active? I don't know, but every appointment that I try to make, I end up explaining because nobody tells me. This distinction matters with medical appointments—especially overseas where I am a DoDea teacher and I carry two ID cards.

In conclusion, though it is hard, there needs to be an organized plan in place before the deployment. All of the papers need to be centralized in a binder or briefcase. There should be cash on hand that is only to be touched in the event of the unthinkable. If I had been overseas when this happened, that cushion should be even bigger. Each online bank account and credit card needs to have two access points and two passwords. One of my credit cards is still not fixed because of the rewards we had accrued in the ten years prior to Phil's death. Take out the extra insurance policy just in case, and talk about the unthinkable—where to live, financials, paperwork, children, etc. Phil and I did do the last bit and that became a crucial component in my walk of learning to live without him. Maybe this blog is morose and unnecessary—and oh, how I hope that it is, but I should have been better prepared. I had 23 years to get ready, but I failed to plan, and in failing, it has made the journey longer and more difficult.

Oh, How Different Today Was Supposed to Be

Oh, how different this was supposed to be. Phil and I planned for the day we were going to see Ramstein this time. We had so many things we dreamt about and wanted to do. As my Family Liaison Officer drove me into an area that I once knew so very well, my heart was assaulted by memories of four years shared here. We came to Ramstein with five children ages 1 to 11 and we lived in stairwell housing now deemed too inhumane to out the big families in, but oh, how we loved living overseas and the adventures it brought.

I will never forget the day that Phil called me at the pool and had one of my employees get me out of the water. I thought he was joking. I stood there speechless. We didn't know where Boarfink was, but that was inconsequential. . .it was Europe. Little did we know that we would be diverted in route to Ramstein. It took five months to get our fast shipment. . .by then, none of the children's clothes fit. We spent nearly three months in a one bedroom lodging room where we put the two boys in one bed, Emily in the other, the babies in play pens, and Phil and I slept on the fold out couch. It isn't like that here now. I am staying in a fancy room with the biggest Air Force Mall attached to it. I am in awe. . .Macaroni Grill plus other restaurants, a BX that is huge and overwhelming, a rock wall, and on and on. None of that existed when we were here, yet we felt so blessed.

I saw the trail I ran on, walked through the emergency room where I spent numerous hours with my children (and where Josh was taken by ambulance after he fell out of a tree by our apartment), and I walked up the stairs where we once lived. Those top apartments are no longer lived in, but I could hear the echoes of Josh and Emily bickering, Tiger saying, "sorry, I said sorry!" after he pinched his brother yet again (he was two), and Patrick getting frustrated at his lack of space. I remembered the homeschooling days when I marked everything in the house, and I remember lying on the king sized bed and reading to the kids for hours and hours. I remember the many trips to Baumholder and the Lanstuhl Allwetterbad. We had one car. . .a big blue minivan. It made me so happy to see Phil driving up to get me after I had been teaching swimming lessons all evening.

I remembered the six month deployments to Southern France and the one month we all crammed into a small hotel room so that we could see Phil's family origins. I do not know if I could ever return to Marseilles, Arles, Avignon, but I remember that Phil and I snuck out every night to get

Vietnamese egg rolls. I remember the lavender fields and mostly, I remember the pride Phil had as it clicked that he was a successful interpreter. The fire for his commission came after one of these deployments. He still, holds the record for over 300 CLEP credits through University of Maryland. He took 15 credits and got a bachelor's degree and proved to the education counselor that, yes, it could be done--a commission after earning a degree like that. He always thought the Air Force would discover him a fraud and take that commission even after he earned his PhD.

We drove by the building Phil worked in. I will never forget the day Phil came home after overhearing his co-workers talking about the man with all tho "damn" kids. From then on, he felt like the Kentucky militia and he and I and the kids became such a tight unit that we didn't need anyone else. We did everything together. . .all of us. We were the Boy Scout leaders, the Girl Scout leader, the Sunday school teachers, the parents involved in school, and we were the family that went to the NCO club every Thursday because the kids ate free. We were the family that took hikes, had picnics, and experienced as much as we could in the seven and a half years here, but Phil and I never had a moment where it was just the two of us.

I got back memories that I had forgotten. My heart did bleed for the life I shared with my Phil. I am sorry that we never had this moment of standing in awe at the changes in our old stomping grounds. I am sorry that when we were here, our focus was often on what could make our kids successful and good and that we were focused on breaking the poverty pit we were mired in. I wish we had taken just a day to recognize that being together was all any of us really needed. Some of my happiest days were spent here. Some of my darkest days, too, for it is here that I lost my health for quite a few years. I would never ever trade the time we had here. I sure wish that we could share it now because it is interesting. I can afford to do the things I wanted to do last time I was here, but I would give it all up for one more moment in my Phil's life even if it were in the project rejects of 3870 T Birch Street where we had a drug dealing free family on one side and some thugs on the other side. I would take the one moment and gladly live for the backwards meals, the hikes, and lying together as a family, reading, always reading.

Ansbach for a Reason

Exodus 4:11-12 "Then the Lord asked Moses, "Who makes a person's mouth? Who decides whether people speak or do not speak, hear or do not hear, see or do not see? Is it not I, the Lord? Now go! I will be with you as you speak, and I will instruct you in what to say."

All along, I have felt like there is a reason for me to be in Ansbach. I prayed and I felt the fire blazing even at Phil's funeral. Few know that I put in for worldwide teaching availability the day of Phil's funeral. I had filled out the application in preparation for a PCS military move in January. The thinking was that we would know where we were going to have our last assignment before going back to USAFA for the rest of Phil's career. I could get a teaching job and move on my own orders. In our last conversation, the what if conversation, Phil told me that if something happened to him to put in my application for worldwide jobs, thus I did.

My application was five days late, but DoDea took it because of the circumstances. I was told all of the positions had been filled, yet I got a phone call in July offering me a job without an interview. I had five days to get everything done. The five days included a family day, the fourth of July, and a weekend. Two generals later, a compassionate doctor later, and many other nice people later, I had my package in. My official passport came in record time and I was in Germany less than a month after being offered the job. I never doubted God wanted me here, but it made me fearful of why I was being called to be here.

Today, I know why I am here. It is as I feared. Really feared. Two more women are military widows. Their husbands are gone far too soon. On a small garrison where everyone knows everyone, and where most are deployed, there is a pall--a cloying smell of hysteria. If the unthinkable could happen to two pilots, then what about the rest of the deployed troops? Extolling people to rely on faith and to not waste time worrying is fruitless and trite. To a young military wife waiting at home and walking through the first long dangerous deployment, to the senior leadership, all is not well. Fear and loss etch our faces and carve grooves into the crevices of the planes. Silent tears fall both in the heart and from the weeping eyes. Words of being strong and bucking up will not work--rather they will push the people in need further away.

What then will help? We need to stand watch and stand together. People are stressed and sometimes the people that look the most put together are hurting the very worst. We need to be lifelines to one another--reaching and watching. Stress is high. It is going to be higher even still. People will withdraw, act angrily, and fall to other coping strategies. We need to be the family that we claim to be. We need to watch for the walking wounded and we need to carry them when we can for we are the walking wounded and we will need to be carried at some point also. I wear the mask of stoicism well. I wear the mask that camouflages the tears and pain in my heart. Nobody sees it--or rarely. We need to be vigilant because as a family, these losses will lead to more losses if we do not reach out.

Our children are stressed. I took the stress test and scored a 584. I had lost a spouse, a dog, and moved to Germany. Many of my students scored what I scored or around that score because they are dealing with military moves, deployments of parents, friends moving, new schools, moving with their families, etc. I asked them in class about if they knew what buttons to push with their parents. Every hand went up. I shared that parents knew what buttons to push also. Under stress, we all have behaviors that we are not proud of. I do not even see mine, but they are there. We cannot pretend that our children won't be affected by the stress of military loss. They are afraid already. They talk to me. They are afraid for their deployed fathers and mothers. Losing two pilots will make it real to them. They will fear more. We need to bond together as a village and watch vigilantly for withdrawal, behaviors out of character, delinquency, self harm, depression, and I could go on. The journey is going to be a difficult trek because summer is upon us.

As a village, we need to open our doors, windows, and hearts. We need to stop hiding. Programs need to be implemented so that people come together and find a way to laugh and forget for just a minute. We need to develop a check in system. I needed that accountability. My people in Colorado and the KAIA group (deployed group) gave it to me for the first few months physically and they still carry me. We may not have the words or the actions to fix what happened, but we need to unite for our military family. We need to carry the widows indefinitely with prayers, cards, actions, and we need to carry our fearful walking wounded. My hand is raised. My heart is open. I am here for a reason. Use me in the lives of the children and families now. Blaze spirit, blaze.

The Military Connection That Ties us All Together

I have Lost My Family--My Military Family

I have always believed in the military family standing as one in time of loss. While that may be true on some level for many fallen soldiers' families, it isn't true for me. I am not sure why, but contact has basically stopped since the funeral of my Phil. It is crushing to think that people come out and play the pretenders for the media and the big brass attention, but that they don't care to reach out when no one is watching.

I didn't know that I had a Family Liaison Officer (FLO) person assigned to me until the day before Phil's things were delivered. I have not seen him or talked to him once since the day after the funeral. Another wife who lost her husband in the same attack is contacted every day. I don't need that, but I feel as if I were to fall off of the face of the earth, not one person would give a damn outside of my children. Why is it that I am being left alone? It has been nearly two months (Tuesday) and I do not merit any contact? When Phil was deployed, not one person contacted me either, but that omission was laughable. This is not.

The one military male friend that I had that was not assigned to our family except for Dover has been warned repeatedly to be careful. Huh? What did I do, say, etc. to lead the brass to say something like that? I have never in my life behaved inappropriately and I can promise anyone that I am not going to start now. Where once I could call him to lean during the hard times, I no longer have that option, but there are no replacements stepping up.

I am feeling better today, but there has been two specific times when I needed the military connection: 1) when I got the autopsy report and the pictures. I should not have had to ask for a person to sit with me when I looked at my bullet ridden husband's body and read about how many bullets hit him, and, 2) When 14 footlockers come in filled with all the things that mattered to my Phil, it should be okay for me to want a military person that I am comfortable with counting his underwear. I shouldn't have to ask for it. I don't want it if I have to ask for it. I rarely need the support, but I needed it the past few weeks. I didn't get it from the military except from someone really far away. It isn't right.

I have always believed in the military family standing as one in time of loss. While that may be true on some level for many fallen soldiers' families, it isn't true for me. I am not sure why, but contact has basically stopped since the funeral of my Phil. It is crushing to think that people come out and play the pretenders for the media and the big brass attention, but that they don't care to reach out when no one is watching.

I didn't know that I had a FLO person (maybe not who I think it is-or maybe I don't have one) assigned to me until the day before Phil's things were delivered. I have not seen him or talked to him once since the day after the funeral. I really am not sure if anyone has been officially assigned. Another wife who lost her husband in the same attack is contacted every day. I don't need that, but I feel as if I were to fall of the face of the earth, not one person would give a damn outside of my children. Why is it that I am being left alone? It has been nearly two months (Tuesday) and I do not merit any contact? When Phil was deployed, not one person contacted me either, but that omission was laughable. This is not.

The one military male friend that I had that was not assigned to our family except for Dover (I think, but how do I know who is assigned to do what), has been warned repeatedly to be careful. Huh? What did I do, say, etc. to lead the brass to say something like that. I have never in my life behaved inappropriately and I can promise anyone that I am not going to start now. Where once I could call him to lean during the hard times, I no longer have that option, but there are no replacements stepping up.

I would say something, but to say something puts a target on my four military children's backs. One is at USAFA as a cadet. My daughter is getting a second master's degree at Purdue at USAFA's expense to return to USAFA to teach like her dad. I am so aware of military protocol and bucking up, but I am adrift. I have lost the family I claimed the past 23 years. I have been a military wife and mom for that long. I moved where we were told to move and I did what I needed to do to support my family. Now....I am a nonentity. That shunning has hurt more than words can express. I am alone.

Standing Up to the Bullies

Many people have heard or read of my Phil's story. A story that begins with a twelve year old boy immigrating to the United States. A boy who did not know English. A boy who at eighteen opted to join the United States Air Force as a way to give back to his adopted country. He was always thankful for the opportunities and freedoms he was afforded as an American citizen. He served honorably and well for 25 years and he gave all he had to give on 27 April 2011 in Kabul, Afghanistan.

Phil was there as an American soldier, but his role, one that he passionately believed in, was educating and mentoring the Afghan military members. He was not in another country bullying or repressing. He was there to help another country through education to stop the oppression against the weak, women, children, and the religiously different people. He stood for those who were unable to stand for themselves. He stood against a bully that still wants to dominate and control anyone who does not believe as they do.

This morning, I was deeply wounded by someone I highly respect. Two days after hearing the unthinkable details of my husband's massacre, I awoke to a message asking this: "But WHY??? Can't we live in peace with each other?" This statement crushed me. My shattered heart re-split. I know this person did not mean to inflict more pain, but as a military wife and as a military mother of 4 children serving now, I want to stand up and talk for what my Phil died for. I am humbled to be a mouth piece for the names that flash across our TV screen. Every name that flashes across the TV screen stands for a soldier who wanted to come home—a soldier who was loved and waited for by someone here.

These soldiers stood for us. In my family, we have taken on the role of either fixing people or educating people. Many of my children are in the medical field. They are in the healing business. Phil, our daughter, and I are educators. We affect change through the education of people. While I am not a military person, I included myself because I believe that through education people's lives and attitudes are changed.

As a middle schooler, I was bullied incessantly. I was quiet, shy, insecure, and I was ugly. I was heavy and I had not only an acne problem, I had allergy issues that led to my being called lovely names such as Linda Leper and Linda Pizza Face. The taunts hurt, but being invisible and undervalued hurt more. I have been blessed as an American citizen to have opportunities and privileges as a female. I can speak and I have independence. I do not fear that my family is going to be killed if I am saying or doing something that someone else considers wrong. I may make bad choices, but the choices only impact me—not the people around me. I do not live in fear.

As a woman and a mom, I would hope that if people would stand up to injustice against me...against my children. I would hope that someone would come in and help my society establish itself so that I could live without fear. Yes, as an educator, I would hope that the bullies would respond to education and intervention. One of the reasons I love teaching PE, it is about teaching youth to work with a team that includes weaker players. I love teaching cooperation and teamwork, but what happens when a bully escalates violence and oppression?

At the elementary school level, it is easy. The bully is sent home for the day. Parents are involved. The bully receives feedback on the error of his ways. Understand, the bully usually continues until someone stands up to hi/her. The bully is often secretive and driven in his/her actions. At the world level, the terrorist is the ultimate bully because he seeks domination through the most extreme forms of violence. He often does not perpetuate violence against his own people, but against people who are shifting attitudes and mores of the repressed people he has for so long caused to live in fear. The terrorist bully is a secretive bully. People do not see the vile evil lurking in the shadows of his eyes. The terrorist often is like a chameleon. He comes across as a friend, an ally, a person working towards the cohesive community of cooperation and peace, but below the surface, he is undermining and plotting. This evil runs so deep that it is hard to fight. Education alone will not always work.

Having said that my family is comprised of people mostly in the education or medical fields, fields that are non-combative, what happens when the bully doesn't back down? What happens when the bully continues to take lives and inflict pain not only on the people around him, but on the people there to help? I am thankful for the people who are willing to stand up to the bullies of this world. I am thankful for the military men and women who are willing to say to the bully, "enough is enough." Though these military members do not want violence, nor do they seek it, they are willing to respond to the violence around them. They are willing to try to educate the bullies, but when the bullies respond with more violence, they are willing to stand up. I am so thankful that they are.

Through the course of hearing about the events of 27 April, I learned of a man who also was not serving in a combative role. A weatherman. A family man. A man that was not even in the same room where the evil was playing out. This man responded though he could have run away. This man lost his life as a hero. He didn't ask to be a hero. It wasn't his job. It wasn't his responsibility; he could have run out the door to safety, but he chose to stand up to the bully in front of him. He is my hero...

Another military man that I recently met (and I do not know him) through the circumstances of the husband's death is in a role that few would want. It doesn't matter what that job is, but here is what does matter. What he is doing is making difference. He stands up to the bullies, he gathers information about the bullies, and he has the back of every military family out there. His job was to let me know all of the events that happened in that room. I know it wasn't easy, but I wanted the information...needed the information...He stood with me against the bully because he found the information and he gave me the information.

While the military members have many roles, some combative, some non-combative, the ultimate role of the military person is to stop oppression and to stand for what is honorable and right. I am thankful that people throughout history have stood for my rights. I am thankful that people stood up to the bullies that repressed women, children, and dare I say, American citizens. I am a proud American citizen who says, yes, I want peace. I pray for peace, but if there is a bully, I hope that someone is strong enough to stand up for me. I hope that someone is willing to give all so that my children and my children's children do not have to live in fear of violence. I stand for what is true, right, and honorable. I stand for all even as my Phil gave all.

Phil's Things and the Cold Awful Day

I am going on a rant. I rarely let myself do this because it isn't productive, nor do I feel good when I am done, but there is something really fundamentally wrong with making someone wait and wait for 14 footlockers containing the remnants of my husband's life. No phone call. No e-mails. Just a date.

I did ask to have the time clarified and narrowed down. My e-mail was ignored. You know how that makes me feel? Non-valued. I get that I am just a military dependent and that duty has already been done, but I am a person. I am a person whose heart is bleeding. This just isn't right.

Really? I am supposed to wait around all day waiting for footlockers that thought of brings me to my knees. The only thing that keeps me from bolting (and I still might) is that it might impact my children. I don't want the military tattle-taling to my military children. Sigh. Can you tell that I am feeling really, really ugly. . .discombobulated?

Did some things for me today (translation. . .cost money). I bought a smaller bed and sheets (the kind is just too big for me), but more importantly, I bought cute clothes so that I can be look decent (clothes actually fit. . .I lost a bunch of sizes since April) as Sasha Fierce on my pink bicycle. It just made me happy to be making some small steps.

A True Hero

Many of us in life rarely know someone who is a hero of a caliber like Captain Nathan Nylander. Nathan chose to leave a safe area and run to the rescue of his fallen friends, one of whom was my husband, Major Phil Ambard. Nate could have chosen to leave the building. Many people did, but Nathan stood true to the end and it cost him his life in the process. Although his gun jammed three times, Captain Nylander did not flee. He stayed true and present to the very end. I can't fathom the depth of fortitude it took to respond to the vile evil playing out around him, but Nate stepped up to the plate.

While I will never have the opportunity to see if my courage will be sufficient in a wartime situation, and I am not sure if I ever see myself in a hero role, there are day to day heroes. So often I race about oblivious to the hurting needs of others around me. In their quiet desperation, they do not ask for help and I do not see the unspoken plea. I have learned by being totally broken and bowed that sometimes a kind word or kind act is the simplest form of heroism. In my darkest hour of need, there have . been lifelines given in the way of a simple instant message, a phone call, a meal, etc. I may not have looked like I need a hero, but those people stepped up to the plate for me.

I have learned that people do not always cry out for a lifeline. I don't, or I rarely do, but I am desperately clinging to a thread of hope in a better tomorrow. People around me are much the same. In their darkest hours, they may not be able to utter any language but a cry from the soul. I need to be watching and willing to help. I understand that I am spent and broken beyond repair, but I am still able to reach the rescue buoy to my drowning friend. By being afraid of doing the wrong thing, or saying the wrong thing, means that I am willing to watch someone else drown.

As I gasp for my own breath of air, I sense the pain in others. I may not be able to stand up to vile reprehensible bullies like Nathan did, but I can reach out. I can be a lifeline until real help comes. I can stand up and I can walk with someone else who is just as battered and broken as I am. In the process, I just might find my own footing and my own sense of self. My own pain may be allayed if only for a second. I can in no means ever be a hero in a Superman cape like Nate, but I can perhaps make a small ripple of difference in the murky pond today. I choose to look beyond my own pain and loss to finding hope through providing a reaching hand to my brother and sister today. I may be only one, and I may be weak, but I choose to show up. Nathan chose to show up. It meant all to me and it meant all too many other people. I use Nathan's heroism to compel me to be the person I am being called to be—one who lives beyond my fears.

Speaking Out About Afghanistan

I have never spoken my mind about Afghanistan like I have been doing recently. I am so tired of people thinking that we are warring and are somewhat responsible for the loss of life. Phil was there as a trainer and advisor to make life better for the Afghan people. He was not an aggressor. Our military is trying to educate, help, and set up programs so that oppressed people might have an opportunity. As a mom, and as a woman, I would hope that all of my children would grow up with certain rights. He wasn't strong arming. . .he was EDUCATING.

I am not educated enough or articulate enough to speak about this, but understand, my husband believed in what he was doing and he took pride into going into the schools and working with the Afghans. He spoke of making a difference and he prayed to make a difference. When people say that they want the war to be over, I get frustrated at the simplistic ignorance. As a woman, and as a mom, I hope that someone looks out for my basic rights. I hope that someone stands up to the bully in the room. When a person is willing to die for religious beliefs, very little can be done to combat the intent behind the violence. The argument should be whether or not the culture and people want the change. Ask the women and the children. Ask the Christian man living there. The extremists are the only ones being heard right now. They are heard through the vilest, most reprehensible and cruelest forms of dominion.

In the Bible, God used the little guys to stand up to the bully time and time again. First, there was little David who stood up to Goliath with a sling shot. He slays the big ogre because he acted. If one looks at Joshua, God used the harlots to hide him so that he could be successful. The component in each case is the two men who lived by faith. I believe. I trust, and I obey. I know that Phil did not want to die in Afghanistan so I am making it my mission to educate and bring a face to the names that flash across my TV screen every night. Each name is a loss and the loss diminishes us all.

We Are Family - I

Last night someone said to me, "We are your family now." I don't think that he realized just how much those words meant to me. I have felt like I have lost my Air Force Family. The only exception to this is the people in Afghanistan that are still walking with me. The people in Afghanistan and the people here do not know me. They didn't know me before the loss of Phil damaged me. They choose to stand with me now when times are tough. . .when I am not so easy to be around. They choose to love me in spite of myself.

The Air Force that my Phil served always seemed like a family to me. In fact, for almost thirty years, I felt that the military was my family. . .my home. I felt safe and loved. I never once thought that the friendships and relationships would be severed when Phil was killed. He died honourably. In fact, in the military realm, he died the admirable way. Yet, upon his death, the Air Force family stood with me when the media was watching, but then they left me standing alone. Family does not do that.

Family says, we love you any way. They spend time with a person even when the person isn't a bundle of laughs. People in family do not have to be told to spend time with family. They care. Family stands together and they do the right thing because it is the right thing to do even when nobody is watching. Family makes a person feel included and does not ignore a person trying to hide out.

It is interesting that the army knows this. Yes, they have had more losses, but isn't even one loss too many? Does this mean that Phil didn't matter to his military brothers and sisters outside of Afghanistan? Does this mean that the Air Force only valued his work ethic, and like his own mother, can't be bothered to even attend his funeral? It hurts.

As a military spouse, I lost my entire adult identity in one fell swoop on 27 April. I lost all I gave my life to with the exception of my faith and my children (who the military owns also). I relate to the military. I feel like a social outcast, but I want the military connections. When people include me and call me family, it makes my heart bleed a little, but their kindness gives me hope that I still am important to my family. That I still matter.

Forever Linked

We are forever linked through the tragic events of 27 of April, but here is the aspect you don't know. . .I choose you all. You would have been my friends if I had met you in real life. You know, when we all had a life. Maybe we would have . . .been too busy or too enmeshed in our busy lives to have appreciated the strength that I see in all of you, but there is a reason we are walking this journey together. WE have to stand together because we are so strong as one. I feel that I can make it through any day if I have you ladies standing with me. I know you understand more than any other person the disbelief, the loss, the confusion. I know that you all do not judge me no matter how I feel or what I say. You will forever be in my heart.

Sometimes people become friends through their darkest hours and greatest need. Many people may claim to know us well, or they even may be related to us, but they are not walking the same uneven path. When my Phil was killed with eight other people on the 27th of April, I was forever linked with the other surviving spouses and people who were there. I did not know any of these people. I may have been a friendly acquaintance if I had met them at a time previous to our loved one's death, however, this tragic event led to a bonding that very few can understand. We understand when we talk about the hurt of losing a spouse or a colleague in such an inhumane manner. We understand the fear of the unknown, the friend who is an enemy. We understand the bereft feeling as the institution fails us. We understand seeing our colleague, our friend, our son, our spouses so broken that nobody should have that image etched in their heads.

It is a lonely club. It is a club that no one would elect to join. We are twined together with unbreakable strands of cord. When one or two is weak, the group carries him. So many nights people have stood with me from Afghanistan. They talk to me and tell me that they remember, yet lifetime friends and family have pulled away. They do not understand the loneliness or the loss of self-identity. Only the people who have seen the worst can fully understand the need for our loved ones to be remembered and that we still need to talk about them. They do not judge as each person careens back and forth striving to find a new normal.

There have been people who have stood with me and carried me. These women have inspired me and pushed me to be a better person because I did not understand the great need I had for the human touch and friendship until they responded. These women rescued me even when they did not know me well. They took care of immediate needs like food and mail/car/transportation needs, but they also gave me glimmers of hope for a brighter future by throwing me a 50th birthday party, putting together my Sasha Fierce bike and giving me plenty of pink to be fierce, bringing me coffee, and just being a friend. They listened, made me laugh, and they didn't ask or expect me to be any different than I was day to day—up and down like a yoyo. Four months later, these women still carry me. They get it. They have never lost their spouses like I lost mine, but they truly get it. I did not until this happened to me.

Time does give me the luxury of erecting walls and developing a new normal. I have forever changed from that shy quiet girl into a woman who stands up and writes and speaks about loss. While many do not understand why I publicly put my thought out there, I put them out there for people like me—people with a big heart that do not know or see the pain in others. I strive to honor Phil's memory by standing with and walking with others that suffer greatly. My heart was shattered into a million shards that April day, but I believe that by reaching out and being the friend that others have taught me to be, I will be whole again. I look to that day and I reach for that moment. Until then, I am learning and I am striving to be the friend that others have taught me to be. I will fall short, but I will be better than I was yesterday one step at a time.

Why September 11th Means so Much to me This Year

September 11, 2001…I remember where I was and who I was with. Ten years later that day still touches me and still sparks my outrage and sense of nationalism. On that day, I was away from my family. I was in Dayton, OH for training. I was the Youth Center Director for Hill AFB. I was in a school with people I did not know. I left class to use the restroom and I saw three people standing around a very small TV screen. I flippantly asked what they were watching. As they silently shifted so I could watch the image of the first plane crashing into the first tower, my heart dropped. My life changed that day. My sense of security and safety in my own country altered forever that day.

In the days that followed, the human spirit began to emerge. I drew close to the people I was in training with (one of whom is still a close friend) and I found my patriotism that lives on. The picture of the firemen hoisting that tattered flag over Ground Zero still touches me. Phil was no different. September 11th gave him a mission and a desire to change people who sought to maim our spirit by destroying landmarks and more than that, killing of people for no other reason that ideology. Phil sought to change and create new attitudes through education and mentorship.

He never felt like he was worthy of recognition. He never wanted people to know that he was an immigrant because he thought they would think less of him or think that he had malicious intent based on his origins. In church, or anywhere else they asked service men and women to stand, he wouldn't. He felt that honor belonged to those who served in combat zones. He thought he was a blue suiter who the military could live with or without. How wrong he was.

In the spirit of 9/11 and in the spirit of the American people, resiliency and a sense of neighborly help emerged. We became connected as a nation and as a people. Ten years later, people have lost that sense of outrage and connection. My Phil gave his life standing for his adopted country. Phil lost his life doing what he was compelled to do that awful, awful day. Phil stood for change through working side by side with people who say they want change. Phil knew that there would be enemies; he just never expected them to act like a friend. Phil wanted to believe that people's attitudes and beliefs could change once they were working side by side.

Shortly after Phil died, he was brought back to the United States in a flag draped numbered box. For a man who did not know a word of English at 12, and who became a citizen at 18 in order to serve our country, his life was being played out in the media. His life in the military was never more defined than that moment when he was shot in his military uniform. His life mattered to me and to his family for much longer than that, but his life and death as a military man is directly impacted by 9/11. There is a You Tube video that came out with the images of bowed heads and flag draped boxes bearing the bodies of nine people who lost their lives on 27 April. The music played on this clip, "I'm coming home. I'm coming home. Tell the World that I'm coming home. "Yes, Phil was coming home to the land that he gave all to the land he adopted. His spirit lives on in the tattered flag that waves above Ground Zero and in the faces of the grimy, fatigued firemen who are looking up. I look up and I see…I see the human resiliency and the human connection. I reach for that tattered flag because it holds all I hold dear.

United for Nine

United for the 9, I ran on. Though quite sick, the prayers of many allowed me to live my faith and finish. Though I was far off of the time I should be running, I am standing. I cried once at the end. I booked the last two miles and I just felt like I had the arms of angels surrounding me. This feeling is fleeting, but today I felt comfort and help in spite of the very sick body.

I cared only that I could honor the 9 fallen airmen. I didn't need a speedy time to prove that my loyalty was any less. I stood as part of the tattered blue uniform that covers me still. I am the flag that waves proudly for my country.

I prayed for my many friends today. I prayed for hurting warriors, deployed soldiers far from their families, and I prayed for something I have not been able to pray for yet. . .I prayed that my heart could see that not all Afghanis are bad people and for God to help me with my fear and xenophobic tendencies. I never felt that lack of trust before my Phil was taken by someone he trusted and considered a friendly ally, if not a friend. I have suffered and felt crushing pain in this area. I am not going to lie. My trust is not miraculously back. It is going to take time. It is going to take me being open to Afghanis. I will continue to step in faith and I will continue to look for a future when I can honestly say that I have chosen to forgive because forgiveness is a choice. I will get there. I am just not there today.

I run on to the rays of hope that I see. I run on to a new normal, but still my blue family is a part of me always. Waving in my heart, I see a flag flying and soaring. I see a future. I see hope. I stand as one heart to heart, arm in arm, together as one with my family wearing the tattered blue uniform. We are one today, tomorrow, and yesterday. Don't forget me.

The Uniform That Holds Us All

I run to my family clad in blue. I run to the arms of the military men and women standing for my county. They are my family. For thirty years, my adult life has been defined by being the strong military wife and mother. While my husband pulled on boots and a series of Air Force uniforms, my job was to keep the home fires burning. My role was to support and to be the stable parent at home.

Phil spent a lot of time away from home as a military man. He would walk out that door and know that I was at home and that I wouldn't fall apart. My strength and flexibility would hide the tears from prying eyes and from our children who looked to me for clues about how I felt. No matter where we were, when the military sent my husband to far off places or said that it was time to go, I found a way to make the separation seem like an adventure. I looked to the future to find strength from within.

With the loss of Phil, the adventure this time is gone. I fall into a deep rut sometimes because I am looking for direction, also. For thirty years, I affiliated my adult life as a military spouse and I let Uncle Sam dictate where I lived and for how long. It is strange and foreign to me to be making my own choices. I may fall, but I am walking by faith. I may regret choices, but they are still made by faith.

I still walk in the shadows of my military family. I am not quite a member of that family any more, but I have this need to stand with them and to affiliate myself with them. My heart is red, white, and blue. I may not be a part of the in crowd any more, but I stretch and lean towards my brothers and sisters in uniform. Can they see me? Do they know how proud I am of my family? Do they know that I stand with them? That I weep with them in times of loss? Do they see my pride in our fraternity? I stand proud.

I see the uniform and my heart breaks. I see the men and women behind the boots, and I see my Phil. I see my children. I see my friends. I see the uniform and I want to clutch it to my buxom and hold on for dear life. I am a part of the ragged uniform that holds us all.

The Bell Tolls for Thee

The clanging bell tolled on and on this morning at the Catholic Church. For five minutes the clamorous din filled the courtyard. People walked on as if nothing was out of character, yet when the five minutes ended, and the funeral hearse opened its doors, people paused. Some crossed themselves, others cast their eyes quickly to the ground, but it was eerily silent. John Donne once penned, "Do not ask for whom the bell tolls, it tolls for thee."

People rarely are privy to the mark they are leaving in the world. Over time the watermark become indelible and permanently fixed to the etched surface. Lives are like that. Before a person enters our lives, we cannot imagine the need or want for that person. Once we know a person, share with a person, love a person, our hearts and our very being are changed. We are changed, thus when death occurs, we change yet again.

Death of a loved one brings a loss and sense of overwhelming despair because normal is no longer normal. Each day is different. Each reaction. Each dream. My life changed in a blink of an eye on 27 April. I had been content in the quiet shadows of Phil's life. I didn't mind that he shone so brightly because I was a part of him. When he died, I was thrust front row and center to speak and to write about a man who sparkled and left his water mark. I had two choices-to cower in the corner or step up to the plate with my knocking knees. I chose the latter and in doing so, Phil's death forever changed me.

While the bell has long since finished tolling and resonating for Phil, the resounding echoes bounce off the walls of my heart and push me to a change that I think Phil would have welcomed. I think that he would have enjoyed seeing me standing so strong and confident. I think he would smile at my Sasha Fierce persona and I know that he would laugh at the pink polka dots and the bubbles. In my heart, the bell tolls on. I continue with the grace of God to push on and to use the gifts that I was given and that I learned through Phil loving me.

I take those lessons into my day to day life as I move from my home to Germany. I choose to embrace the strength he always had no matter what the obstacle. I take the lesson of wanting happiness for myself because he wanted that for me. I step forward into a budding relationship even though I am terrified beyond belief. I choose to continue this journey as a woman of God. I only can hope that I can honor the man that Phil was and will forever more be. Let the bell toll on. Let the clanging din be etched into the silent grooves of my beating heart. Always and forevermore, I am changed because of the love you had for me.

The Courage of One

Courage and internal fortitude are often born of circumstance and the split decision to act. Many people imagine that they would react in heroic manners when called to do so. Many people look for opportunities to shine in this area by selecting jobs that give them an opportunity to act in crisis situations. Few people realize, however, the opportunity to be a hero on any given day. Heroism may not be the grand epic act that makes the headlines, but rather, it may be a simple act that escapes any notice at all, but the action may change the a life or a process.

Nathan Nylander was a hero in everyone's eyes. He chose to respond to an evil monster shooting our military troops in a room next door to where he was. In the process, he gave his own life. Most people will never have this opportunity to be a Superman, but people can learn a lesson from Nathan. People can choose to respond to the something happening around them. Most people want to protect themselves and not to be the center of attention when it might cost them money, time, personal security or status, or recognition.

Nathan did not choose to respond and react for medals or recognition. He simply responded and reacted because it was the right thing to do. Many other people chose not to react or respond. Nathan, however, stepped up to the challenge. Many people ignore the injustices going on around them because it might single them out for the same injustices. Many people ignore the bullying or abuse of power going on around them because it may bring that same abuse or bullying to them. In middle school, I was bullied. Verbal taunts were terrible and a part of my everyday life. Other girls ignored what they witnessed thus silently condoning the behavior of the two who saw fit to use their social status at my expense. Sometimes a simple act of fortitude might be saying enough is enough.

Sometimes heroism can come in action to change policy, raise money, or to give of a time and talents. Volunteering to be a scout leader, raise money for worthy causes, sending letters, or mentoring/coaching others is the opportunity to be an everyday hero. Granted, people do not recognize the heroism, but the involvement leads to positive change and reactions. Involvement leads to making a difference with a positive impact on others. It is answering a need without the desire for recognition. Again, it comes down to choosing to react or to do.

In my own life, I have been a lifeguard for years. My job has been to save lives. I do not consider that heroic in terms of true heroism because I was trained and paid to react. I didn't have to enter a room where I was shot or a pool with sharks. I simply had to use my physical capabilities to help people. I consider it far more heroic to choose to stand up to the bullies of this world with my written words and through the use of my spoken words. I don't have to speak out on my journey, however I choose to because I know that many people are learning through my journey. I know that I am putting myself out there on the line when I talk about broken areas in our military system as it pertains to widow/widower support. While my act is nowhere near that of Nathan Nylander's, it is still a conscious decision to react to a need.

Complacency and inertia lead to many people barely surviving each day. Because of the comfort in status quo and the fatigue of daily living, people wait for others to respond. The question should be, if not me, then whom? If each person responded even in the smallest of manners, the world might change. If altruistic acts were the norm versus the rarity, then we might live in a society where war and social injustice no longer reigned. We might all live a happier and fuller life. True altruism means giving and responding without calling attention to the act. Action is all that is required. Nathan Nylander, acted selflessly and immediately without a thought to his own safety or recognition. His heroism has compelled this girl to examine her own life. I will never have a heroic act on the caliber of Nathan's act, but I will act.

My Military Family

My military family has never meant more to me than since my husband was killed in action in 27 April 2011. After 26 years of being an active duty family, the military is all I know. My identity and sense of belonging come from being a part of this group. Having lived away from my home town for so many years means that I am closer to my military family members than I am to my own family. When Phil was killed, military members all over the world carried me through my darkest hours. They have e-mailed me, sat with me, helped me logistically, sent me things, and they cried with me. More importantly, they shared Phil with me. Military members have carried my four military children, also. My children are stationed all over the world, yet they have been wrapped in the arms of support and faithfulness by a family that knows too much loss.

Veteran's Day has always meant a day off (or at least a brief remembrance of the people who have served in the United States military). Phil never thought that he deserved or had merited any recognition. He felt that he was only doing his job. The military family knows what that means. Long separations with multiple time zones separating them, too many missed family events to count, danger and having to consider not being able to live long enough to retire, combat boots and ABU uniforms, running in the wee hours of the morning, carrying a gun, and a family that gets used to a missing member. Military families are strong because they have to be strong. Children and spouses are expected to move every few years, deal with these long separations, and live not complaining about any of it. Veteran's Day honors the military person serving, thus it honors the family waiting behind.

Veteran's Day also honors the commitment that Phil made to his adopted country. He did join at the age of 18 for citizenship, but he served 26 years. He didn't have to. In fact he could have retired long before now. He chose to stay the course. He would have stayed in as long as the military would have him. He didn't have to do this. He felt an incredible sense of loyalty to the country which had given him so much. He felt nationalism that drove him and compelled him to encourage many, many people to join the military. Phil was not a recruiter, yet everywhere he went, he mentored adults and extolled the virtues of the military lifestyle. He convinced four of our children to go that route. When he donned his military uniform, hat, and combat boots, he became a soldier, but his heart and his life was that of a true soldier because he believed in all that is good in our country and in helping the oppressed and unrepresented in other countries. He stood for what is right and true. Phil believed in service and education to change the world around him. He didn't just believe, he acted, and in his action, he gave all.

Many civilians do not understand the military family. They do not see the conversations that we must have about the "what ifs", nor do they see anything beyond the images that flash on the TV screen of the bodies arriving from Dover. How can anyone understand what it is like to have a knock at the door and to open the door to uniformed people standing outside? How can a civilian understand a death after months and months of being apart? That we have nothing that smells like our loved one nor do we have recent memories of time spent with our loved ones? How can the average voter understand what it is like to raise five children largely alone and that my military man missed so many milestones and family events that he couldn't even remember them all?

As I hear the words, "Phil is not forgotten," and that his service is remembered, I know that we stand arm in arm, heart to heart, together as one in loss. This unity means all to this girl. This oneness is the reason that I am teaching overseas on an army post. I need and want my family, my military family, around me because they stand with me. They understand how I have lived my life and how I live it still. This means all to me. They are the only people who truly understand what it is to live the way that we do—temporary roots, strong connections, loyalty, a sense of duty to our country, and going on in spite of the inherent fears of putting on a uniform or loving someone in a uniform. They are me. I am them. We are family.

Happy Veteran's Day. I stand with you, my brothers and sisters especially those still serving in harm's way. You are loved, remembered and not forgotten. EVER. For my sisters who are trudging the path of loss with me, always, always, you are my family. I carry you as you carry me during the dark days. For my four military children and a special military friend, you mean all to me. Thank you for being willing to live the life that you are willing to live. I am deeply appreciative of the freedoms I am afforded because of people like you. I am proud to stand next to you. My military family, always you are loved.

The Tightly Woven Tapestry

Recently I met a friend from high school in Stuttgart, Germany where we enjoyed many hours of talking about days past as well as our lives now. Our threads of life are forever linked and woven tightly into a multi-hued tapestry. She and I could reminiscence about teachers, boys from high school, and we could share some of the tears of adulthood. We could commiserate over a shared past. The time we spent together was never awkward or strained. Silences were as comfortable as talking about our math teachers in high school. Today, however, I was reminded of how much the world has changed.

While this girl and I have a prolonged history that will never be written about in books, people can find out more about me than I was ever aware of. Through the use of Google and other search engines, people can think they know me. Someone told me today how many matches there were. . .thousands and thousands for me. I caught my breath. My life is even more public than I thought. I am not famous. I have not been arrested, detained, nor even had a speeding ticket, yet people can see a thinly woven piece of my tapestry. Not only does the running show up, but so does the work I did for St. Judes and the National Adrenal Foundation. Throw in teaching and some awards. Pile it high with the events of April, and people would think they would know every facet of my life. How wrong they would be.

Close friends know stories about me that would make me laugh or hurt. Close friends know that it is more than polka dots and bubbles that make me happy. Close friends can tell you about the awkward girl, Linda Lou Loser, who sat in class her junior high years, bullied and invisible. Fat and ugly. Taunted and rejected, but they can also tell you the story of a girl who discovered running and tell people stories that nobody will ever see in print. They know the tightly woven compartments of my heart that I do not let the public into. They know that no matter how many Google hits there are, it is but a piece of the puzzle.

These same friends will tell you of a girl who prayed diligently for five years, yes, five years, that she live beyond herself to shine brightly for Jesus. Jesus never needed me, but he knew the desires of my heart and the days that Phil had on earth. He was preparing me through my own prayers and desires for this very moment. As I fell into my faith and the calling that I found with the loss of Phil, those friends understood innately why I moved to Germany and why I can face each morning with hope and a smile. The Google articles are a small part of who I am. I am much, much more than that. I am so glad that I am.

Heroes do Not Always Wear Capes

People Magazine honors heroes in our world once a year. This week, the week of Christmas, it is only fitting that this magazine honors the lives of nine soldiers gone too soon. While I always knew that my Phil was a hero to me and our five children, now the world knows that Phil's life mattered. Why is it that in death, people find reasons to honor the life of service that many heroes gladly give?

Military men and women often fade into the background. Many people have many thoughts about the military presence throughout the world, but few think of the sacrifice these men and women gladly give. While it is a choice for our men and women to serve, this choice goes deeper than the surface. My husband, Phil, joined at 18 to get citizenship in a country that he loved. He had grown up in Venezuela where the opportunities went to the wealthy, the connected, or the corrupt. Phil never ever took for granted the opportunities and freedoms this country afforded. To the end, he was loyal and true to the red, white, and blue flag that represented all that he held dear.

When Phil pulled on his combat boots and buttoned his uniform, he stood for all that was true and all that was noble about our country. He was willing to stand up to the bullies that threatened to destroy or undermine the foundations and tenets this country was founded on. While he did not want to die, and, oh, how he did not want to die, he was the flag. He was a thread in the fabric of the stripes that bind our country. While as a lifelong United States citizen, I often took for granted the safety and freedoms of my country, Phil never did. He believed in the true immigrant population of service, hard work, and loyalty. He never had a sense of entitlement that many of us have. He chose to serve because he felt compelled to give back to his adopted country.

Servicemen give much more than wearing a uniform. They give up many family events and family connections. Military people are often deployed far away from home. In 23 years of marriage, Phil was gone almost half of it. He missed so many birthdays, anniversaries, and life events that he lost track. I became the glue that held the family together while he was absent. I sacrificed career and connections to follow him throughout the world. A choice, yes, but that choice goes deeper than the surface when the motivation to serve is more than a pay check. Family members must move and must sacrifice for the person choosing to serve. It isn't easy for the children or spouses either.

This year, Phil would have been in Afghanistan getting ready to come home--to have his happy reunion. Phil would have worked Christmas like any other work day. He wouldn't have complained and he wouldn't have thought twice about the 12-14 hour days. Phil would have buttoned his uniform and but on his combat boots. He would have greeted the maintenance people and the security guards by name and he would have spoken to them in their native language. He would have offered them gum or candy because that was who he was. He saw people and he recognized the innate good and the possibility in people. He was a hero long before People Magazine saw his worth. Heroes do not always wear capes; sometimes they wear combat boots and wear an ABU (military) uniform. Sometimes they are the flag and they bleed red, white, and blue.

We Are Family - II

Today one of my sons won a very prestigious summer internship in photo journalism in DC this summer. I never even knew that he was interested in that area. I have always known that he is smart and interested in many areas, but he was my closest child to Phil. Phil and he spent hours together and he soaked up the time like a sponge. Where most children can't wait to leave home, most of our children looked for ways to come home. This has changed since Phil's death and I can't fix it. While four out of five of my children were closest to me before Phil's death, his death changed this, too.

Instead of my children calling to talk about their successes and failures, they retreat to other places. I am no different. If this award had been conferred while Phil was alive, he would have shown the public a very sedate humble father. At home, however, he would have been dancing and singing (yes, singing) all over the house. He would have been talking the accomplishment to death and laughing that the internship was in something that meshed both my mother's and my interests. More than that, he would have been so very proud.

Many people do not realize why we isolated ourselves so much as a family. We learned in New Mexico that having five children meant that everyone looked at us like we were trailer court trash and they talked about our family ad nauseum. We had commanders suggesting we get a TV set and giving birth control advice even though we did not use any form of public handouts with the exception of the free breakfast/lunch program that the school automatically enrolled us in. No matter where we went, even when we went to church, people were always weighing in on our big family and Phil's enlisted status (senior airman when the fourth child was born). Yes, we were a noisy family. There were a lot of us and all of my children had terrible ear infections which meant they were loud.

My children did not grow up with things. They grew up reading and being read to. They went to the park. They were expected to help and do their homework before friends. They went to church, scouts, and sports. Phil and I were leaders or coaches so that the children could participate in these activities. The only child who not to share a bedroom or wear have handed me downs was our only girl, Emily. We ate rice and beans and went on family hikes. I worked at being the manager of the base pool in the summer so that we could have Christmas and school clothes. We never felt that we could ask for help, so we didn't, but the stigma of having a large family as a young enlisted family changed Phil and I. We retreated. We pushed our children hard.

A B was not good enough IF there were missing assignments or last minute preparations. An A wasn't good enough if there were missing assignments. Our children did summer academics with me (45 minutes writing, 45 minutes math, 1 hour reading, and a thirty minute exercise program of their choice before movies, TV, etc. Yes, we were the mean parents. Yes, we were overly diligent in checking up on our children and having friends over to our house versus the other way. In our house, we closed ranks around each other. WE were one another's best cheerleaders. We were, we are, we will always be family.

The issue is who do I share the children's accomplishments with? It isn't as if anyone else will understand just what these milestones mean to a family that truly had nothing for many, many years. Who will understand that each accomplishment means that all of those naysayers from Holloman and Ramstein who thought we were trailer court trash based on our financial status and our big family were always wrong? Who will dance around with joy when the children surpass the parents in success? Who will share the joys and sorrows of being a parent? I do not feel equipped to be the single parent dancing and singing with joy. I want to talk about it with somebody and have that somebody understand just what these accomplishments mean. We were, we are, and we will always be a family even if the person dancing and singing for joy is singing with the angels.

I Hope That my Thoughts do Not Bring Disservice to Our Military

Crap. . .I am turning into a whiner and a complainer this evening. The body hurts and I am lonely. Today, the Stars and Stripes made me really question the way the assassinations are being looked at. While most people have heard of the four French military people assassinated in Afghanistan because the French want to pull out, what blows my mind is that the father of the assassin is claiming that his son had mental problems. Huh? While I buy that anyone who shoots people is insane, a red flag went up. How many more times are we going to say "mental issues" in terms of trusted allies turning and shooting our military men and women? How many more times are we going to turn a blind eye to the fact that if someone was truly insane, he/she wouldn't stop to distinguish between NATO and Afghan troops. Is there collusion? I don't know. All I know is that the more this happens, the more I wonder why we are protecting and acting like the assassins are singular. What is it exactly that we are gaining by perpetuating this myth of no Talbani connection? These are my thoughts and I am sure that I bring a great disservice to our military, but I am still pro America. I just am tired and confused. The more I know, the less it all makes sense.

Who exactly are the investigators trying to protect? What exactly is there to gain by labeling the assassins as insane? Is if for morale? Is it for public opinion? I don't know. It doesn't bring my Phil back, but the reasons given for the assassination will never make sense to this girl. Especially now.

Valentine's Day and the Love I Share

Valentine's Day is a day where people in relationships celebrate the love they have for one another. This year, however, I am celebrating the people who have walked a very dark and twisted path with me. I am bonded to this group of people with threads that cannot be broken. The invisible ties that bind us, bind us forever.

I now have sisters that I was not raised with. Pain and loss forged a shared unity that is deeper than a common mother or father. From the start, our hearts found each other. With no language but a cry, and with pain as the glue, these friendships will forever stand. If one of my sisters needs me, I will go to the end of the earth for them. They may not even be aware of the depth of my compassion and empathy, but here is what I know. When nobody else gets me, and when the whole world thinks that I should be getting on with my life, there is no judgment from these ladies. WE all fall. WE all weep. We all struggle mightily, but we are bound forever by an act of violence we will never understand.

I have another set of forever friends. These friends wear the invisible scars of the survivor. They were the comrades who worked, ate, laughed, and lived with our united nine. Their perception and sense of wellness was forever altered. The sense of security and rightness ended with the broken bodies of their friends. Fear. Pain. Loss. They wear those battle scars, yet nobody understands unless they too were a part of that evil day. My loss is visible and perhaps more understandable, but my soldier friends have been forever altered and maimed in a manner that few understand. I stand with them and love them today. . .always.

My best friends are people that were on the fringes of my life before my Phil was taken from me. They sensed my unspoken needs. They carried me through my darkest hours and they continue to carry a girl who hides very well behind the mask of smiles. Like a house of cards, it is all mirrors and doors. Underneath the gilded walls is a scared, lonely, and heartbroken girl. These women and one man saw my bravado for what it was. They offered me so many hands of love and friendship that soon I began to see some sunlight. Soon I began to crawl up the muddy slope to a life without Phil. While I am starting to understand that it is possible that my family and friends could not deal with my pain and their pain, I am deeply humbled and tied to the people who stood and walked with me.

Then there is the man I am taking small steps with. I am not sure what he sees in this broken girl, but he reached out to me in my most broken state. He gives me the space and love I need to process and to slip into dark days. He allows me the freedom to love my Phil, recognizing that I am capable of loving in a fully different manner. I am not the same girl I was when I was married to Phil. While this is never how I wanted to find out, I am stronger and more resilient than I ever thought possible. I step forward knowing that it is I who have been blessed and that I have a caring God that is providing for the broken Linda who continues to put band aids on her heart.

I reach to those in my life this Valentine's Day. I can't begin to articulate the commitment and love I have for all of you, but the bond of life is there. I stand with you. I walk with you, and I will carry you if you need it. I know that you would do the same for me. You are forever loved by this girl.

Death Has No Rank

Today, I was reminded of how rank conscious many people are in the military. Even young elementary aged children know where one's parents rank in terms of status. As I was talking to my runners today, we were sharing the differences between the army and air force. We then shared the different bases we had been at. Phil and I lived in army housing as an enlisted family in Landstuhl, Germany. I lived at Dugway, UT in army housing. One student commented that the air force knew how to take care of our families and I made some joking comparisons between some pretty nasty air force housing and army housing. One of my students said, "But your husband was an officer."

Well, yes, Phil was, but before getting his commission, he was enlisted for 16 years. He started as an airman basic. I was then asked if I knew any of the famous military officers. I wanted to ask why they thought that my husband, a major, knew these people, but the sad fact is that I do know most of them. I have met them, hugged some of them, and talked with them. Another student who had Googled me said, she knows everyone. At times, it certainly feels like that, but the one thing these teens do not understand is that while Phil and I respected the rank and the hard work that went into obtaining that rank, rank did not mean that a person was likable or compassionate.

I know that had Phil died as an airman basic, and if all of the men in that room had been enlisted, their deaths would have been but a blip on the television screen. Why is it that by virtue of a commission and time in the air force does my husband merit attention? I am so appreciative of where Phil is buried, the interest in his story, and the fact that the advisor deaths call for people to look at safety procedures for our military troops, but what if he had been an A1C with three children? What if he had been a radar operator? Would my family have been so blessed to meet and be the recipients of the many kind people and gestures of ranking officers? I hope so because many of the high ranking people I know are wonderful compassionate individuals, but some are not. I have had generals host my family, drive my family to airports, and bring me food. I have had generals e-mail me and send me cards, but I see only the person behind the act. Good people are good people. Kindness has no rank or merit.

John Donne once said, "Do not ask for who the bell tolls, it tolls for thee." In death, we are only people who were loved. We are only people who will be sadly missed. Phil was loved and appreciated long before he earned his rank. I loved him when he had just turned 21 and I met him at the Mountain Home AFB swimming pool. I wouldn't have cared what rank he was. He was my Phil. He was always my Phil whether he was an airman basic or a major. He was a wonderful person, husband, and father. And, oh, by the way, he just happened to have earned some rank. In death, he is equal to all.

The Girl I Found with the Air Force Times Interview Yesterday

Do not gloat over me, my enemy! Though I have fallen, I will rise. Though I sit in darkness, the Lord will be my light. Micah 7:8

I had an interview yesterday that caused me to take pause and actually realize something about myself. All this time that I have lamented about losing hope and living in the darkness. Somewhere, somehow the iron shroud is rending apart. There is light and hope seeping in. Even though I didn't see it or expect it this month, my sense of humor is coming back full force. I like that girl. The one who sees good and expects good, and the girl who can laugh when her world is imploding.

The interviewer asked me to talk about Phil and my feelings toward the assassin and the military investigation. I truly do not think about or consider the assassin. He no longer lives which may be the reason that I can compartmentalize so well. While I still am very passionate about the inequalities of justice in terms of what is meted out for our troops vs. the Afghanis, troop safety, and my umbrage and outrage over the feeling that we are catering too much to a nation that is using us for our resources versus the actual desire to change or want us there, there is no amount of justice that could bring my Phil home.

April has been a very hard month for birthdays, Phil's assassination, and the most unexpected thing of all, getting dumped for the first time ever on Phil's birthday. I had begun to take small steps forward and this person was supposed to be with me on the 27th. His timing was terrible, and it added to the weight of the month. I found myself just living in a deep dark pit of despair. I actually asked God to take me home, but of course, life does not work that way. I realized as I was talking yesterday that the fourth is always going poke my heart because of Phil's birthday, but I began to laugh. My heart is going to hurt on that day. Why not heap all of the bad aspects of my life together and just have one pity party day? The fact that he went back to an old girlfriend and that integrity was an issue? Heck, no, I don't want him. Keep him. He is all yours. Facebook stalk me? Have fun with it. The privacy settings will change after the 27th, but my friends will still love me. It is funny to be 50 and having to learn the game again. I think I will keep laughing.

The interview showed me that I have begun to make plans and decisions for myself. I am beginning to look at a much bigger calendar than tomorrow. I am considering my school options which will then lead to career options. I feel like all of the prayers, experiences, and people in my life have brought me to the place God wants me to be in to be an advocate for military families and military loss. While this is not the life I ever once considered, I see were my marriage, my children, my friends, my jobs, and my talents are leading me down a very different path. I need and I feel compelled to be involved in the military dealing with families walking some path of loss. To get there, it is a hop and a skip education wise because I have so much school. The key is action. I am there. I am ready. The fire is blazing!

Lastly, the interview showed me anew the people who have stood with me and walked with me. Help has come from so many unexpected sources. Just last night, many people messaged me, encouraged me, or sent me e-mails. My best guy friend called to see how I was doing. My daughter in law sent me messages just letting me know that she was thinking of me. I have been blessed by the reaching hands of God through many people even when I could not feel hope or happiness. Is it strange to feel happy albeit lonely, ever so lonely? Maybe. Phil's life and love are me. We loved each other well and for a long time. Were we perfect? Heck, nobody is, but his love made me the woman I am today. I can be happy and I can be confident in a future that I may very well live alone because I do know what it is like to be loved not only by Phil and my children, but by so many wonderful people in my life. The interviewer tore the Band-Aid off. The skin below was laid bare, but guess what? My broken heart did not break anew. My broken heart did not bleed or hurt. My heart beat steady and true and the rays of light shone through the mending pieces of my life.

Can I Say that it is Well With my Soul—

The Faith that Carries me

I Choose Faith

As I have written before, it is easy to claim to have faith and belief when life goes according to plan. It is hard to really believe and have faith when one is walking through turbulent waters that roil and crash into us. When the unthinkable happens in people's lives, the faith a person has is defined. People watch to see if the person who has faith will cower and turn a cold shoulder to the once claimed faith. For this girl, though my faith is tenuous at times, I reach for the beacon of hope that I see shining occasionally in the distance. I may cower under my covers on certain days and I certainly have the never ending pain of my shattered heart as a constant reminder, but I truly, truly have to believe that my Phil's life mattered and that I will see him again.

Yesterday, I had a briefing on the events that led to Phil's death on 27 April. Some of my worst nightmares were realized. Enduring three hours of details and information did send me into a dark corner where I wanted to hide, but I never once raged against God not did I ask why. On this earth, the question of why will never be answered. I choose to believe that somehow, and in some manner, that God is working through the vile evil that played out in that room in Kabul, Afghanistan. I choose to believe in a life beyond this life even when it hurts so bad that I can't see beyond the next minute of my life, let alone years without the promise of Phil in it. I believe that he is in the everlasting arms of my Lord even when I am broken and crumpled on the ground.

I think one of the hardest aspects of this is the loss of my best friend. It is lonely. There is a feeling of drowning without a lifeline. I have lost a feeling of my own self worth because after this many years of marriage, I know who I am with my Phil. I do not know who I am without him anymore. I didn't have time to prepare myself for his death, so when it came, I was caught totally unaware. I had isolated myself in our relationship, family, and day to day activities. When Phil died, I truly had to rely on my faith and I had to learn to see the people reaching out around me. God provided lifelines even when I was too weak to grab them. I was drowning, and at times like yesterday, I am still drowning, but though I was drowning, I was being carried by the prayers and words of many people across the world.

It is humbling, deeply humbling, to be thrust into a position where my grief and loss is being played out for the world to see. I fall down and I second guess myself at every turn. I am so afraid that I stand paralyzed in indecisiveness. I do well for a few days and then I feel like I am falling right back into the morass of the chasm of my pain. Through it all, and when I am questioned, the answer is, I still believe. It is well with my soul.

You see, I may not know how God is working. I may not feel the peace and comfort of my life situation, but I do believe that all things work together for good. Through this vile evil violence, I believe, and I see it being played out, that lives are being touched. I see people watching my faith and how I carry myself, but the strength does not come from me. I am being carried by many people and I am being carried by my Lord. I believe. I have hope. I know that all is well with my soul and that all will be alright even when I can't grasp it today.

Forgiveness is a Choice

Forgiveness is a choice that is not always easy. In the vilest of circumstances and in our darkest hours, it isn't always easy to make a choice to forgive. The choice to forgive is often a static choice minute by minute. I struggle with my humanity in this area. While I think of the shooter rarely, I find myself struggling with the idea that not one Afghan was killed or stood up for our men and women that day.

I could forgive the shortcomings of our American troops should they have frozen, but why is it that I am mired in the chains of thinking that someone should have stood up to the monster shooting our troops that day? I understand that the culture is different, but my husband (and the other men and women that day) were in a room educating, advising, and being an equal peer to the Afghan troops in that room. Why is it that I feel that in a room of peers that it shouldn't have mattered if it was Americans or Afghans being targeted?

Why is it that I get stuck on anger that if the situation was reversed, and an American had chosen to shoot only the Afghanis, that worldwide there would have been a cry of outrage that none of our troops had tried to stop the senseless violence? I get stuck in this area. I also find myself struggling with the understanding of how this one man could get weapons into the airport without internal help. Yes, maybe I am speculating, but the end result is nine people that are gone way too soon.

I don't ask why my husband or why God couldn't have changed the outcome because I believe that God blessed my husband's life beyond his wildest dreams for 44 years. I believe that those gifts were given because God knew that my Phil's days were so finite. I do not ask why Phil died in such a horrific manner or why it happened in such a public way because I can see God's hand working through Phil's life song. Yes, it hurts and I would have done anything for this not to have happened to Phil, but I lean on the everlasting arms of Jesus to give me strength when I cannot find fortitude of my own. I will never understand the timing or the events of that day, but forgiveness is a choice that I can choose to make. A choice that I may have to make multiple times throughout the day.

Right now, this second....I am going to choose to forgive even though I cannot fathom what can lead people to help or silently condone a vile offense.

I am Awake. I am Alive.

"I am awake. I am alive." I really like the band Skillet right now. I have been stuck in this dark pit for two months. The only thing I have known for 23 years is being a military wife, a mom, and then whatever my job needed me to be. I can outperform most people because I have a high threshold of energy. The interesting thing is that I have discovered that I need people. I need the human touch. I am discovering some things about myself. I don't like some of the facets of myself that I am discovering. Other traits have emerged that have taken my breath away.

First, I discovered that I am stronger than I think. While I am still afraid of my own shadow and reestablishing a life without my Phil, I am discovering that I am capable of more than I thought. I have considered and started to pursue things I wouldn't have considered ever in my life. Mainly, living abroad.

It would be easier to stay in Colorado. I still might, but I am looking at the big picture. I am no longer the young girl I once was. There is something appealing to starting over where no one knows my name. Where people only know me as one, not as part of a couple. I would give anything to be a part of that couple we were, but I know that to be healthy, I need to be where I can stand on my own.

Phil was well known and liked. I walked in his shadow. I didn't mind. I liked being his wife. I liked being a military spouse. I have realized this week, that when the military person is gone that the spouse stands alone. If I were to move, I would always be known as a one. I have never been as well liked or as popular as Phil, but I have had a strong cadre of loyal supporters and friends. I am okay with that. What I am not okay with is the gossip that surrounds me because people judge levels of grieving. If I were to stay in bed all day or need people more, then I would be judged worthy.

People do not see the need in me. I am not good at asking for help. It took being totally brought to my knees this week to post how low I really was. For the first time ever, I confronted a situation in my life with someone. I grew as a person through asking for help. I am inept in this area. I can't promise that this will become a familiar habit, but I am going to make a bigger habit to reach out when I need people.

I love my job here. There has never been a doubt that teaching PE (physical education) is my dream job, but at the end of the day, I have to come home to an apartment we shared. I have to see people who knew me as part of a team--a team that worked well together. I have to contend with people who see me as invisible now that Phil is not part of that team. I have to see "the pretenders" who shine when the media is present, but who have retreated when there isn't a camera.

I am not sure of my future. The road may lead back here. Right now, Sasha Fierce here is going to continue to take steps forward. There will be many falls back into the sucking quagmire, but I am continuing to grasp the golden strands of hope that occasionally flit across the darkness of my heart.

Hope does spring from the whispered prayers of my feet and the simple acts of kindness. Some of the kindness has come from strangers or unexpected sources. I have been touched in many ways. I have been carried my FB (Facebook) friends. I have found joy in running again. I find solace in rediscovering the minimal independence I had in my 20's. I look to a future where I will carry my love for Phil in my heart, but I look for a future where my loss is not defining who I am as a person. While my love will never be forgotten, I choose the life that he wanted me to have should something happen to him. The unthinkable happened. I wish with all that I am that it hadn't been my Phil. I choose to honor him. I choose to live.

Sometimes My Faith Is Tenuous at Best

Sometimes all I can see is the darkness of my pain and loss. I am not going to lie; my faith is tenuous at best. The waves are crashing all around me. Crushing Darkness looms all around and I am covered in a shroud of hopelessness. Oh, I am lost. I am adrift. Today is one of those days.

On those days, I tend to circle my own wagons and I withdraw. I first allow myself the freedom to sit and not have to be strong for anyone else. I let myself crumble. I can't do this too often. I have to find footholds to claw myself back out of the abyss into a promised day. I don't know when I will have more than a moment of happiness or hope, but I do know this. I am being carried. I can see the hands that grasp my drowning frantic clutch. Even though I would like to succumb, I know that I cannot.

I must press on. I must be the person that I am called to be no matter how hard it is to face my own future. I look in the mirror and I barely recognize the content and even keeled person I was for so many years. I am all over the map right now in terms of making it through each and every day. One would think that I would be more stable since I do have faith, but having faith does not make me immune to human emotions. What I do with how I am feeling is my choice.

Yes, I am weak, oh so weak, but I know that through the ashes of my life something can shine if I am patient. I want the dull ache in my heart to go away. I am not sure if the pain will ever go away, but I get out of bed every morning and I believe. I trust. I believe and trust in the tomorrow I cannot see. I believe in me even though I am often petrified and rendered immobile by my fear. I believe that God is faithful even when I know in my heart that I will never understand the events of 27 April. I believe. I hope. I want.

It is Well With my Soul...Or, at Least it Will Be

Fear has been the overriding factor in how I have felt lately. Today, as I ran, I thought of my favorite hymn—a hymn that I had played at Phil's Memorial service. The man who wrote the words, "It is well, it is well with my soul," had just lost his wife and his daughters in a boating accident. There the man stood, broken and bowed, yet he could write that it was well with his soul.

While the waters roiled around him and he clung to the ballast at the bow of the boat, he found comfort in his faith. Faith is easy when life is going according to plan and when things are easy. Faith is not easy when the unthinkable tragedies occur. While I stand so broken and bent, like the broken shards of glass that litters the silt filled sea bottom, something beautiful to the surface will someday arise. Those slivers of glass will become smooth and beautiful. Someday, I will too.

I also have to ask myself exactly what it is that I am afraid of. The unthinkable has already happened. I would have given all for it not to have been Phil, and I may never understand the will of God, but I do grasp for the unseen lifeline. I have grasped the elusive fraying rope in the course of my tears numerous times. Sometimes it is an instant message at 0300 telling me to get some sleep and that prayers are going up for me. Sometimes, it is a unforgettable birthday weekend or someone picking me up for church. Sometimes it is someone sitting on the step with me and carrying my broken heart after I saw the autopsy pictures. I may not know what to ask for, or what to want, but God is answering the prayers my heart is crying out. I may not have the words. I may not have the faith, but out of the ashes of my life, I cling to the beacons of light I have seen. The hope that I can occasionally feel.

Do I think that the dark days are over? How I wish that was so. I think tomorrow is going to be really difficult. I do want the details. It can't be any worse than the scenario in my head. Here's the thing. I would give anything to change the course of that day (to include offering my life), but that day is over. I will never ever understand why my Phil was called home. I will never fully be comfortable with the course my life has taken since that day. Even if what I hear tomorrow is worse than I think, I do, with the grace of God, believe that somehow the angels were there weeping as the evil played out all around them. I believe the angels offered a lifeline and that my Phil was carried to the loving arms of the Lord.

I will cling to my faith; no matter how tenuous or broken it is, because faith is the hope of things unseen. I may stand on a sinking boat, but I will stand with the confidence that God is not going to let me down. If the worst happens here on earth, I will rely on the promises of the life beyond. I may be the broken shard of glass being tossed about in the roiling crashing waves, but there will come a day that the sharp edges will be smooth and beautiful. I will be able then to loudly proclaim that all is well with my soul

"So let my whole life be a blazing offering. A life that shouts and sings the greatness of our King." Wow. This line was in a song during services today. I love the idea of being a blazing offering because it is easier to hide and to shroud myself in complacency. Let me move beyond my tears and fears.

Beacons of Light

Needing and wanting a run because I feel the best when I am out running. When I run, I am able to allay my fears, cry my tears, and I am able to fully trust in my faith that sometimes waivers, but never falters. I may be scared by the buffeting wind and the crashing waves, but when I can't see the beacon of light showing me a calming haven, I will trust. I will trust that I will escape unscathed. Maybe I will be battered, torn, and broken, but I will emerge a stronger and more confident sailor. I press on.

It is frightening to be at the mercy of fate, or so it seems. If I didn't have confidence in a bigger plan, I would be hiding. I would have crawled into a cave and I would never want to face another tomorrow. While I still may be in the middle of my hard times that weigh crushing my soul and very being, I do believe and I do have confidence in a future that is bigger than the life I have on earth. Even if I am lonely and in this deep pit of pain forevermore, I believe that my Phil is firmly wrapped and nestled in the arms of the my Lord.

I know that many people cannot fathom this faith in a God unseen, but I have to believe and I DO believe that there is a bigger plan. While I know that there will never be a minute that I will understand the events of April 27th, nor will I understand the evil vileness that led to the events of that day, I do know that beauty can arise from the ashes. I am not going to understand in my lifetime, and I would never have chosen, nor would I ever be okay with the events, I believe. I have to believe in the bigger picture. Without that belief, there is no hope.

While my hope is minimal at times, I am starting to see glimmers of a life without my Phil. By moving to Germany, as scared as I am, I am saying that I am ready to spring into a new chapter of my own life that does not include my Phil. While I would give anything--to include my own life--I have to start anew. I have to figure out my place in a small world that does not include the best of who I am. I carry my Phil and the lessons he taught me deep within my soul, but I have to press on. If I chose to hide, the lessons I learned from a man who embraced all of the opportunities life gave him, would be for naught. I choose to honor Phil and the life we had together by leaping into a future I never for saw or wanted.

Forgiving or Moving On

"Lord, I am not worthy to receive you, but only say the word and I shall be healed." This one line in the Catholic mass that I still fall back on and pray on a daily basis is this line that is recited right before the sacrament of Communion. I utter this line throughout my life because I am unworthy and I do fall so short. Right now, I am struggling with forgiveness. One would think that I would be struggling with forgiveness towards the shooter or towards the military, but that is not the case at all. I am struggling to truly forgive people who I thought were our friends that have let me down. I have begun to look at them as pretenders—the ones that perform for high ranking individuals and for the media.

With the shooter, I know that he is dead. I know that he has had his judgment day. I didn't know him and though I struggle with the singular aspect of his friendliness towards my Phil, I never saw this man as anything other than a reprehensible individual that chose a dark path that led to the biggest loss of my life. If Phil had lived, he would have struggled to understand the shift in his friendships and in the way people responded in unexpected manners. Today, I was deeply wounded by someone I trusted and with whom I was a good friend to.

I gave him Phil's autopsy report and pictures which he promised me that he would hold on to and never show anyone. When his marriage imploded and then he returned to his wife, for some reason he saw fit to give those pictures and report to his wife. He didn't tell me. I feel like it was a total betrayal on so many levels. He could have and should have told me and mailed it to me if he didn't feel that he could have given it back to me. Second, I was his friend. I stood with him and I would continue to stand with him even if he couldn't stand with me. Friends are loyal and true. I stand on my promises and I stand toe to toe loyal, true, and there for my friends.

Other people who were friends never called. Never e-mailed. I can't un-friend people easily, but I think the biggest hurt that I have had is the people that have been friends long term (like 15 years) that have not e-mailed or called. Again, sometimes saying the wrong thing is better than not saying anything. At least it shows effort and a connection. It is easier to forgive a person who is well meaning but says something inappropriate than it is to forgive the silence that drags on and on and on. It is like a double whammy. Lose someone you love and lose your friends with it. I have made new friends, but I have not heard from many old friends. :(

As a Christian, I do strive to be worthy and true to my beliefs, however, is it ever okay to end a friendship? I went to dinner tonight with the couple we had been long term friends with. It was a pleasant meal, but the friendship is deeply altered and changed. I will never have the confidence I once had with them. If I move beyond this (and the forgiveness that I can begin to feel toward their struggles with loss), then why is the second situation dealing with Phil's autopsy report so much more reprehensible? Am I unworthy because I can't forgive this major indiscretion and loss of a friendship? Trust is broken.

As I have said before, unexpected death brings major trust issues to the survivor. I struggle to trust even myself. When someone that you relied on and leaned on does this, or when people you counted as friends do not act in a manner that a true friend acts in, it further erodes self confidence. My trust is shaken to its very core. I question myself and the picture that I am portraying. Am I so needy that people either want to avoid me or they want to sleep with me? There never seems to be much of a middle ground in some people. I had two aging smoking hippies (with multiple tattoos and teeth missing) who hit on me today as they were moving my boxes. I am further than ever away from taking a risk on a dating relationship because until I can trust most people again, I just can't.

I do have a small circle of friends that I totally trust. These ladies and one man were not even in my life in April. A few of the women were women that I had met one or two times. These people have become my circle of trust. That trust and loyalty runs so deep that I would stand with any of them no matter what the situation or when the situation occurs. I would give a kidney, hold a hand, cry with them, etc. Many of these friends are walking the same walk as I am in terms of dealing with loss or being a survivor that had a front row seat to the events of 27 April, but not all of them are. Some of my circle are choosing to be there in a different manner. They choose to e-mail, throw me a 50th birthday party that will always be unforgettable, e-mail me, call airlines and raise Cain on my behalf, buy me socks because the movers grabbed my socks, and the list goes on and on. It is through those kind and generous people that I have learned what friendship is. I have started on the path of healing and trust. I may not be worthy, but I continue to pray that God will only say the word and heal the heaviness in my heart and I pray for clarity in forgiveness of people who have fallen short...who have betrayed me....who are no longer in my circle of trust. I pray...

Send Some Mercy Down

When I saw the uniformed people standing in the office of my principal, I knew that the worst had happened. While they kept urging me to sit down, I just couldn't sit in a chair and behave in a civilized manner. I sank to the floor in a corner shrinking from the all too harsh of reality. In the blink of an eye, my life forever changed. My dreams were crushed and defeat overtook the confidence and joy I carried in my life. In the almost four months since, I have been hard pressed to dig out from this deep morass, but I have found some foothold and glimmers of hope. This morning, I was thrown right back to that dark bleak April afternoon.

I woke to a message about a friend I had recently visited with. This friend had walked with me during my dark times. Although her life had not been easy, she still stood with me. She was happy and her life was full. Janel died of a brain aneurysm Monday (yesterday). I don't understand. My heart cries out to God. I cannot go on.

While I understand that God is not punishing me and that heaven is the ultimate reward, why them and not me? Why now? I am crushed and hiding under the covers. I cry out to God but it feels as if he has forsaken me. I clutch the remnants of my faith and hope to my breast and I am desperately scrambling up the muddy slope. I can't go to the bottom again, but I am almost there. I need for God to send some mercy down right now in the form of a promise. I am beaten and bowed. Broken and spent. Send down the rain to cleanse and heal my broken heart.

In The Arms of an Angel

As I ran on the whispered prayers of my feet and bleeding heart, I heard the song, "In the Arms of An Angel". I started to think about the awful briefing of the events of that day. Over and over, the investigator kept talking about the sounds and the views of that room. Gun shots were so deafening that the military people were assaulted not only by fear, but by the noise that temporarily robbed them of their ability to judge where the shots were ringing out. The haze of the gun powder mingled with the acrid smell of gun powder and spilled blood, further made the scene to unspeakable to fathom.

Imagine being crouched under a desk and watching one's friends and colleagues falling. It doesn't matter if the time was five minutes, ten minutes, or even the fifteen minutes that the investigator kept using. A lifetime passed for these military members. A lifetime. . .fear flooded all but maybe the first person hit. Phil was not the first person hit. It kills me and pricks my heart every time I think of the fear and the pain he must of felt. I wonder if he knew how much I loved him. How much I wanted to be home. Did he think of me? Our five children? Did he find time to right his soul with the Lord?

I cling to the hope that there were angels there in that room as the unthinkable played out around my Phil. I hope that he was cradled in the arms of an angel(s) before he could feel the horror and pain of those minutes. If angels can be around us even when we are unaware, then why is it so difficult for me to imagine that angels were in that room?

I know that many of my preacher friends would disagree with the fact that Phil can be my guardian angel. See, here is the thing. I derive comfort from thinking that Phil is walking with me and is with me. If it isn't so, then there will be a day when I am face to face with God, and I will understand. I do not understand this vile reprehensible event that yanked my Phil from my life in such a violent vicious event. I don't understand why we never got to say goodbye, why I didn't get a trip that was planned just for the two of us, why now. I just don't.

Phil was special to a lot of people, but to me, he was my best friend. My fears were allayed when I was with him. We had 23 years. I thought that we would grow old together. He loved me, so why is it that I don't feel him with me? Why don't I see him when I close my eyes? Feel him in the whisper of the wind on my skin?

Is it so wrong to have hoped that he is walking with me? That he is on my heart still? My Phil would never have willingly given up his life. I need him today just like I needed him over 23 years ago when he entered my life. Can't he be an angel walking with me or holding me at night when my heart is crying out because I miss him so much?

The Promise of Fall - I

My favorite season is fall. The world around me literally explodes with color. Red, orange, and yellow assault my senses at every turn. As a runner, I love the beauty and the nip in the air. Fall beauty comes at a price, though. The beauty explodes as the leaves are dying. It is as if the leaf is singing a swan song, per se.

When I look at my Phil's life, in particular the time we spent in Colorado, Phil's swansong was sung loud and clear. He touched so many lives in a very short time. Not only does he hold graduate degrees from two universities in CO, he coached, volunteered for numerous organizations, worked in many schools, and taught at the Air Force Academy. I don't know anyone who made the end of their life count as much as Phil made his life count.

He never saw his life that way. In fact, Phil was often a reluctant participant. He often did things because he felt that he should do them. Like many of us, he could have a bad attitude, but he always showed up ready to play the game. He always camouflaged his attitude to give a full effort. He would say that others deserved more recognition or that he hadn't done that much, but Phil was one of those people that led by quiet example and an unbeatable work ethic.

What few people realized until after his death is that he was a driven man. He was driven by the humble roots of an immigrant boy who could not speak a word of English at the age of 12. He was motivated by the family that he wanted growing up. Having five children was Phil's idea of family and connection. He always craved that security and wanted that unconditional love. He was further motivated by a sense of loyalty and duty to his adopted country. Phil did not need to be motivated, urged on, or prodded. He did the things he did because it was the right thing to do. He performed because he believed in the things he was doing.

At the end of Phil's life, he shone so brightly that the rest of us paled in comparison. His colors exploded with promise and possibility. While we stood in awe, Phil was marching forward. In the cusp of the season of fall, I see promise. I see Phil's life song and I am looking to sing my own. While I may never have the brilliant red, yellows, and oranges, I look to my own fall. I look to my own explosion of beauty in the possibility and potential of my season.

Today's Hope

I felt a hope and promise today. It is hard to explain, but something clicked. I just felt like I am where I am supposed to be and I am doing what I am supposed to do. Even if it was just for today, I am not cowering or second guessing myself. What a novelty to say, all is well. Not only is it well with my soul, I am starting to see a future.

Phil instilled in me a sense of confidence because he always loved me for who I am. He did not look at my running as "abnormal" or my dislike of driving as anything but a quirk. He always, always believed in me and was proud of me as I was of him. As I ran today, I heard our song for the first time since he left in January. As the words wafted through my ear bus, "They say we're crazy...nothing's going to stop us now..." I wish Phil were walking with me, but I know that he would want all that is happening for me. He would be thrilled that I am in Europe and about to start another school year. He would be talking about it to everyone he knew (and embarrassing me tremendously).

Even though he is not physically with me, he is walking with me. I miss the life we had together and I never ever thought that I would even be considering a life without him or with someone else. I am not sure if I will be able to let someone else in. It comes down to the fairy tale. If I can't love someone as much as I loved Phil and in a different way that I loved my Phil, then I will be alone all of the days of my life. Today, I felt very discombobulated.

Two men sought me out today. One moved in a little too fast. That is not going to work for me. I am still stuck on feeling unfaithful, disloyal, and confused. I need some time in the friendship phase. I need time to process and work through how I feel about moving on in this direction. I can make jokes all I want, but the bottom line is, I am lonely and I would like to have someone to do things with and to share my life with. I don't know if it is possible to live that kind of life twice in one's life. Maybe not, in which case I will live my life alone. If is possible, I think that it will take slow steps into that direction. I think that it will sneak up on me.

I feel the promise of contentment and peace today. Isn't that something to be thankful for? I am thankful for the many friends standing with me. In my darkest hours, it is as if you know. I do know that there will still be times when I am caterwauling backwards, but today I took several steps forward. I feel good about that. It is a little scary to be living a life without my Phil, but I know that he would be right here applauding my steps if he could.

There Will be no White Flag above my Door

I am at the end of my fraying rope today. I am feeling the weight of the world on my already bent body. I feel the control slipping away and I am clutching at any fraying tenuous cord to cling to. I have felt this way before in different jobs, but this is different. I am going it alone. I don't have Phil to pick up on the hitch in my voice or the stoop in my shoulders. He knew that I need a Whole Foods Sante Fe sandwich, some Rocky Mountain chocolate, and a kind word or two. Those simple gestures helped me make it through the nights when all seemed lost.

Today was my first day of teaching. None of my rosters were right. I had classes of 50 students and one class of 12 students. Add to that, I am ill equipped with middle school equipment to foster games that are well liked and promote skill development and cooperation. I know that on some level this has to resolve (I hope), but knowing that I am going to be out for so much this fall, I had hoped to have my organizational skills have everything up and running smoothly. I am beyond overwhelmed by the task ahead, but there will be no white flag above my door.

I needed a kind word...a smile...a friend. I am alone. Running helped. Really helped, but still miss my friends. I miss Phil's secure arms just holding me when I felt this way before. I have never been a reactionary person. I have never wanted to sit and cry my eyes out. Tonight, I just might.

Tomorrow will be better, I am sure. I just need to hold on to the faith that God is not going to let me down. He will not have brought me this far to drown. I believe even as I am sinking. I am reaching for the fraying rope in front of me and hoping that the knot will hold. I believe...I hope...I will not wave a white flag today, tomorrow, EVER.

Faith and Hope as Small as a Mustard Seed

I have discovered something about my faith, it is strong and it is there always. I may not be able to articulate it, but when I am cowering in the corner on my knees thinking that all if for naught, a sense of peace and promise fills me. I may not always be able to see the glimmers of hope shining through the pitch dark skies, but somewhere and on some level, I feel it. In my darkest hours, there have been people who carried me to those glimmers of light.

My faith may be a mustard seed, but when I look back at where I have been, I do see how God has provided for me. I wish, and oh how I wish, that I could be talking about the blessings in my normal life. It is funny how my life is being defined as before when I was happy and content and now walking in fear, crushing grief, and doubt. As I walk the treacherous path of my life, I sense a hope born of my faith and of the ways that God has provided for me with friends, a job, my running, and I could go on. I know that though I may not always see God's hand working, it is there steering my rudderless boat however many days I have.

I cannot pretend to understand why God could not have stopped the events of that awful, awful day. I will never fathom why my Phil and the other eight people that day died. In my wildest dreams and fears, I never ever saw Phil dying in such a malfeasant unspeakably evil manner. I never saw my nightmares be as terrible as the reality of what happened in that room on that day, but I have to cling to some hope that there were angels there weeping as the sinister mad gunman chose to assassinate nine people there to train and change a broken country. I have to believe that since I wasn't present when my Phil died, that he was carried home in the arms of an angel.

When my children were little, they used to watch a TV series called "Touched by an Angel". Our family was blessed enough to meet the characters when we were in Utah. I like the idea of an angel of death walking the last moments of life with a person...removing them from the evil situation or pain before the event plays out...allaying all fears and tears. In reality, life and angels probably don't work that way, but I have to believe that God is faithful and that God provided for those men and women. If I live my life in error, I have lost nothing because I have gained the will to travel on. I believe thus I can have hope even if my hope is as small as the tiniest mustard seed.

The Prayers I Uttered

For five years, I prayed the same prayer diligently. I prayed that I would live beyond myself and to glorify God and the faith that I have. I thought that the adrenal issues were the challenges laid before me. Running and speaking about Addison's disease was just a warm up to the main event. I have changed and I am changing still.

Many of you know the quiet shy librarian Linda girl. I am not her any more. I am answering the small nudges and the giant pushes to do the things I do not feel equipped to act on or to do. When Phil was killed, it was mere hours later when the media began to call and to wait for my reaction. I have never been so crushed, defeated, and broken as I was during those days. I chose to speak for all of the names flashing across the bottom of the screens of TV's every night. Each of those names is a person who was loved, missed, waited for. Each of those names was a person who anticipated coming home for the joyous homecoming reunion that never came. Our homecomings came with meeting a numbered flag draped box bearing the remains of our broken loved ones. Our homecoming came with black boxes being delivered (and with elements of our loved one's belongings missing) to our houses.

I do not feel like I am the most gifted writer or speaker. I fell into this role primarily because of my very large family. Phil was the poster airman for his adopted country. He started as an 18 year old immigrant airman basic and worked his way into a commission and his dream job of teaching at USAFA. Together we raised five children, four of whom are serving our country through military service. He instilled in all five children the sense of loyalty and giving back to this country where many people have a sense of entitlement.

I have lived my life in the shadows. I have been content in the fringes watching others stand out. When I prayed to live beyond myself, I saw a life touching lives with teaching and I saw my life encouraging others in an active lifestyle. I always wanted to write a book. I never thought I could speak up and speak out. I write and I am the voice. I speak for those who cannot or who are too broken to speak. My life is not the life I imagined. I would give anything, anything to have my Phil living with me growing old together. I am thankful for the 23 years we did have together. I see all of the blessings I was given to produce the internal fortitude and charisma to live my life the way I am being called to live it--I am being called to a purpose driven life that is beyond any vision I can see, It is humbling and terrifying, but I stand for all who have suffered military loss. I stand.

But Then Comes the Morning

I felt really cut off from the world this weekend. When I rented my house I did not think about how isolated I would be as the only American living in my town. There are no stores, restaurants, gyms, etc. My village is picturesque to be sure, but I have discovered I need the human touch and companionship. I still do not have internet which means that reaching out to those I love during my time of need has become very difficult. While the internet will eventually be rectified, the loneliness causes me to descend into that dark hole of despair.

The despair is so deep, so crushing, and so consuming that it is hard to imagine hope or happiness. I have felt both since Phil has died, but I have never been in a spot where I didn't feel like I didn't have someone to call or to connect with. I am struggling, but I do believe, and how I believe, that if my prayer was for God to take me where I was needed and I put in for world wide availability and I got Ansbach, Germany, he would forsake me. I need to believe...have faith...that morning will come.

Night is always the darkest. The cloud of oppressive ebony presses and crushes my will and my faith. I think of Jesus hanging on the cross and crying to his father, "My God, My God, why have you forsaken me?" I feel that sometimes, but I do not carry the sin of the world. I do not hang from a cross betrayed by all. I was given love. I was given the family I desired. I have been blessed for 50 years (or most of it). Many people never find what Phil and I had. I should be content no matter what my lot, should I not? And, if, I am alone and lonely for the rest of my days, morning will eventually break. With the morning rays come hope of something. I may not see the something, but I believe.

Morning rays of sun always makes the darkness of night seem so far away. Somewhere through the dark billowing clouds will raise a beautiful rainbow. It will happen; I know it will. With my despair, I will reach, I will cling, and I will believe that if not today, someday soon. My faith will stand the test of time. I will pray for a glimmer of hope in the form of connections. I will hope that my internet is repaired very soon, but if not, I will let my faith carry me. I believe in things unseen. That day is coming when hope and faith will collide to give me that rainbow; someday soon, I hope.

Full Forgiveness. Is It Possible?

Forgiveness is a choice. I have written about this before, but something triggered my thoughts in this direction this morning. I read a post about a sermon on forgiveness. It is easy to mouth the words of an accepted apology, but what happens when the act is so vile and egregious that it steals every dream for the future a person has? What happens when the act is so vile and horrific that it hurts to even talk about?

For me, my world came crashing down on April 27th. In the days that followed, I could barely wrap my arms around the loss of my Phil, but little did I know that I was to hurt even more. As the details unfolded about the awful events of 4/27, I could not make sense of what I was hearing. Not only was my husband assassinated by someone that he considered a friend and with whom he talked with on a personal level, he was shot more than anyone else in the room. Though the gunman did not survive what if he had?

If he was alive, I am certain my outrage and resentment over his vile act would consume me. I rarely, rarely think of the shooter. I figure that God has dealt with him, judged him. If I were eye ball to eye ball with this man, could I forgive? I am not there now. I may never be, but I do desire to be the person who doesn't just voice an acceptance platitude for an apology. To really accept the apology, I would have to act and I would have to trust. I wouldn't react in anger, but I would be very wary, very quiet, very internally conflicted.

I think that the worst part of this event in my life is how xenophobic I have become. Why is it that I no longer trust any Afghan? This is not the Afghan people's doing, it is the act of one man who chose to act reprehensibly. I struggle with acceptance of a struggling people. I struggle with wrapping my arms around true forgiveness. I know that Jesus forgave us even as he hung on the cross. I want to be more Christ like in forgiveness, but I struggle. People have told me that I need to forgive fully. I accept that the gunman's fate is in the Lord's hand, but I am not there in terms of full unequivocal forgiveness. Maybe in the future, but not now. I will start with the smallest steps. I will pray and I will choose to work towards full forgiveness. I want to be able to forgive. I long to be the person that I am called to be, but though I believe that God is working to perfect his work in me, I am far from where I need to be. That does not mean that I won't get there, I am just not there fully.

I think that it is naïve to expect that people can forgive completely immediately. I am a flawed human. Though I lack anger, should the assassin have lived, would I invite him into my home? Would I reach out? Would I TRUST, the essential ingredient in full forgiveness? I am not going to stand here and tell people that I am capable of that at this point. I may never be, but I will not be bitter, full of hate, and xenophobic forever. I am working towards putting my negative thoughts per se towards one individual who made a very evil sinister choice that day. I am working towards believing in the Afghan people as a whole, believing that inroads are being made by the training, mentorship, and financial resources we are providing. My hope is that the children in Afghanistan grow up to be more global than their forefathers. Maybe then, forgiveness in the form of trust and mutual respect will be a reality.

Faith is Not a Crutch During my Hard Times

I know that many people reject their faith when hard times occur because they wonder how a loving God can allow tragedy and loss in their lives. I, on the other hand, derive a sense of peace and calmness with my faith and I cling and clutch it to my heart more tightly. During the good times of my life, God has often not been central to my day. He has been more of an afterthought. In my loss and in my deepest need, I have had to believe that there is more to life than our numbered days on earth. It is central to my belief that death is the start of eternal life in heaven

Now, I am not going to lie and say that I feel any joy whatsoever in my loss of Phil. I will never wrap my arms around that day, but if I thought for one second that I would not see my Phil again, and then I might as well quit living now. I don't believe that and because I don't, I am compelled to continue speaking and writing about what I feel here in my living state.

I feel an overwhelming sense of lack and loss in my life. I am used to not being alone. I liked being part of a well oiled machine, but I feel guilt. I feel guilt that I took for granted our time together. After 23 years together, it was easy to make Phil less of a priority. I always knew that at the end of the day he was going to be there. It takes my breath away every time I think of him lying in fear in that room with the evil monster that chose to take his life and the lives of eight other comrades. Did he know that even then, he was carried in my heart? Did he know that my arms were wrapped around him as he took his dying breaths?

I can't go to his moments in that room without physically hurting. In agony, I supplicate and call to my Lord. In my own feeble state, I am fixated on those moments, yet I know that Phil's life was about so much more than that. He touched lives and he lived so much in a short amount of time. God knew his days were numbered, and while I believe that God has the power to intervene and stop evil, I believe that if this life is just the start and not the end, I am thinking with my own human frailty and selfishness when I cry out and ask why. Jesus wept. He wept when his friend Lazurus died.

I weep because I miss the man who was as much a part of who I am as I am myself. I weep for my loneliness and fear. I shrink when I consider that maybe I will feel this way all the days of my life and that loneliness will be my new reality, but I step forward to what I see God calling me to do. It is interesting that I have developed a sense of purpose out of my loss. This quiet and unassuming girl has been thrust into a role that I have never felt comfortable doing. I am, or was, very shy. I have changed. My choice was to cower in a corner or speak out about the hope I find in my faith and about the true feelings that everyone experiences in loss.

Military loss is so hard. It robs all of society of men or women in the prime of their lives. All of them are young and vibrant. Death is unpredicted and sudden. Often the death occurs in the most violent fashion possible. Many times the last breaths come on foreign soil and family members deal with loss in a very public manner. We are left to spend the immediate future flying to Dover to greet a numbered flag draped box that bears the broken remains of our loved ones. WE are left to deal with more paperwork and briefings about the unimaginable than the normal person. It is overwhelming how many things keep coming up. It is as if the bad times will never end. Through it all, I would love to have had a tee shirt that smelled like my Phil or his camera which was taken for the investigation, but I don't even get that. I hadn't spoken to Phil in the three days prior to his assassination. I had deleted his voice messages never thinking that those would be the last words ever uttered.

So, when people ask me how I can hide behind my faith, it isn't hiding or cowering from reality. I fall to the comforts of my faith because those arms wrap tightly around me and provide for me a ray of hope in my darkest hours of need. If I can stay within my faith, I can visualize and feel a sense of calming security because I will see my loved ones again. I will see Phil again. I cling to that faith because God does know what I need. I may cower and cringe at the purpose and direction my life is taking, but I am stronger and more resilient than even I could have seen. I see that I have and I am being given what I need to step forward one tiny ril at a time. I believe. I choose to believe and grab that lifeline. Oh, how I need that life preserver!

These Hard Times

Self-Medicating and Drinking?

Why is it that doctors want to throw sleeping pills at me and friends want to get me drunk? Self medication is only temporary. I am afraid of the lingering dependence on external sources to provide comfort. I don't want to put things into my body that will numb the pain temporarily. I want to find a way to work through the pain to finding the new normal that everyone keeps talking about.

It is official. I now weigh what I weighed in college when I ran collegiately. No wonder I can't keep my clothes on. I am eating. That is always the first question. Am I depressed? No, I wouldn't say that. Am I down and sad? Yes, but I have found humor in some of the dark days. Do I see hope yet? I am not so sure.

My life is moving on. How could it not? I have five wonderful children (a beautiful bonus daughter in law) and the hope of being a grandma some day. Can I see being alone the rest of my days? No, but I can't see myself taking a risk of putting myself out there either. I had a good marriage. We were always friends first and foremost. We liked spending time together. I am not sure if that is fair to anyone else. Having said that, I am not ready to become a nun (as one of my sons suggested). I am also not sure when or IF I will ever be ready to date or put myself out there for someone else.

I don't sleep at night because my heart yearns for Phil's phone call and touch. He was the calming force in my life. He was who I wanted to run home to. My heart always sped up a little at the thought of going up the stairs and spending the evening with him. It wasn't always bells and whistles, but at the end of the day, I wanted to share with him and to be with him. The quiet companionship, the shared history, the caught breaths, and the fun times will be sorely missed. I will sleep again, but when I do, it will mean that I am moving on. I am not ready for that yet.

The Gift of Time and Guilt

Guilt is such a powerful, paralyzing emotion. It is counter-productive and insipid in the manner that it robs an individual of their ability to move on. I am mired in guilt right now. I was faithful, true, and committed to my Phil for 23 years, but I was guilty of not making him my priority. The gift of time never seemed like such a big deal until there was no more time left.

For years, I rushed about my petty pace day in and day out. First it was the children. I put everything I had into being a mom. I don't regret that, but somewhere along the way, I became a mom first vs. a wife first. Some of that was self preservation since Phil was often deployed. Some of it was that we had so many children (I don't regret that either). Some of it was just the passing of time. Regardless of the reason, I grew comfortable within thinking that we always had tomorrow for that trip to Venice or time together. When we finally scheduled a trip away without our children after 23 years of marriage, it came too late. Our trip was scheduled for October.

Second, I think that when people first start dating they want to spend every waking minute together. I got caught up in work and running. Phil and I became second priority to each other. How I wish that I had invested the time that I invest in other people into my spouse. Granted, I was not off hanging out with friends or away from the home, but I worked way too much. I think that Phil might say the same thing. If I had one more day, it wouldn't be filled with running around. It would be filled with sitting and enjoying just being together.

As an English teacher, I had my students do an elegy project where they had to write about what they would want to do if they knew they had one week to live. Often, their answers were a ton of traveling. I, today, would like that isolated cabin in the woods where there would be no phone calls, electronics, TV, or outside distractions. I would like to spend that week talking, laughing, crying, playing; loving...I would like the gift of time.

The gift of time isn't something that one can get after a person dies. I am so regretful of not investing more time. I always thought that there would be another tomorrow.

This Isn't How my Life Was Supposed to go

Why is it that I feel like an unwilling participant in my own life? I feel so inadequate and ill prepared to walk the path in front of me. I don't have any answers, any vision of my future. The fear and the second guessing of myself is a constant companion. I want to live a worthy life and to make a difference, but I so often fall short. I would not have chosen the door I am being shoved through.

Four Days of Blackness

After the dark moments of Wednesday, I have decided to trust God and not to lean on mug own understanding. I am not saying that this is easy, and I value integrity above all, but even the truth is not going to change what happened to my Phil. I so appreciate the prayers, comments, people sitting with me, listening to me, standing with me in my dark times.

Support has come from all over the world. In one of my worst hours, I had prayers going up for me from Afghanistan when I should be the one praying for our soldiers. I had a good friend sit with me after getting a very dark e-mail from me the day I got the report. I had written, "Got autopsy report. Very bad. Physically ill." He was there within an hour. I had another friend take me to the Airport and who made me feel happy about an upcoming event in my life. She gave me something to be excited about and to look forward to. I have a friend here in Boise that I have been friends with since second grade. She has sat with me, listened to me, and shared her daughter. I had another person e-mail me about a regulation and valuable information. I am humbled. I look ahead.

Here is the thing that I have noticed the most. As much as I hurt, there are people hurting more than I am. I have hope. Many people lose the glimmer. . .that spark. In my pain, I finally recognize the broken hearts all around me.

It makes me wonder how I can be a better friend. I so often fall short and I too often think only of my needs. Living out loud and living a life that is worthy is what I strive to do. Running is a large part of this plan. I like who I am when I run. I process and deal with anything that causes me pain or even happiness. When I run, I run on the whispered prayers of my broken heart and my plodding feet. I run on because if I can run, there is hope that one day things will be better. Sometimes, running is all I have, but still I run on to the one golden strand of light bursting through the dark clouds.

As I Prepare for the Footlockers to Come Home

Tomorrow promises to be a barrel of laughs for someone--just not me. I am not sure why the military thinks that someone needs to be with me to count underwear and socks of someone who can't wear them again. For the record, even if I have a friend doing the inventory, it is damn intrusive. I know, I know. . .I so very rarely swear. I will do what I made my children do when they were growing up. I will pay a dollar to the vulgar pot. I'm just saying. . .

Wondering when the hard times will end. I have to wonder when the days will stop bringing so many negative surprises and gouging wounds. When will the darkness be over? Tomorrow promises to be hard. I want to run far, far away. I am sure the military would chase me down. Interesting. . .for 23 years, I felt like a nonentity. I didn't need or want their help. I find myself clinging to my friends that are standing with me. I can't walk this alone. I am so thankful for all of the people who carried me. I wait for the day when my first thought and my last thought are not of my Phil. That day seems so far away tonight

Really? The Gossip Has Already Started

I don't know whether to be flattered or offended, but I am laughing. I hear that people are betting about how long it will take me to get remarried. 6 months? Are you kidding me? That would entail dating again. It would also entail me to get moving like yesterday. I am not ready yet (need the friends more), but even if I were, I am old and really scared to join the dating game. I didn't do it well the first time. I am not slutty Linda, for the record. It would make things easier, but I want the whole fairy tale again. If I can't have it, then I will stay single and celibate. I know, more information than a person needs, but I am choosing to laugh versus being offended.

It is interesting, though, that for 22 years (after the first year of our marriage) Phil and I were boring. No one gossiped about us. Become suddenly single and everyone warns every single man that is my friend to be careful. I did not change my moral compass because I am single. For the record, my singledom was not a choice--duh.

Add to that the perverts that hit on me. I have had more than one married men hit on me. What's with that? I had one woman hit on me-- uh, my home team did not change because my husband died. I have to laugh because what else is there to do. Phil would have laughed right along with me. :)

Finally, my relationships with couples change, too. It is strange. When I was part of a couple, people did not worry if I talked to their husband or if we hung out as a group. I find that many of the couples we knew backing off. I am the third wheel. I get it. The greatest joy in groups that I get is when I run marathons and I run into my running friends. It isn't like that (except for the savage maniac).

Lost and Adrift

Lost and adrift. Disappointed and hurting. I don't much care for the pretenders. When one feels totally boxed in and bound by rules and expectations, people think they can behave any way they want to behave. It is wrong on many levels. I may not voice my thoughts to people (except through writing), but it doesn't mean that the story doesn't come out. That the pain doesn't etch deep canyons through my already broken heart.

Dealing with the Questions of my Students

As a PE teacher, I am the most popular teacher in the school. I walk the halls and rend fistie fives (fist bumps) at every turn. My students knew my Phil because Phil coached alongside of me and he was my sub when I was gone (he was getting his PhD). When news of my husband's death hit the students, the students took it hard. The day I returned to work, all 750 students wanted to talk to me about my husband (and to give me hugs). At the elementary school level, students do not have the filters in place that people develop as they age. They do not have the filters that stop them from saying or asking certain questions.

A first grader came up to me and said, "I am really sorry about Mr. A. Did he get shotted or stabbed?" I looked at him and said, "Mr. A was in the Air Force. What do you think?" The little boy thought for awhile (we were outside running together). He looks at me and says, "Mr. A got shotted. My dad is in the Air Force. I hope that he doesn't get shotted." I had to smile through my tears. He was voicing his internal fears about his own dad. He didn't mean to hurt me, and really, he didn't. He just voiced the nightmare he had about what could happen to his dad.

As a military mom and as a military wife, I get that. I often don't let myself think about the danger my family members are in. One of my internal coping mechanisms to keep fear at bay is to not think about the worst possible scenarios. I think about reunions and the day to day loneliness of my loved ones being gone. When Phil was killed, I really didn't think that there was any possible way that it could have been him. He had me convinced that he was in a safe area, just away from me for a year. I now face fear in my own life.

I not only fear my decisions and choices, I fear for my children and the other military people who are deployed. On some level, I cling to my belief that God is in control. I believe that he knows each and every hour and minute of our lives. He has counted the hairs on our heads. If it is our time to go, and I do believe this, then I could walk out of my front door and have something fall out of the sky.

For me, then, the chaos of my heart is caused for the goodbye that was never said. When a person is lost after being gone for four months and they are killed far away, there is nothing left that smells like them. All of the personal debris of a person's life is put away or is out of reach. It took two months to get Phil's things back. I still don't have it all. When his clothing came back, it had all been sanitized. I clutched the shirts to my breast hoping to find his smell. I didn't have a used coffee cup in the sink reminding me of a shared morning. The last time he touched me was the wee hours of the morning the day he kissed me goodbye and told me that a year was not all that long. Forever is that long.

I am appreciative of every person who has shared memories of my Phil because it gives me back something that was lost on April 27. When people take time to contact me even though they do not know me to share stories and friendship from half way across the world or to drive out of their way to meet me and to spend time with me, I feel like my reset button has been pushed. I borrow that phrase from another military person who is still in Afghanistan. When my reset button is pushed, I am given back some of the joy and pride I had in my Phil. My tears are lessened and I am blessed because my heart is filled with a contentment of the life Phil led and the life we shared. I was blessed for 23 years to have known and experienced the love of my life.

When Will I Stop Cowering in Fear?

Since I made the decision of where to go to college and what dorm to live in, I have not made any decision independently in terms of where I lived. I have allowed the military to dictate where I live and for how long I live there for the better part of thirty years. I always had flexibility and the attitude of adventure. After Phil's death, however, that adventuresome spirit has been replaced by an all-encompassing sense of fear. This fear permeates every pore, every part of my essence.

I cling to indecision. I make decisions and then I promptly second guess them. I took a job in Ansbach, Germany. I don't know anyone. I am leaving a job that I love. I am forgetting to look at what led me to this decision. The factors that led to my decision are still in place, yet I find myself terrified to leave what I know. I had my car appraised for sale at Carmax today. I don't have time to get my car to the port, nor do I think that my car will do well in Bavaria. I feel a total sense of running amok without a charted course.

I have discovered that at 50, I am less confident in my own abilities than I was at 17. I am afraid to put myself out there. I am afraid of making mistakes and I am afraid of change. Mostly, I am afraid of loneliness and being alone. It is a terrible feeling not to trust one's decisions. It wouldn't matter which decision I made (and lack of action is making a decision), I would feel this caged in helpless feeling. Why is it that I can't precede with confidence and faith in things unseen?

I never felt this way (except for driving—laugh) with my Phil. I saw each move as a time to have new adventures, to meet new friends, and I always figured that even if things were terrible, we would eventually move. When I look at this move, then, what is it that makes me cower in my fear? What is it that roots me unbidden to one spot? Why is it when I look at the girl in the mirror, I see and smell fear pouring from her pores?

I am left to wonder how long it will be before I can face myself and how long will it be before I can take a stance without wavering. In the meantime, how can I make a decision in this magnitude and trust myself. Even small decisions are hard. I know that my window to move is now. I know that I need a break from Colorado Springs, but I am under the covers shivering in the dark of night. I need to embrace and develop my Sasha Fierce personality and stand up. Stand up to change. Stand up to the woman that I am called to be. I just do not know where to start.

Figuring It Out

One of the ways I derive a feeling of closeness to my Phil is to talk about him. I talk about him more now that he is gone than I did when he was alive. It wasn't that I didn't love him, I just knew what we had and I derived a sense of security and wellness from the friendship, companionship, history, and love that we shared. Now that he is gone, I am clutching for a sense of normalcy and closeness to him. It is incredibly lonely at times.

I am so cognizant that people are probably getting tired of me talking about Phil. I am trying to be normal, but even I do not know what normal is any more. It is as if people expect me to be rebounding and for my life to have moved on. I have many friends standing with me, but it is me who feels one dimensional. I am stuck in the pit in which I cannot escape. When I talk about Phil, write about Phil, I am clutching those special memories.

I feel him slipping away from me. I have already forgotten his laughter, the way his fingers felt, and the way he ran. I thought that those qualities were implanted on my soul. We had twenty three years. Shouldn't he be indelibly etched into my heart and memory? Granted, the last time I saw him was over six months ago, but still, shouldn't the memory be stronger?

As I clutch at trying to retain him to my life, I see people who are uncomfortable with me talking about him. I sense their eyes glazing over. I feel the thoughts that I should be further along, or maybe they are just uncomfortable with my loss. I feel egocentric and adrift because I am not ready to let him go. I feel incredible guilt because I have even started to consider dating again. I can see the big picture in terms of dating, just not the smaller steps. Though I am not dating yet, it is the whole idea of feeling untrue and insecure in myself. I keep wondering if the fact that I can't live like a nun means that I didn't love my Phil enough. More guilt.

Then, there is the insecurity in my own abilities to make a decision. I don't trust my own thought processes any more. My hope and trust has been shaken. I can't see my own value. I am 50 years old and I am ill prepared to stand alone. For years, every decision was dictated upon Phil's military career. I followed. I am being called now to stand alone and to make decisions. What if I make the wrong choices?

As I move to Germany, I feel so much fear that I am paralyzed. It isn't that I am afraid of living in Europe. I embrace the newness and the challenge. I look forward to being in an environment where people did not know us as a couple. I see a day when I can have a social group that is mine and that never knew my loss, or if they know of my loss, it isn't the only facet of my life that defines me, but I am afraid of losing what memories we had. I am afraid that I am being unfaithful because I am moving on. I am leaving the last place we lived. I am leaping into an unknown life. It is terrifying.

Part of the fear is that Phil was my safety net. He knew so many languages that traveling with him was fun. I always knew that no matter what happened when we were traveling, Phil's command of 7 languages would get us out of the problematic situation. Traveling was all fun. I could be the planner or the wingman, if you will, because I felt security in his presence. Even when I traveled without him, I knew that Phil was just a phone call away and that he could fix whatever came up. Now, I know that there is nobody could help if I was cowering in a bathroom stall in Germany weeping because I was unsure where to go, what to do, or how to do it. I need to embrace this independence, but it is so foreign to me, so uncomfortable, that I am stuck in indecisive rigidity.

People see a strong resilient person when they look at me, but I am floundering. I am clutching and trying to navigate my own life. I am trying to move on past my loss of Phil. I am trying to be a friend that doesn't always make everything about her. I am trying to figure out who I am without Phil. I am striving to be the woman God called me to be. This is not easy. I have one foot forward and one foot back. Some days I can look ahead. Some days I caterwaul backwards. I want to have a life that is not totally mired in my loss. I want to have people in my life that are there because they like me. I want relationships to be based on a give and take status quo vs. my always sucking the life out of every event. I want Phil in my heart always, but I also want friendships and companionships that are separate from that. I want to move beyond my fear. I hope that the push to Germany brings me there.

I Can't Go to the Places I Once Went

I haven't been able to go to the Y (gym) since Phil died because it is a place that was our home away from home. I work as a swimming instructor for my second job. Recently, someone asked me to fill in for her while she was on vacation. Today was day 1. I am out of swimming shape, but it felt darn good to sluice through the water today. Water is healing for me.

There were some moments, though. I didn't cry or break down, but my pasted on facade shifted. First, I had at least ten people talk to me about how much weight I have lost. Them: "Wow. What kind of diet are you on?" or "You need to eat when your husband is gone. Do you have an eating disorder?" (Two people). Uh, no. I am on the grief diet. I did tell them that. You should have seen the jaws drop. I probably shouldn't have responded that way to the eating disorder question, but, still. . .

Then there were well meaning parents, staff, and kids who wanted to know where I have been. They hadn't put two and two together. I had people boo-hooing on me. I had to endure hugs in a swimming suit. Awkward--laugh. I had one man that kept staring at me. He was wearing a military shirt. Finally, he apologizes for staring, says that I look familiar, and then keeps throwing out places we might have known each other. I said, "TV?" A funny look crossed his face and then he kept apologizing. I am fine, but at almost three months later, it is still there.

Regrets?

This week I tipped a card that I never thought that I would show because I have friends that are hurting. People look at Phil's and my marriage and think that it was perfect. Many areas of our union were perfect, but I am a flawed individual. Phil was not perfect. It is easy in death to turn a person into a saint and to have guilt and denial of the cracks in a relationship. We had them. We just didn't show them. I talk about it now because first, life is too short for the regrets. Second, it is too easy to leave a marriage (not necessarily divorce).

If Phil had been sitting across the table from me last night, he would have been incredibly sorry about two things. We never had the opportunity to go away without our children in our entire 23 year marriage. At first, we were bogged down by parenting duties and financial restraints. As time went on, we forgot about wanting that time with just the two of us. In the latter years, I asked for that time alone, but it wasn't until Phil got to Afghanistan that he began to see that our marriage needed it. Every marriage needs a grounding place away from children. I wanted it and needed it, but we never got that time. I enjoyed my Phil's company. I would have liked to have had time where we were not just talking about the kids or the day to day responsibilities. I would have like sharing laughter and play again.

Another area that he would have sorely regretted (and I am guilty to the nth degree) is that he pulled away from me every deployment. It would start as soon as he knew he was going. Phil would become moody and distant. He did not mean to be that way. He pulled inward because he had a hard time saying goodbye and being away from his family security. Phil grew up without having the security of knowing he had two parents who loved him. He grew up with emotionally shut off parents. His home life growing up was so horrendous that it is amazing that he was such a loving father. I loved that characteristic about him more than anything else. Here is the problem, though. His role models for marriage were so terrible that I understood when he told me that he couldn't be my friend at one point in our marriage.

He couldn't deal with being away from us because of his own abandonment issues. In order to get through the time apart, he emotionally sealed himself off. It happened this time, also. I know he loved me, but I was surviving the year apart and imaging the trip to Venice and then the PCS move to where we hoped would be Europe before we returned to USAFA. I responded to him pulling away by becoming very introverted. I have been a lone ranger for years. That works until someone is not able to come home. If he were here, I wouldn't let him pull away so easily. I would fight harder for that connection.

See, here is the thing. I loved Phil. He loved me. No questions about that. We were an unbeatable team. I would be with him until the end if he hadn't been killed. I didn't want to walk the path we had with anyone but him, but we did have areas that we should have invested in. We didn't fight, but we didn't always talk about what we needed either. I feel incredible guilt that I allowed him (and myself) to be okay with the distancing. I know it is easier emotionally to box one's heart in, but I for one, and I am sure Phil for two, needed more in terms of intimacy and closeness. Phil was my best friend. I ran to him, but I shouldn't have been okay with just waiting for him to come back.

What happens when a person doesn't come home? I have struggled to let people in. For the first time in my life, I have been honest with what I am feeling and with what I need (to my friends). I write about my feelings and I post them because I know that it is helping other people. For someone that always, always stood alone and hid behind a quiet placid façade, this has not been easy, but I write things I would never say out loud. I am choosing to let people in and I will never again allow myself or other people close to me to withdraw because it is easier. It isn't easier and there is a cost to every relationship when that is the coping mechanism. If Phil were sitting here today, I know that he would agree. He would choose us.

Slipping Backwards

My life is spinning so fast that I need for the world to stop. I need to breathe the air. I need to find footing and to find solid ground to stand on. Forever is a really, really long time. I would like to close my eyes and have that sense of stability and comfort that comes with a long time relationship. I would like to stop second guessing my every move and decision. I would like to feel that things are going to be all right. Right now, I see a bleak lonely future. I don't like what I see.

For the past two days, I have found myself slipping backwards. I have been teary and really frightened. Today I ran and I considered why I am feeling this way. My life has been upended. Everything I know, and everything I held dear, is now but a lifetime ago. In any move, I feel a sense of being discombobulated, but I embrace the adventure. My adventuresome spirit is lying dormant right now. I am doubting my decisions and I am clinging to what I do know. The problem is that by clutching what I am familiar with is that it is now an illusion that I can never attain. I do need to move on in terms of doing the unthinkable and embracing new challenges, but I stand treading water frantically while the looming tidal wave is bearing down on me.

I know that once I get through the raging waters, I will find a calm garden in which to rest my weary head. I just need that Eden now. I need to find that foothold to spring into the self I knew for so long. I recently turned 50. It is so strange, so foreign, to feel as insecure and lost as I did at 15 and 27. I cry because I lost myself when I lost my Phil. I lost the piece of me that I liked the best and I am not sure if I can ever get it back.

While I recently have rediscovered my wicked sense of humor, I am looking to regain that quiet peace that comes from loving myself and from knowing who I am and where I belong. As I ran out the door today, three young boys came running up the stairs with my newspaper. A shocked surprised look crossed their young faces and then a delighted, "Mrs. A! Mrs. A! You live here?" I will sorely miss being Mrs. A at Stetson. I love those kids and they loved me. I will miss being Mrs. A, Phil's wife. This girl needs to figure out who Mrs. A is when she stands alone. I may sink. I may flounder, but in the end, I am going to claw my way to the surface and I will take a heaving breath and know that it is okay. For now, I am holding my breath as the waves crash all around me.

Linda Lou Loser

Dear Linda Lou Loser (no, I don't want a jillion messages telling me that I am not a loser☺),

Sasha Fierce here pink polka dots and all. You are stronger than you think. You can do this one step at a time. One mile at a time. Don't forget to breathe and enjoy the ride. Don't forget, polka dots make everything better. Promise.

Sasha with the girlie pink bike

All of my elementary students know my first name and that I use the 3D triple L symbol across my forward to laugh at myself and my goof ups in sports. I throw like a little girl...I use the moniker and the symbols in jest and to teach students to laugh at themselves and to not take mistakes so seriously. What they do not know is that the Linda Lou Loser evolved from a painful lonely early adolescence. As a shy, quiet overweight girl who was ALWAYS picked last for every team (even dodge ball and swimming which I was really pretty good at), I knew that people saw me as Linda Lou Loser (maiden name started with an L). They didn't have to say anything. I knew. I saw it when I looked in the mirror. I felt it.

Here is what my peers did not see, however. I had a raging fire to overcome from within. I had spunk. I had drive. I didn't know when or if people would see me differently, but I could believe in myself even when nobody else could. Along my painful teen years, I developed a wicked sense of humor that few see. I hide behind laughter to get me through the dark times. Sometimes my humor is not appropriate, but the more stressful a situation, the more I try to find something funny to look at. I have five living testimonies to my personality quirk in Patrick, Josh, Emily, Alex, and Tiger.

Many of you know that I had a few rough days this weekend. I am overwhelmed and frightened of the unknown. Logically, I know that I feel this way every move, but usually I have someone walking the move with me. I remembered something today. 15 out of the last 18 months that we spent in Europe, I spent alone with five children, a naughty dog, and working so many hours that I didn't see how I could continue to press on. Phil was deployed and then he went to Officer Training School (OTS) and tech school. I didn't have a lot of phone contact during parts of this.

I had to figure out moving (TMO), lodging, transportation, high school graduation, the dog getting back to the states, a son's major knee injury and surgery, and a son's reporting date to USAFA as a cadet. Mind you, I was working over 13 hours a day. I survived it when I didn't think I could by taking each minute one second at a time. I prioritized and I pressed on. I press on now.

I may not see the security at the other end. I may not feel peace or know where my life is taking me, but as I ran on this morning, I know that I will be okay. I know that lurking under the placid façade that I have worked hard to put on, lurks my alter ego—Sasha Fierce with the polka dots and the pink bike. Sasha here will be okay. She will find her way. Through the raging roiling waters, Sasha will pedal furiously until she figures it out. She may trip, stumble and fall. She may even hide behind the humor of Linda Lou Loser, but Sasha knows that all will be well with a lot of faith and a giant leap into the unknown.

Trust, I Don't Even Trust Myself

As I get ready to spring from my safe secure platform high above the raging waters into the roiling dark watery abyss, I am feeling unmoored and uneasy. I find the tears flowing again and I have a sense of wanting to clutch the life I have. As much as I want the life I have, however, it isn't but an illusion. I want the life I shared with Phil. I want the security that comes with being loved and loving someone back to the same degree. It never mattered where we lived; home was where we were together. As much as I love this place, "it is haunted".

Phil was his happiest here. He never expected to be a professor or that anyone would see his worth in the military. He still thought like an immigrant who struggled to find his way with a strange language and customs. Although to the outside public, Phil was incredibly successful, he never thought that way about himself. He had just finished his PhD, a second master's degree, and he had five successful children, he never felt like he could hold on to what he had until he came to the United States Air Force Academy. It was in mentoring and teaching young cadets that Phil found his way. He found his niche and his confidence.

Before Phil left for Afghanistan, though, he began to feel uneasy and unmoored. He wanted security and promises. In fact, few people know this, but Phil really wanted a chance to be a parent again. We were in the process of adopting when Phil suddenly got cold feet. He wanted to wait until he came back from his deployment to continue pursuing that dream. He just felt too young to be done with children. He knew, as I know, that the best and most successful area that we had as a couple was parenting five remarkable children.

Before Phil left, he became really withdrawn. He insisted on doing things he had never done predeployment before. He got more life insurance. He wrote me sweet notes. He cleaned up his mess, and he wrote out many details of our marriage that he took care of. People ask me if Phil knew. I don't think so because if he had any inkling, I believe, I know that he would have made time for that trip we always meant to take together. He would have called me more often.

I never thought that he was going to come back home the way he did—in a flag draped coffin to Dover, Delaware. I thought there would always be another day, another hour, another minute. I see my glaring flaws. My lack. I wish, and oh, how I wish, that I had been better at putting him first. I thought that I would die first. I was okay with that. I was almost six years older than Phil and I am the one with the medical issues. I wish I had been first, but that was not the plan.

Having a person yanked unexpectedly from life after six months of them being deployed out of one's life is probably the absolute worst way to lose someone. There are no goodbyes. I have nothing that smells like him or even any of his things out around the house. I find myself trying to remember his smell, his laughter, his touch. My world was always okay when I was wrapped in his arms.

The interesting aspect of my loss is the physical pain that I felt for the past few months. I never expected grief to make my body hurt. I ache...everywhere. For awhile, it hurt to breathe. I truly thought that I would just not wake up one morning. The other area, the one that is costing me the most right now, is the loss of trust in my own abilities to make decisions. Yes, I am making decisions, but I am so unsure. I am so ill prepared to walk it alone.

There are many aspects of trust, though. I don't know if I will ever be able to trust anyone enough to let them into my life in terms of another man. I have never been like this before. I can logically see it as an extension of Phil dying suddenly, but I can't wrap my arms around trusting someone enough to get that close. While I was recently surprised by feel attraction towards a male, I picked someone who is unattainable and who lives far away because it is safe. It is nice to think about without having to deal with the emotions that would come with touch and emotional intimacy. I don't know if those days of being able to put myself out there will ever come. I do know that Phil and I talked about it. I would have wanted him to date and find someone if I had died first. I would want him to be happy. I know he wanted the same for me which is the very reason I am stuck. I loved my Phil. I wanted the life we had. I wanted to grow old with Phil.

Moving to Germany may seem like a huge step and maybe even a questionable step, but I am stuck here. I do not know who I am without Phil. My whole paradigm has shifted. Many of my best friends I did not know, or I was not close to, when Phil was killed. Some of my oldest friends couldn't handle the loss of Phil and they have disappeared fully from my life. My job, my dream job, is the hardest thing for me to leave, yet I know that for me to become emotionally well, I do need to step forward and to find my own place. Phil's place of refuge and success was USAFA. I do not know where mine will be, but I continue on my journey. I step now into freefalling through the unknown.

I am Invisible

One of the strangest aspects about being my age is that I am invisible. I hate that feeling. I am not very confident in myself right now. In the words of Emily (AT THE AGE OF THREE), It's lonely down here! I hate eating alone and going places alone. I am working on it, but it SUCKS in a big way. People rush past me and don't even see the woman in front of them. To them, I am invisible. . .unworthy of a kind word. As a young girl, I often had attention I didn't want or seek out. In middle age, being alone is like a death knell. My value has decreased as if I suddenly lost my worth. In my marriage, it seems, I gained value by being with someone.

Being alone puts me into a category that sets me apart. It doesn't seem to matter that this aloneness is not of my doing. People who do not know me well innately withdraw from me. It is as if I am sending off the black aura of neediness and want. It is hard to eat alone. Go to movies alone. I can't even imagine a vacation alone. I clutch at human companionship through Facebook because I am scared, alone, and grasping at figuring out who I am without the love of my Phil.

While some people are comfortable in their own skin and doing things independently, this has never been me. There have been times when faced being a lone ranger better than I am now. I actually like being a lone ranger, but that feeling dissipates when one considers the finality of death. Forever is a really long time. I sometimes want to crawl into a dark hole and stay there. I can't do this of course, but this path is hard. Treacherous.

People treat me differently now, also. Military wives often don't want to talk to me. There are a few, and communication from some of them has deeply humbled and touched me, but many women turn away. I know that when they see me they face their own nightmares—their own fears. It hurts. Men see me as fragile and wounded. I am that to an extent, but I have never been a clinger or a person that demands from others. My friend Suzanna, who is walking the same walk, had to deal with her husband's birthday coming and going today. Only one of Jeff's colleagues reached out to her today. Maybe they did not know what to say? Here is the thing, though. I would rather have someone say the wrong thing and try, than to not acknowledge my Phil or the events that were important. While people quickly move on, I have not. My family has not. People closely tied to the event have not moved on. We are slowly healing, but band aids can and do get ripped off sometimes.

This weekend I ran the San Francisco Marathon. Phil picked this marathon to be my 55th marathon by 50 while he was in Kabul. He wanted me to repeat California because we had our last family vacation to San Francisco in 2004 when Patrick was a senior at the Air Force Academy. It was terribly hard to run past the places we had so much fun. I cried when I ran by Fisherman's Wharf and at the finish line. I have lost so much. We used to joke around about being stuck with each other because of the children and all of the special memories that we have shared. Am I ever going to be able to go on vacation by myself? Eat alone without feeling like a loser? Go to a movie and not be uncomfortable?

It would be easier to find companionship if I wasn't looking for a different fairy tale again. I feel old and beaten down by life. My moral compass hasn't changed. Maybe I will have to spend the rest of my life alone. I hope that it doesn't hurt or loom so broadly soon. My heart is crushed. I ache with longing of the life I once had. I don't know that I will ever understand why Phil was called home so soon. My best part of me died right along with him. I sometimes can't (or should I say that it is oppressive to) look at my future. It looms dark and sinister. Forever is crushing the hope in my heart.

Fading Memories

Memories are fading and it bothers me. I have already lost the sound of my Phil's laughter and the way his caress felt on my skin. I remember his fingers, his back, his smell, but I am sure that in time those remnants will also fade. I clutch the photographs to my beating heart, but photos bend and fade. They can be reproduced, where my memories are lost in a hopeless cavern in which nothing can be retrieved. I hate that I feel that I didn't value us together enough not to keep those thoughts and memories, but I can't find the shared pieces of our 23 years.

In my heart, I search for ways to reproduce what I felt, but it isn't possible. I travel to places we have been only to cower and hide in a lonely room. I find myself running and looking for ways to outrun the pain and loneliness. It does help, but I still carry that longing and incredible sense of loss. It just feels like the world lost someone who really mattered. Phil mattered not only to me, his five children, but to many other people as well. He used his skills and talents to make a difference and to span the world. 44 years of life was a mere drop in the bucket. There was so much more he could have done, that he wanted to do.

When a life is cut short, people wonder at the senselessness of the death. Survivors often feel guilt that they are still alive and living a life that involves laughter and fun with the pain. On many levels, I am there. I do have fulfillment in many areas of my life, but there is a huge gaping hole. I do not have anyone to share my joys or my trials with. I do not have human touch in my life, and I do not have a confidant in which I can share all. I cannot show my true all to anyone. I hide my insecurities and pain behind the biggest wall I can erect. While I have many friends who have carried me, it is the sharing of a life built on shared memories, common direction, and passion that I miss the most. When the children act up or someone hurts me, who am I going to turn to?

As a survivor, I find that many people make Phil into a saint. He was a good man. A really good man, but he was not perfect. I am not perfect. Well meaning people end up making me feel like the wrong person died. I know that they do not mean it the way it is coming across, but I already feel some of that. My life is so provincial as a PE teacher and as a runner, and I am still figuring out how I want to live out loud, but Phil's life has compelled me out of my ennui to speak up and to be a voice for military families everywhere. This is out of my comfort zone. I find myself changing and moving in a direction I never wanted to move. I wish, and oh, how I wish, that Phil could be a part of this journey with me in a different way.

Loss can define a person by one of two ways. First, there are people who never move beyond the anguish in their hearts. I understand this. I often feel broken, too broken to face anybody or anything, but I really feel called to react in another way. I need people to see that the military family is global. We stand as one in time of loss. Arm in arm, heart to heart, there but the grace of God go any of us. I use this platform to spring ahead into an unknown unwelcome life. I use this platform to spring into a purpose driven life. I will answer the call. I will go where I am being called to go even if it is painful and difficult. I will speak and become an activist in terms of putting a face with the names that flash across the TV screen nightly because each of these names represents someone who was being waited for at home and a person who was loved by someone. I stand, not just for my Phil, but for every soldier, man or woman, who died defending me, standing for the oppressed, or defending my friends. I stand as part of the military family today.

Feeling Crushed and Broken Today

Right before daylight leaves or comes to the day, blackness turns to a deep dark purple blanket that covers the sky. It is in the purple gauze glimmers of the promises of the daylight are lost or are gained. The loneliness squeezing me is almost more than I can bear. Seven months ago today, I lay wrapped in Phil's arms and felt that all was well in my world. Moments later, I watched him waving goodbye for the last time.

I knew that a year would be almost more than I could bear, but looking at a lifetime without sharing it with my Phil is almost more than I can bear. I am stuck in the cold grip of a reality that seems too much to face. I am so ill equipped to walk this walk alone. I am scared, unsure, and broken, perhaps beyond repair. Where I once faced my life with a sense of adventure and ease, I shrink and cower in the shadows. I want to feel a sense of wellness and confidence again. I am just not sure how to get there.

As I ran on for miles and miles today, my heart wept tears of loss and frustration at myself. I wish I was lying wrapped in Phil's arms again when I felt the "all is right" in my little corner of the world. I never needed popularity or the adulation of many; I just wanted and desired the concept of family and of home. For me, home was my family. It didn't matter if my whole world fell apart if I had Phil and my children. With the death of Phil, my world was thrown asunder. All I see now is the pitch dark shroud that crushes all hope in tomorrow. I am waiting for the twilight or the sunrise that promises to come. I can't see it or feel it, but I hope for it today.

Loneliness is as Cold as Ice

Loneliness is strange. I don't know that I have ever felt it this acutely before. I think I would remember the squeezing of my heart if ever I had been this alone. I have been a mom since I was 21 so every time I lived alone or had Phil deploy, I had someone to entertain me and to turn to. Human touch (even a nice word) is important in everyone's life. I just never thought I needed it. Oh, how I do.

I need more than people reaching out to me, though. I need to feel useful and I need to be a friend back. When Phil was killed, I knew hope first when I was first able to see beyond myself. As I helped a few of my friends and I stood with other widows who were hurting, I realized I was not alone and that I was needed. That hope. . .that connection, as it were, drug me out of a dark quagmire that threatened to consume me. I have that need now.

I have the need to be useful and to be a friend. I have the need to have someone care about me here. I stare at the four walls of my hotel room after I finally sit down for the day and wonder about a future that involves solitude and quiet. For a quiet person, this silence is daunting with how encompassing and oppressive it is. My joy is being robbed bit by bit.

I love Germany. . .truly, truly love Germany. I am just so alone in the world. If I dropped off the face of the earth, how long would it take for anyone to notice? I am not suicidal, nor do I have a death wish. I have miles and miles to go before I sleep. I feel it and I know it with my very being, but I am just asking the question. Feeling removed and feeling invisible is not a good feeling.

I am older than (I think) everyone on post. At fifty, I am too young to be experiencing this emotion and this loss. I clutch at the ease and the companionship I had my entire adult life before Phil died. I feel different than normal people (at least how I once felt).Everyone is married. It feels as if I am the only runner on post. For an army post, how come nobody is running in the morning? In Landstuhl, every morning no matter what, the GI Joes/Janes were out running and chanting. I miss the familiarity of that routine. One would think that with all of the Special Forces, I would see this. Not so.

As I strive to find normalcy and connections, I am trying to stay upbeat and positive. I know this is where I am supposed to be. Know it and believe it. If God pushed me through this door, can't he provide a local social network for me? In the meantime, I am really looking forward to meeting up with my friends in Ohio soon for the AF Marathon. To feel like I am part of a bigger group, to feel a connection, and to be a supportive role in a group is what I truly desire. I need to see and feel something other than the dark cloud of being totally alone.

Death of Yet Another Is Pushing Me Backwards

I am struggling a lot this week. The death of a long time friend plunged me back into a pit of uncertainty and fear. Add to this darkness, the discombobulating feeling of loneliness and being totally overwhelmed by moving, the military, and a new country, and a person can see the picture of me broken and on my knees. I am struggling to find the footholds and the glimmers of hope in the ashes of my life.

I am human. Not only am I totally crushed by the weight of the losses that are mounting up, I feel jealousy and want for the family reunion I never had. I was waiting, always waiting for Phil to come home. I never thought the wait would be forever or that we wouldn't have a goodbye. His life was not ended in a normal way. I don't have anything that smells like him. I don't remember the touch of his skin on mine. His voice is gone. What more will I lose? As the months since Phil's death add to the time he was deployed, I long for that happy reunion, the phone call, the connection. I long to share my life with him, my fears, and my total fatigue.

While I know that God is faithful, and that I will never receive more than I can bear, I feel crushed under the weight of loss and uncertainty. I want to feel something besides longing and darkness. Today, I broke again. As I sat weeping, things started to go right. My quiet desperation turned to lull and a peaceful oasis in terms of a person walking with me today. I needed the human connection, and Heather gave it to me.

I am not out of my dark pit, nor am I done with the terror or the rush of longing for my quiet simple life, but I see that God is reaching through people and circumstance. I wish I could see how God is working through the circumstances of my life, but I can't today. I do know this, even in my dark times, and even in the weight of loss crushing the hope in my heart, I believe. I believe in a much bigger picture than what I am experiencing here. I believe in the cross and all that it stood for. I believe that I will have a reunion with Phil. I hope that happens in the near future, but if that is not to be, then I pray that I can stand firm on the promises I cling to even when I can' see them or feel them. It is lonely and cold here, but I believe that God is faithful. I stand firm today. . .tomorrow. . .

Please Pray

I am hurting right now. Will you pray, please? Sundays are the worst for me. What only one of you knows is this. I can't even go to Catholic mass right now. It is too painful. I do go to services every week, but I am struggling a little. I am heading into a really tough window of time. First, Phil and I never had been away on a vacation without our children. He married me with three young children by a previous marriage. He never wanted to go away without our family until he deployed to Afghanistan. This was our honeymoon--23 years late. I leave in two weeks because of a promise I made to him on Easter Sunday, the last time I spoke to him. Our daughter had just returned home from Afghanistan. He made me promise to take her if anything happened to him. I should be so excited for this trip. This trip is all he talked about and wrote about for months. My heart bleeds, but I am stepping in faith.

As soon as I get back from the "dream vacation, a cruise out of Venice, I have to deal with a four hour briefing on what happened in that room on 27 April. It is bad. Really bad. Our anniversary follows on 27 November. I need two or three gathered in his name to pray with me. I am trying to walk this time by faith. I want to be the woman God is calling me to be by living with the purpose and mission he has given me. Sometimes, my purple rhinestones fall off of my tiara and I crumple to the ground. I drop my sword and battered shield and hide for awhile. I am doing that now. Please pray.

Sometimes I am Such a Little Girl

I am not sure why, but in the past two weeks this non-crier has been crying a lot. My heart is bleeding. I just keep clutching my fading memories and wishing that it had been me instead of Phil. It hurts really badly to be the survivor. Sometimes I feel shattered beyond repair.

While I can see how God is working through the black ashes of my dreams, I am living a life I never envisioned for me. I am terrified of failing and falling short. I have never started a job needing this much time off or so in the front row. I want to cower and hide, but alas, the death of Phil in April has taken my comfort zone away. I am an unwilling participant in my own life.

The tears start when I least expect them-at church, running, and when someone is nice to me. I am bleeding. I am broken, but still the kindness of so many people touches me. It humbles me in my cowering state. I want to be the person everyone believes in and I do cling to the promise that in my weakness there is strength. My fortitude must lurk under the shadows because I do not see the strength that others see in me.

I just want to live a worthy life that has meaning. I want to be a good employee even as I shrink from the events of 27 April. I know that I need compassion and empathy. I know that concessions are being made. I am on my knees knowing that there is nothing left except the will of mine which says to hold on. I am clutching and clinging. I am looking through the blinding smoke to a future where maybe I am not crying or feeling so alone and broken. I may not see the light, but I do know that it is here. I know that beyond the darkness something bigger looms. Can I see it today?

I need some hope. I need a promise. I am beyond missing Phil. I ache for him. I want to see him one more time. Did he know how much I loved him? Wanted him? Needed him? He was my life. I waited when he was gone. . .I wait now. I strive to be the person that he would have wanted me to be. I want to live out loud, but can I when all that I feel is pain and loneliness? Can the small steps mean that I can do this alone? I wish that I understood why Phil. . .Why 9 good people on 27 April. I will never understand, but I wish, oh, how I wish that I had had that Venice trip with Phil. I wish that he knew how much I loved (still love) him.

I step forward out of necessity. I embrace a future that I never envisioned or wanted. I hope that I honor his life by how I am living mine and the words and actions that I do. I want a promise for tomorrow that my loss will only be part of what defines me. I want happiness and I want a life that doesn't involve little girl crocodile tears. I can deal with the pink polka dots, but the tears leave me feeling bad. I want strength to stand in my weakness. I stand now.

Death, the Grief Process and Me

Recently a well intentioned close family member told me that he thought I needed professional help in dealing with my grief. Here is the issue. He no longer knows me. He remembers me as a young insecure girl. I am no longer that girl. I am a woman who though broken and bowed, had discovered a purpose in her life. I didn't pursue this mission, I sort of fell into a role of being a mouth piece for military family loss. In embracing this role, I have found a purpose to my life and my loss. I honor Phil by

185

speaking up through my writing, running, talking, and my faith. My family does not understand that in action, I am healing.

I may not portray a grieving widow the way that most people think a person who is suffering loss should grieve. None of us are the same. I do not need pills, alcohol, meaningless sex, or self destruction. I need to run, write, spend time with my friends, and I need to pray. This works for me. For me to go to a stranger to talk about my loss would be excruciatingly painful. It would be work and I would hate each and every minute of the talking, yet when I am the most in need, I run, talk to God, write, and then find a way to connect with the very friends that get me. Who understand that I use humor to make it through another bad moment? Who understand that what I am not saying is sometimes what I should be talking about.

Somehow, my family has never seen my strength or my resilience. For this reason, I have chosen to live the life of a vagabond. I love my family dearly, but I feel so different in terms of what is considered normal. If I am outside and if I can retreat when I am my weakest, I will be okay. I write about what I am feeling because nobody else is doing that. I am being compelled to write as part of my healing process. People are all so different. Where others find it liberating to talk to an unknown counselor, it literally makes me want to vomit. I honor Phil by living out loud through my writing and my speaking.

I see how others may perceive that I need something more, but again, the grieving process is different for each and every survivor. One person who understood my deepest need right from the day I set my feet down in Dover, DE, is my friend, Robin. She knew that if I ran, I would work through the pain in my heart. I would run on the whispered prayers of my plodding feet and my beating broken heart. A stranger then, yet she understood. People all over the world understand, but many of the people who knew me prior to Phil's death do not understand. I have always been quiet and somewhat shy, but in no means was that a sign of weakness. Phil always told me that I was the strongest woman he knew. I didn't see it. I am starting to see it now.

While I would never ever imagined this life or that I would be stepping up to speak and give a face to families who have suffered the loss of a loved one, I know that this is what I am supposed to be doing. I feel compelled with all that I am and who I am to speak, to write, and to give honor to the names of the people who flash across our TV screens. These names represent people who were loved, who wanted to go home, and these names were people who had people waiting at home for the homecoming that will never happen. In a blink of an eye, our loved ones were yanked away from us. We do not get the goodbyes, nor do we have the clothes that smell like our loved ones. We have often been separated through the deployment length. We all waited for those televised family reunions. Ours never came.

I am the voice of so many people. It does not make me weak or strange, but it does give me a way to honor my Phil and a way to work through my feelings. Writing and running may not be the way that most people grieve, but we are all different. Others do need to talk to a stranger because it is a safe haven to work through the emotions. For me, and there is no right or wrong way to cope, it is running on the whispered prayers of my feet. It is the writing and sharing of my feelings, and it is the friends that stand with me, make me laugh, and who listen when I need it the most. You are my family.

27 Is Just a Number

I used to mark the 27th of each month in terms of how long Phil and I had been married. We would have been married 23 years on 27 November. Now, I mark the 27th of each month by adding up the months Phil has been gone from me. Four months is the marker today. Four months, or one third of a year.

I still wait for a phone call that never comes. I am not sure how to train the heart not to leap when the phone rings. The silent longing is still there. Though I am doing okay and taking steps to move forward, I still see where the wounded heart lies. I can hide behind my mask and my shroud of strength. For the most part, that resiliency is who I am. Who would have thought? However, the resiliency and the natural joy of life that I feel don't replace the sense of loss or of belonging.

No matter where I am in the grieving process, I would be remiss if I didn't say that the events of 27 April don't cross my mind every month. Like a bad anniversary, my mind and heart jump to that dark day. While I am not dropped to my knees, I feel the want and need to talk to Phil just one more time. I fall into this pit of hoping he knew just how much I loved him and of wondering what I could have done better as a wife. If either of us had any inkling, I know we would have talked more frequently and e-mailed more frequently. There is the quiet regret born of a tragedy neither of us imagined.

The Wounded Fissures of my Heart

I find myself walking every night. Lord knows that it certainly isn't for the exercise, but rather it is to run away from sitting alone every night in a hotel room. It is hard to explain. I never really felt alone even when the kids were grown up and out of the house and Phil was deployed. I think it might be because the empty house looms large because it is a forever house. The calendar no longer is exciting to look at, because the loneliness is magnified as the days roll by.

I have always been a girl who rolls with the punches. I don't react and I laugh off most things. Since Phil's death, I find my self-control in terms of the placid demeanor slipping. I feel out of control in my own life. I am not talking destructive behaviors or decisions; rather, it does not take much to make my voice crack and waiver. It takes very little for my eyes to well with tears. People do not see my weakness, but, oh, how I feel it.

This week, I got hammered with school starting. My class sizes vary from over 50 (2 classes) to a class of ten students. It is crazy. I lack the equipment I would like to have for the games that promote a quality middle school program. I am lonely and afraid. I think that is normal in my position, however it is terrible to be 50 and looking at forever all alone.

I had been really excited for 50. It is interesting that turning 50 and Phil's death has thrown me into an all out middle life crisis. I didn't see it coming. It is scary looking at opening doors and trying new things. I never thought that this life would be mine. Never wanted a new life. I am now considering things that Phil was never into-camping, canoeing, back packing this summer, parachuting, hmm, should I go on? I wish that Phil was here and that I was leading the comfortable life I always dreamed we would have together, but I am tired. I am ready to step out and do something to wake up again. I want the self-control and the laughter to return completely. I want to be able to shrug off the terrible days and roll my eyes at how bad things are. I want to feel peace and contentment in my life again.

I am a poser, or a pretender, right now. I slip on the quiet mask that few see underneath. It is only through my writing and my friends that know me best, can my cracks be seen. Those almost invisible fissures can break at any time, but for right now, they are holding strong. I may be weak, but in my weakness I find strength. I am discovering that my quiet fortitude leads to resilience and empathy. I just need to keep moving forward and taking small steps to insert the iron born of fire into those tiny gaping holes in my heart.

I am a Lonely Little Petunia

"I am a lonely little Petunia." To give away a private memory, Phil called me a variety of pet names. One of them was "his little Petunia." As I ran on today, I heard that song that he downloaded come up. It made me think of Phil. How poignant because we should be a Parent's Weekend watching a football game and bragging (and Phil was obnoxious about bragging about his family, but not himself) about our five children. We should be at USAFA with our Tiger boy (forgive your mom, Tim). We should be laughing and enjoying the long weekend.

I find myself lonely for the lapsing time. If only, if only. I wish that I could return to those earlier days where the frenzied pace of parenting and being a wife seemed to never end. The responsibilities mounted and I felt incapable of doing it at times, yet I pressed on. There was never a day when I felt that I had done my hours exactly right. I always beat myself up about the things I had done or said or that I hadn't done or said that I should have. Yet, those days live on in my heart. The days of sticky fingers, temper tantrums, story time, backwards dinners, games, and I could go on and on. Those events filled our days, but they live on in my heart now.

A petunia is one of the heartiest flowers. It is often overlooked. Most flowers stand taller and larger in nature, but the petunia lasts through the touch times. The petunia is loyal and true. The flower has many variations and colors, but it stands up to colder temperatures, heat, and growing conditions that other flowers would wilt in. I am not the showiest of people. I am often overlooked, but I am true. I am loyal, and I am standing the test of time. I may be standing in the shadows of cold loneliness, but I am blossoming under the crag in which I stand.

Wanting and Wishing for the Life I Had

It is sobering to wonder if the best days of my life have already come and gone. I look ahead and the loneliness looms so large that I want to drop to my knees right now. I cannot see anything except the billowing dark clouds on the horizon. I don't have anything that I anticipate or want so why is it that I am standing in an eddy of swirling currents without a beach to rest on?

In my adult life, I have had children to moor me. They are grown up. I feel far away from them right now, also. Like Phil would say, we trained them to be independent and no news is good news, but as a mom whose children were my biggest investment of time, energy, focus, and most of all, love, it isn't easy when the day comes when they pull away and begin their own lives. I lack Skype and the internet right now, but really, even if I had it, it seems as if Phil's death created a bigger distance between us. I think that it is possible that they do not want to make me feel worse by sharing their pain just like I do not want to crush them with my pain, but still, I do not have those tight connections.

I miss having someone to laugh with, hang out with, and share those memories and minor complaints about the kids. I miss having someone to wake up next to (even if he did hog all of the covers). I miss being able to talk football smack and someone to share my day with. I miss eating with him. In our 23 years, it is true that I grew complacent in the day to day details of living and marriage, but I would love to have that closeness and companionship.

Three day weekend are terrible. I can barely get through the weekend, but to add an extra day on just makes me feel like a sad lonely loser. I can't imagine another year like this let alone another thirty. I just don't understand. I know that all things work together for the good of all who believe. I believe that. . .really I do, but in the darkness it is easy to lose site of the big picture. I often do.

If God is faithful, and I do believe that he is, can this be all there is for me? I am clutching and clinging to a rope without hope of happiness. I am looking and wondering what will fill my time and my life. I imagined the dream house in Washington State. I saw Phil and me in rocking chairs watching our multiple grandchildren playing in our big backyard. I never saw going it alone. I knew that the day would come when one of us would die, but I thought that it would be years from now and that I would go first. If only life could happen the way that it plays out in our heart. I stand today lonely and cold. Wishing and wanting.

I Need a Do Over Day

I need a do over today. For the first time in years, I had one of those teaching days where I wanted to throttle my students, the little miscreants! I couldn't get the little punks to do anything but make disrespectful comments. I have been gone one week, ONE week. Where are those nice 7th and 8th graders I once had?

I so rarely have an off teaching day that when I do, I beat myself up over the day because I have this unspoken need to try to fix things and to make people happy. I have been the most comfortable in the corner serving people. I don't need to have people looking at me or to be popular, but I am happiest when I am serving or being a loyal friend. I feel better when I look outside of my wants and needs to help others.

When people ask me how I can do the things I do since Phil has been gone, I have to answer it is because I know without reservation that this is one area that God is pushing me to the plate to embrace. I speak and I write to bring honor to EVERY military man or woman whose names flash across our television screens. Every name was a person who wanted to come home and who was being waited for at home. Every name was a person who was loved and who loved back. Every person died for us as a collective whole.

Strength is not something that people are always born with. Strength is what happens when times are not so good. Strength is forged when a person feels that they have lost more than they have left. When a person is finally able to reach one finger to start anew, the person has become fused steel. The person is able to stand up to the battering winds that rip at their confidence and joy. That person is able to laugh with the resilience carried in their heart. I know because I have it. I wouldn't have thought so, but I am seeing it each and every day.

People do not realize that my faith is gathered through the whispered prayers of my plodding feet and my beating heart. Faith has compelled me into a realm that I never had. This realm is the land of resiliency and strength, I may drop my sword and dented shield to cry for awhile, but I know that I will be okay. I see the many ways my life has grown since April and I stand in awe. I wish Phil could see these characteristics in me. I know that he would be slightly intimidated, but very proud.

Today, the polka dots did not work. Today, Sasha fell to her knees, but tomorrow is another day and I will rise up like the bubbles in my heart. I will step forward and I will embrace each new challenge as a challenge to fortify my internal resolve. I look to the new dawn breaking as my promise. It is coming. I can handle those slightly naughty middle school children. They need me in their lives and I choose to be in theirs. I can do this. I know I can!

Today was the Day I was Supposed to Leave Colorado Springs to Meet My Phil

I will not bow. I will not break. I will fall, but I will not fade. . .Today is the day that I should be leaving Colorado Springs to begin the long journey to see Phil in Venice. I should have been the girl in the flirty navy polka dotted dress boarding the airplane with excitement in my heart. I should have been running to Venice and into Phil's arms. He should have had his happy reunion and he should have seen the happiness in me.

Phil would pull away before every deployment. He would shut me out because it was his way of getting through the lengthy separations. After 23 years of marriage, I knew that characteristic. It still hurt me, but I stood with him and supported him because he supported me during my weaker moments. This deployment was no different. He pulled away from me seven months before his actual deployment. He forgot my birthday and he became more and more closed off. This deployment was different, however. He saw what he was doing and he recognized that it was hurting me.

He told me that he would make an effort this time, and he did. He called me every few days and sent me e-mails. He also tried to send me flowers on Valentine's Day. He had never done that before. He bought a bunch of cards to send to me throughout his deployment and he bought jewelry and other trinkets to make me happy. What he didn't know was that it made me happy that he was thinking of me because I thought of him all of the time. He was my first thought in the morning and my last thought at night. He still is.

It was Phil's idea for us to have this trip without our children. I had tried for years to get Phil to take me away on the honeymoon trip we never took. It wasn't until he got to Afghanistan that he wanted this trip. He wanted a dream vacation and he didn't care how much it cost. His enthusiasm and happiness over this cruise made me smile because every e-mail and every phone call he talked about it. My enthusiasm burned brightly because it was stoked by the billows of his joy.

I wish we hadn't waited so long to take time just the two of us. I wish that I had fought harder to make Phil keep a stronger connection when he was deployed. I wish that Phil could know just how much I loved him, needed him, and wanted him. I wish that he could see the happy girl in the blue polka dotted dress coming through customs and walking straight into his arms. I miss him.

I know that I will be fine once I get going on this trip, but I need to get there first. Like many things in life, the fear and anticipation leading to an event is sometimes worse than the actual event. I pray that this is how it is on Thursday when I walk the gangplank on to the boat. I pray that Phil is somehow with me and Emily as we embark on the vacation he wanted and deserved. I step forward to honoring his memory by taking the vacation he wanted for the two of us. I will carry Phil always in my heart and in the woman I became because of the love that we shared.

The Next Chapter and the Changing of Linda

Attracting all the Weirdos Out There

Why is it that people assume that because I am single that I must be desperate? Come on. . .I felt like I was back in high school with the drama (never liked it then, either). There I was running a marathon. I was sopped to the skin because it was very hot in Minneapolis. I kept running because so many people were on the course supporting me. I came up on another fellow runner that belongs to a club (3,000 of us) that I am a member of. I had never seen him. Since I do not often run in my club gear, I identified myself by my number and I encouraged him. I gave him no other information because I talked to him less than a minute. I ran on to the finish.

When I completed the marathon, the medical people latched on to me. I looked and felt bad. The medical guy walked me around for 15 minutes which is all the time this yahoo needed. He sees me and makes a beeline for me in his ugly printed orange shorts that didn't quite cover his tush-- EW! He says, "Can I give you a kiss? I saw your shirt. I could make you feel better. I am married, but she doesn't understand my running." EEEEEWWWW.

I told him that I wouldn't be comfortable with that. He then asked again. The medical guy looked at me and asked me if the runner was bothering me. Uh, hello. Yeah. I spoke up and said so. That got rid of him. Like my friend Marius said, you should have asked him if that line ever had worked for him before.

Fun and Fearless at 50 (almost)

I have been blessed to spend time in Boise with some of my oldest friends. The interesting thing is that we are all late bloomers. We were the overlooked and often minimized ones in high school, but we are the resilient, strong, fearless (well, not so much me) women that rock. I like these girls. There is one fun, fearless friend that is giving me a lot of fun with teasing my mom. She rides a Harley, wears leather, and is fun. Like me, she was quiet when she was younger. My mom is in awe. Gotta love it.

I love my job because I look for those often overlooked and minimized children. I look to find a way to connect to those kids. When I get them excited about something physical, it makes me happy. I get it. I truly do try to make a difference and to live out loud. I am not always good at it, but the internal motivation is there. Never retreat. Never surrender.

Small Baby Steps

It is strange to go to movies by myself. I am not so good at being a lone ranger. It Is interesting because I travel solo all of the time to run, but I hate eating out or going places alone. When Phil left, I just stopped going out. I was in the waiting house until he returned home.

I venture out now and it feels so foreign. I feel like everyone is staring at me. Thinking what is wrong with her. I don't mind traveling alone so what gives? The small baby steps begin the journey. . .

You know, I am starting to really enjoy running again. Running has been about so much for me. When I first started running, it was about running away from my life at 15. I hated everything about that shy and insecure girl. I hated being bullied, being ugly (and, yeah, I was), having an eating disorder, what was happening in other ways. . .Running became my control over a world of chaos.

I have pounded the pavement with the whispered prayers of my feet through college, a bad first marriage (and for the record, I take ownership of my own culpability in this failure), five pregnancies, numerous deployments, life changing illness in my own life, and now, through the darkest time of my life. I run on because whether I run for joy or for gut wrenching grief, running meets my innate needs of my soul. Right now, today, I run for the joy of running. It feels good. I feel good. . .

To Be Almost Fifty and Making Decisions for Myself

It is strange to be almost 50 and making decisions about my future. One of the facets of being married a long time to a military man is that my adult life has been dictated by where the military sent my husband. In a strange manner, the loss of control is comforting. I second guess myself and my decisions at every turn. I feel so ill-prepared and unready to make the most basic of choices.

In almost 50 years of life, I have never moved somewhere alone except for college. It is strange to think of leaving the country and taking a job that is a job that I choose. It is petrifying for me to think of moving far from my family and friends. I don't even drive to Denver by myself. I am forcing myself to act and to move because I know that I need to figure out who I am as myself vs. who I am as a couple. I liked who I was as part of the Phil and Linda team. I don't know who I am or even if I like who I am by myself.

Since I was 20, I have been part of a couple and since I was 21, I have been a mom. With adult children and with standing solo through no choice of my own, I need to figure out what I want. To do that, I need a fresh start. I am one of those people that struggles with independence. I do know that the public does not see me in that manner because I travel solo so often, but I am a scared little girl most of the time. It is time for me to confront my fears.

I do not consider myself a weak dependent person, but as I stare down the girl in the mirror, I see only weakness and dependency. I am standing on a bouncing diving board about to take a plunge. I hope there is a deep cool place to land (preferably with lots of bubbles)!

One of the worst feelings I am experiencing is feeling like I am disloyal to Phil because I am making plans for a future that does not include him. My whole adult life has been about him and the children. I am lost and afraid of my own shadow. I pray and fall to my knees. Can I hide for awhile?

Attraction and Confusion

Look to the sky. The tiny shards of my broken heart litter the sky in the numerous stars that shine through the darkness.

One of the most confusing aspects of my loss is facing the conflicting emotions that deal with attraction and moving on by letting another man into my life. While I can say that I am not ready yet, there have been more thoughts in this area. It scares me. I feel totally ill prepared and unable to move forward in this realm. I am trying to make a year without starting into the dating pool because I need to find myself first, but I struggle with wanting intimacy. Not sex, intimacy.

I want the friend that I can turn to. I want companionship and laughter. I want to be able to give back in that area, also. It makes me feel better about myself when I nurture and stand strong for another person. I want the passion and the touch, but I can't put myself there yet. When I do think of that day, I worry about my own moral compass. I have never been the type of girl that puts herself out there. I don't want to change that, but are there really people my age that feel that way that aren't weird? Also, does this make me the weirdo?

I strive to lead a worthy life. I strive to live out loud and to stay true to that ticking moral compass that leads me to answer to my God and to myself. I am not a girl that feels compelled to follow the social mores and expectations of others, but I am a girl that needs to someday have another fairy tale. I look at myself and I fear that loss and loneliness will alter that moral compass. I do not want that. I desire to be the woman that God calls me to be, but I am never going to be a nun.

Taking the Leap of Faith

Losing Phil means that I have had to face my worst nightmares. These nightmares are more than losing my best friend and husband of 23 years. The scared girl that stares back in the mirror is afraid to move forward and to make decisions on her own. During my adult life, I have gladly followed Phil where he was stationed. I gave up many jobs, friendships, and houses that I liked because the military said that it was time for us to go. I didn't voice opinions or disappointments in the loss of control in my own life because I truly appreciated the opportunities and life the military provided for us all of this time. With Phil's death, I am being forced to take a flying leap of faith.

Leaps of faith are incredibly hard for a woman who has never believed in her own abilities to face her fears or to make decisions independently. This week, I took a major leap of faith. I took a leave of absence from my job to take a tentative job offer in Ansbach, Germany—half way across the world. I had sent e-mails to my new principal and the job offering organization. I had five days to get a massive amount of paperwork in that involved needing a general to get it done. I had to ask for help. I don't do this well. In fact, by my asking for help, other secrets came out. I had largely kept to myself how abandoned I had felt by the military family here. I planned to always keep this wound to myself, but to get help; I had to tip my cards.

I had to assume that my life would be okay even if I was jobless for a year. I had to believe that I could go to Ansbach even though I do not know a soul. This is the first time I have decided where I am going to live since I decided what college to run for (that was not a big decision. I went where I got the most money and where I could get away from Boise). Here's the thing, though. I don't even drive to Denver by myself. I am terrified to leap. I am afraid of careening through the dark skies without a safety net. This weekend, however, a group of ladies surprised me for my fiftieth birthday.

One of these amazing women is blind. She is terrified of heights, yet she put herself out there when we zip lined. There she stood shaking, but she still pushed off of the platform. She could not see the safety net, but she believed. I do not see the safety net, but I choose to believe that it is going to be alright. That I will be alright. That the safety net is going to catch me. In zip lining, there are four sets of brakes at the end of the ride. One is harnessed in and there really is no danger. I am confident because I have done this activity five times. I have not moved or made a decision separate from Phil. This does not mean that I can't leap, but I must trust the safety nets in place.

I leap knowing that I will make new friends. I leap towards a future that includes learning who I am without my Phil. I fly towards the hope that I am starting to feel. I embrace the new activities that I am trying. Phil and I were so insular. We had five children. We kept to ourselves and we really did not let others in too close. When Phil died, I realized just how alone I am. I had not taken the opportunities to invest in friendship time outside of my marriage. When he deployed, I played the waiting game until he came home. Knowing that Phil isn't coming home is daunting. Lonely. Oh, so lonely.

People have carried me, however. Two of my closest friends I have met in my darkest hours. They are walking my walk with me. One is in Afghanistan living with daily reminders of the fear and loss of his co-workers. Another lost her husband in the same event. I didn't even know these two remarkable friends prior to 27 April. I found an old friend that I had lost touch with from our Utah days. Lastly, I have Linda's peeps (or Linda's gang, as one will). These remarkable ladies planned a birthday weekend for me, organized my daughter flying from FL to surprise me, and they gave me back my laughter. More than that, they gave me hope. While I didn't know these ladies well before this weekend, I want them in my life. I want to walk with them. Carry them when they need it. I see what I have missed by being insular.

I leap to Ansbach, not because I am running away, but because I run to the light of hope. I run to a chance to rediscover who I am without my Phil. I run to become the strong and confident woman I want to be. I leap with the promise of faith that all will be well on the other side and that the brakes will work. I believe. I hope, and I trust that God is still working through the ashes of my life. I never felt like I could be a voice of anything, but out of circumstances borne from the tragedy of loss, I am standing for and speaking for military family loss. I stand for the resilience and the love I had for my husband. I stand to honor his memory with my strength. I stand strong, scared, and ready to leap. Here I go...

So, This is What 50 Looks Like

One of the most painful aspects about today is that for the past two years Phil had forgotten my birthday. He forgot last year because he was working his deployment to Afghanistan. It hurt my feelings, but I got over it when he waved the white hanky of surrender (I loved that about him and I could never stay mad). He promised me that this year would be different. At the time, I rolled my eyes and thought to myself that he was fooling himself since he was going to be far away. Here's is the thing, though. It would have been different. He had planned for jewelry and he had already bought the card to send to me.

Oceans apart, but he wanted me to feel special and loved on my 50th birthday. While Phil was not a grand slam type of man, he was steady and loyal to his core. He was all about the small acts of kindness. He brought me coffee and a newspaper in bed every day that he was home. He invested in my running. He always wanted me to have the things I wanted. He drove me places because I truly do not like driving. The only other time that Phil tried for the grand slam was for my 40th birthday.

We were stationed in Utah during the Olympics. Phil wrote a moving essay and filled out a ton of paperwork to submit me to carry the Olympic torch. My favorite running memory is being honored to carry the torch in Ogden, UT. That event was a grand slam that I will never forget. The jewelry and the card that he never got to write in is the second grand slam. Having said that, I would pick the small acts of kindness daily versus the grand slams that happen so rarely. I just don't need the bells and whistles like that.

Yes, I know that my Phil was not perfect. He knew it, also. I am so not perfect either, but together we had an unbeatable relationship based on friendship, respect, and wanting the best for the other person. Today, as I turn 50, I honor the man that he was. I celebrate the woman I was when I was with him. I toast that he got it right this year. I will put on my Sasha Fierce persona and I will continue to move forward small steps at a time.

Getting Ready for the Big Move

Wow. No exercising yet today. I have done address changes, credit card changes, met in two places for the pre-move assessment, turned off my Phone as of 10 August, sent letters of appreciation, sent e-mails with questions to my new school, and I am not done. There is so much to do and my window is so narrow. I am looking forward to my massage, dinner with a friend, and watching a bad movie that I really want to see (Bad Teacher--laugh). Good thing I worked out three times yesterday and I have a marathon next week.

It is really interesting to notice the people who have stepped up to the plate consistently for me. None of them live here. None of them did it for recognition; rather they stood with me and carried me because they felt for my loss. Helping me is not their job. Talking to me is because they want to talk to me, not because someone is ordering them to talk with me. It is so sad that after Phil died, people that we had known for years, even from his really young enlisted days in Istres, France, have not called or e-mailed. These so called friends have been to our house as we were to their house. These pretenders were out in mass for the media, but in the nearly three months since, have not called or e-mailed.

I get people assigned to me that do not call or e-mail until there is an order to do so. It wreaks havoc on one's confidence. I initially wanted to crawl into a hole and stay there. Now, I want to make sure that no military wife EVER has to feel so alone. As independent and resilient as I am, I did want to drop my broken sword and battered shield and hide. I wasn't given that option. Besides being thrust into the military, I have had to forge my way largely alone. The loneliness and invisibility has hurt me more than my written words could ever convey.

Why is it then that the people who have reached out are extremely high ranking or stationed far away from here (Afghanistan)? I am so uncomfortable asking the ranking people for help on my behalf, but believe you me; I have no problems recognizing genuine help and empathy up the chain of command. One person, in particular, helped me and reached out to me even when I couldn't reach back. He would stay up all night instant messaging me on my darkest days. He would spur me into action when I wanted to lie down and die myself. It isn't his job. No one noticed his efforts until I started to talk about his consistent outreaching to me.

In order for him to be valued and recognized, I had to talk about what wasn't happening on this end. It doesn't fix the lack of human contact, but it may get someone recognition for doing the right thing when no one was watching. It may also change the checks and balances for other AF widows. I am pretty strong and resilient, but I shouldn't be begging people to have to spend time with me the day I get the pictures of my husband's broken body or the day that I find out all of the details of that horrible, horrible day in April. I leap to a new beginning where I will not wait around for people who I thought were my friends or at least a part of my military family here in Colorado, to reach out. I would rather live in loneliness and loss than to have the pretenders come out when high ranking individuals are around or when the media is present.

I commit to being the voice of change. I promise to be the person who carries and stands with others in the time of loss. I stand with my military children and true friends behind the scenes stepping forward to ease another's pain. As for the pretenders, don't call me. . .I will call you. And, oh, by the way, my phone is being disconnected very soon in preparation for my move to Germany. :)

Thinking Ahead

I did something today that was very, very difficult for me to do. I scheduled reservations in Hawaii for Christmas. Thinking ahead to Phil's favorite holiday and the family being together for the first Christmas in years, is crushing when I think that Phil won't be there. He did not grow up in a home that did anything for Christmas. He initially didn't understand or embrace all of the hoopla. He learned fast. How he loved the noise, the chaos, and the fun of the holidays. He was at his best element when he was whooping it up with our children as we played Bingo for small gift cards, going to the gym, or doing a WII tournament. Phil was as bad as the kids in terms of the noise level and smack talking. While he loved all of the noise and the chaos, there would be times that I would have to retreat to our room for a little quiet.

I am going to miss sharing the holiday with him. I know that I will not be in the place to decorate or cook the big meal, so I am choosing to shake it up a little bit this year. A beach. Water. There is something about water that is so comforting and grounding. Swish, swish, stroke, stroke, eat my bubbles. We will stand as a family and we will carry each other. Christmas will look different because it will be different. There won't be a Christmas tree, socks, or even midnight mass, but there will be a gathering of the Ambards/Shorts and there will be love and new memories. It is hard to think about, but sometimes it is better to plan ahead for the looming darkness and pain coming.

The Changing of Linda

Phil has been gone for three months yesterday. Two incidents yesterday sent me into a minor tailspin where I question myself and where I send myself into guilt obliviation. Yesterday, the funeral home delivered a large framed picture of Phil. The picture is a head/upper body shot. It is so real that I find myself staring into Phil's beautiful eyes and wishing I could drown there once more. The second incident was one that caused me to look at myself and who I was when I was with Phil and who I am now.

I hadn't considered that I had changed the way that I dress. I am a physical education teacher/life guard. While, I never thought about it, I dressed like a jockette. I could wear girlie things, but other than the socks and the pink work out shirts, I really never gave what I wore a thought. When I walked into my school yesterday in jeans, a blouse, and sandals, people noticed. I had many comments about how good I looked and how young I looked. After a handful of these positive affirmations, I began to feel really guilty. Maybe I didn't take enough time to look nice enough when I was married to Phil. Maybe I am wanting people to notice me?

I have spent my whole life until now hiding in the shadows. I have been content to be overlooked and to be a lone ranger. I have never needed a lot in the way of friendships or relationships. I tended to be a one person girl. When this happened, I was thrust into a very public view. I didn't ask for the role of spokesperson or poster family for loss, it just sort of happened due to Phil and I having four military children and Phil's successful immigrant to esteemed professor story. I could have stayed hidden in the shadows, or I could choose to step up to the plate and play.

I chose to play, and in the process I have changed. I have become a more public person. I have embraced girl friends and time spent with them for the first time in my life. I have become more open and more verbal about what I am feeling. I have put myself out there. Phil would not have been comfortable with any of this. As stand-offish as I could be, he was worse. He never wanted people to know anything except about his children's successes. He was quiet and unassuming. Driven and funny. People outside of family never got to see that incredible sense of humor. What a loss.

I would be comfortable in the grey twilight area of sliding through as a nonentity in life, but I feel a calling to stand up and talk about loss in the military and the loss process in general. It is hard for me to speak, but not as hard to write. Thus, my way of talking is to write. Along with this change and with losing my ability to slide under the radar means that I have changed. I am not sure that Phil would like or approve the changes so I feel guilt. My shroud of complacency and a quiet life is shifting.

I have changed the way that I dress and the outward personality, but I have kept the important components. My faith and moral compass are stronger than they have ever been. I am loyal and true to the end for my friends. I would walk to the ends of the earth for them because they have walked through fire for me. I am a better friend because I see the pain in others and I react quicker to the pain. I stand in front of the mirror. While I may not recognize the person I have become, I like some of the changes. I am choosing to embrace my alter ego, Sasha Fierce who loves polka dots. I am choosing to find the Linda I am meant to be at 50. I am choosing to stand up, speak out, and love more deeply. I only hope that Phil would somehow understand and approve.

My Name is Linda and I Did Something Totally out of Character

Okay. I did something totally out of character and not for the reason you might think. I did sign up for Catholic Match.com and I am not even a practicing Catholic at this point. I just need to be able to communicate with ANYONE, you know? I feel ancient compared to the men and women here. I went to the gym to see about runners. They laughed at me. I went looking for a USO. . .nada. This is a very small base. I just want to have friends or at least be occupied online. I don't figure there will be anyone here for me to be matched with. Not ready for that but I do want human interaction. I couldn't ask for males and females to contact me, though. I might get the wrong kind of attention--laugh!

I am not looking for my Facebook friends to say or do anything; I merely am wanting a person to talk to. Even online is better than nothing, plus it is safer. I am not sure that I am comfortable with any of this, but understand that, first; this life is not the one I wanted nor is it the one I am embracing. I live in an incredibly small community where it seems that everyone is younger than half of my children. I am not a bar girl, and my moral compass has not shifted. Where I was once fine with being alone without human companionship, I had Phil to look forward to coming home at some point.

I am a nonentity. I get that the military must call me ma'am, but I feel like a nobody when people do that. I have a name. Why is it so hard for people to use it? When I hear my name, it brings tears to my eyes. I don't even like my name all that much, but being invisible and unimportant to anyone is worse. Living in a small community doesn't give me opportunities per se in meeting anyone. I put out an SOS for a running group. I went to the gym and I posted it on the base web site. Alas, when the laughter stopped, I was praised for being able to run that far. I just want friends.

At the chapel, the Protestant Women of the Chapel meet during my duty day. There isn't a USO or any type of club system, thus my opportunities are fairly limited. What do I expect from joining an online group? Well, it is nice to look at the forums in the widow/widower group. It is nice to see that other people have found hope. I am so far away from people that it feels safe. I couldn't ask for friendships from both males and females without coming across like a pervert, so I will lurk in the forums, I will enjoy the daily devotionals, and I will use my resources. I am not a practicing Catholic, but it is nice to see people of faith reaching out to others, finding each other, and connecting on some level.

While I can't say that I am ready to date yet, I am ready for a friend or two. I can see the big picture and know that at some point that there will be someone in my life, but I have a lot of smaller steps to take first. I am not being called to be a nun. I want to share my life with someone. I hope that I can at some point. It is intimidating and totally overwhelming to think beyond the first steps of being physical with anyone. I can see a kiss or hand holding. I don't see beyond that without getting physically ill and terrified. It is going to take a very patient man who can be a friend first. I don't think that will happen online, but I embrace the idea of meeting more friends to walk with. I am ready to spend time with people and to laugh again. I am ready to run and try new things. My name is Linda. . .Let's do it.

No, No, Thank You for Asking

This week has shown me that I still have men that are attracted to me...just the men that I am not interested in. Is it shallow to want to be attracted to someone physically, intellectually, and lifestyle wise. Add in my faith and belief system and it seems as if I will never be attracted to anyone ever again. People may laugh, but I would rather be alone that settle and I am no longer the type of girl that dates just to date.

In college, in a complete reversal from the shunning I received in high school, I had more dates than I knew what to do with. I was a "nice" girl who loved sports and being active. Even then, men thought they wanted that. I am kind of a handful, though. I am spunky and I need my running time. I do not make a good docile woman. This does not work for every man. I can run over the wrong type of man (and I have hurt people in the process). While many men are attracted to my addiction to adventure and sport, many want the tamed household goddess that I will never be.

The men asking me out this week are sedate overweight men. Most are aging hippies which also does not work for this very conservative girl. I like the clean shaven GI Joe look. I am hiding behind a true fact. I won't date people that I work with. I just can't. All of these years of working as a supervisor have taught me that it is a bad, bad idea to date someone at work. It isn't going to happen.

So, where am I with the whole dating thing? Well, I don't know. There has only been one man since Phil died that I thought, hmm, he is kind of cute. My T.A. (trained assassin) is not someone who is in my life, nor will I ever see him again, but for a moment I thought, wow! He's cute. I need someone who will give me lots and lots of time. How much time? I don't know. I need to feel safe in a friendship. I need to laugh and I need to ease into the comfort of the friendship before this spunky athletic girl can move forward.

I miss the smell of a man. Weird, I know, but I like the way men smell (not dirty men) and I like how safe I feel in the arms of a man. Those two reasons are not enough of a reason to compromise what I am looking for. I want someone who has faith (and practices that faith on some level), is athletic, genuine, intelligent, fun with a sense of humor (because mine is so inappropriate), and someone who can give me room to grow into a new relationship. I am a catch, yes, I am. I may not believe it on every level, but some guy is going to have a lot of fun with me. It just has to be a missing puzzle piece. I need someone different from Phil to sate different needs. I will do the same for him. Time will pass, I will heal, and I will be ready.

Today the Joy Came Back in Running

I gave myself the same gift that I try to give myself daily; I ran. I have run for thirty five years. While some days are harder, some days are like today and I run in that magical zone where I do not feel anything but pure joy. Running is a time for me to center and to come back to a calm middle ground no matter what else is happening in my life. I can't explain it, but I am not a very emotional person on the outside, but my heart feels it all. Through running, I can live my joy, pride at an accomplishment, or deal with my gut wrenching grief.

When Phil death was still so new, I could run and cry. I would never be comfortable showing that much emotion in a public place (or even at home by myself). I have those dark moments when God and Phil feel so far away from me...when darkness enfolds me within its clutching embrace, but running brings me back to the faith that is central in my life. In my darkest days, and during those times when I might rail to God about the injustice and unfairness of taking Phil, I find myself coming back to looking at a bigger plan, a plan that I thought and hoped would be longer at this level. I find comfort in the plodding prayers of my feet and the tears in my heart can fall.

Running also helps me to sleep. While grief is different for everyone, I developed insomnia after Phil's death. I think I aged ten years in a span of six weeks. My face is now an open canvas to the joys I have had in my life, but the planes of my face show the deep emotion of loss. My eyes have a depth that gives away the pain, or so I have been told. Running brings me a joy that gives that layer at least the top billing.

I don't know if anyone else falls to running as I do, but I do know this, I will run on until my dying days as long as I am able. For many years, I was told that it wasn't "normal" to run like I do, but I believe with all that I am that running is a gift that God knew I would need at various times in my life. Never more than now. I am so thankful for finding joy again...first in running. I don't know if I will ever have joy anywhere else, but for today, I am feeling happiness at the day. While the miles rolled by, I experienced a sunrise, five German towns, a forest rife with fall colors starting to explode, and a centering that brought me back to knowing that someday all will feel right again. I run on to that day.

Change and Adaptability

Change. Whether or not I wanted my life to change, it altered in a very dramatic manner on 27 April. The events of that day made me a different person and it showed me that I have a resiliency and adaptability that I never before had discovered in myself, yet I am human. People that I thought were friends or that maybe should have stood with me let me down. I had always believed that the Academy was a family, a united family. What I discovered however is that like any family, the Academy has hidden flaws. Maybe in the petty paces of everyday living, airmen stop short of being a friend in when times are tough. Maybe the Air Force in general has forgotten how to be a family in times of loss, however the time for the whining and waiting has ended. The time for me to stand up and be the change for the next person is now.

I hope that the Air Force Academy never loses another person, but as a mom of three Air Force children and one Army son, I think that the possibility still stands for loss in the line of duty. I pray that my children's lives will not be asked of me. I beg God to take me versus them, but I know that history is already written in the eyes of the Lord. What can I do to impact change for the next person who suffers loss? What have I learned?

Sometimes the simplest act reaches the most shattered part of the heart and for a moment soothes the ache within. I have had people reach out to me at 0300 in the morning, strangers sending me cards, a general handwriting a note and taking the time to find me once I disappeared off the radar, rides places, surprise birthdays, polka dots, a box of goodies, and I could go on and on. My Facebook friends from Boise to Afghanistan to Colorado to Switzerland have stood with my most unlovable self. They may have been worried about saying the wrong thing, but they said something. That to me is step one. I may say or do the wrong thing in someone else's hour of need, but to do nothing hurts far worse. At one time, I felt so alone and so abandoned that all I could think about was running away from my life. I think I might have done that and in the process discovered a mission of change.

I am affecting change my blogging and posting it everywhere. While my intent is not to hurt anyone, I know that I might be stepping on a few toes. Here is the point, though. Blogging and posting equals education and awareness. I was told over and over to ask for what I needed. In my darkest hours and in my time of greatest need, I no more could have asked for help than I could have helped myself. I was broken—shattered really. I wasn't sleeping or eating. I was consumed by the vivid images of my husband's broken body. People rarely can help themselves during these dark days, let alone ask for help.

People are good about stepping up to the plate initially. The Air Force Academy could not have done a better job with the funeral. I was and am still deeply humbled and appreciative. After the funeral and I am talking immediately after the funeral, people did not call or visit. Over four months later, it is still that way. If a person can't handle the sadness, send a card with these simple words on it, "thinking of you now." Again, my change is through education and awareness through my blogs.

I am done (and if I am not, call me on it) expecting or wanting help from people who are unable to give it. I ask for the report. I stand up and I stand with other Air Force families who have lost loved ones in the line of duty. I am here whether it be 0300 in the morning or a visit to Europe. I have learned from my friends and family that have stood with me. I cannot change what happened in the past, but I can change my attitude about what happened in the past. I choose to leap to my next role. I choose to adapt and overcome. I will start right now, right this minute.

Morning Has Broken

I felt really cut off from the world this weekend. When I rented my house I did not think about how isolated I would be as the only American living in my town. There are no stores, restaurants, gyms, etc. My village is picturesque to be sure, but I have discovered I need the human touch and companionship. I still do not have internet which means that reaching out to those I love during my time of need has become very difficult. While the internet will eventually be rectified, the loneliness causes me to descend into that dark hole of despair.

The despair is so deep, so crushing, and so consuming that it is hard to imagine hope or happiness. I have felt both since Phil has died, but I have never been in a spot where I didn't feel like I didn't have someone to call or to connect with. I am struggling, but I do believe, and how I believe, that if my prayer was for God to take me where I was needed and I put in for world wide availability and I got Ansbach, Germany, he would forsake me. I need to believe...have faith...that morning will come.

Morning rays of sun always makes the darkness of night seem so far away. Somewhere through the dark billowing clouds will raise a beautiful rainbow. It will happen; I know it will. With my despair, I will reach, I will cling, and I will believe that if not today, someday soon. My faith will stand the test of time. I will pray for a glimmer of hope in the form of connections. I will hope that my internet is repaired very soon, but if not, I will let my faith carry me. I believe in things unseen. That day is coming when hope and faith will collide to give me that rainbow...someday soon, I hope.

Hope Floats - II

I have written about hope floating before, but as I continue to step forward and outside of my comfort zone, there are things that I intrinsically know. I know that I am stronger and more resilient than I ever would have given myself credit for. I would have thought that I would have not been able to go on alone. When Phil was killed, however, I needed to be strong. He was killed in the most public manner possible. People were looking for me to fall apart and disgrace Phil's service to the military. My own family wondered if I could stand up under the weight of a loss so unthinkably tragic that very few know how to deal with even the thought of loss like this.

Even in the beginning of my darkest hours, I had to deal with the media. Most of the media took their cues from me. I chose to talk because very few people do talk about military loss and its impact on the family. Our loved ones dies an unexpected death in the prime of life. We were the family members at home waiting, always waiting. We kept the home fires burning while yearning for the day our soldiers came home to us. Home for us is where our soldier takes us. It is a feeling carried in our hearts, thus when our soldiers die in the most unthinkable way, it is hard to wrap our arms around the magnitude of the life altering changes brought to our lives.

We have given up the close family networks born of close proximity and time. We have given up the established long term friendships as we move base to base. We have given up the normal days preceding death usually. We do not have clothing items that have the scent of our loved one or daily reminders of a life lived with our soldier. We were waiting for the happy reunion that never came.

This trip, the dream trip that Phil and I put off for 23 years, was very hard to start. I couldn't even pack my suitcase until the last minute. Phil deserved his reunion. He deserved to be on this boat overeating, laughing, and spending time with me. I deserved him coming home to me. Life is not always fair or predictable. I didn't think that I could laugh and enjoy this trip, but I am. I am finding joy in simply moving forward one step at a time. I see sparks of light echoing off of the lazy waves. Hope is floating.

I do not know what my future holds. I may be alone, but maybe not. I may experience great joy, but maybe not, but right here, right now, hope is floating like tiny rills rising to the surface. I am moving and reaching to my future. I believe in me.

The Planes of My Face

I had to laugh last night when one of the widows told another widow, "I am glad you are young. I thought they would all be old!" Well, I was the oldest person in that room. It is interesting how that shift from being one of the young ones to be one of the old ones happened. I never felt old or even noticed the wrinkles on my face until April. Everything changed in a blink of the eye.

When I look at my reflection in the mirror, I see the etched grooves on the visage of my face. These etched grooves show everything from the sorrows to the joys in my life. That line there? That is the one my Josh gave me many years ago when he was a challenging boy. This one? That one belongs to Emily and incidents like the YMCA parking lot. I could go on, but every parent knows that there are many sleepless nights and moments of worry that do not stop when a child leaves home. In fact, I have less control and influence now. The grooves become deeper.

The caverns of grief spill out amongst my freckles. Although I do not cry easily, my face, to include my eyes, betray my soul. The planes have shifted. I see my loss as plain as day, but I see something else. I see the spark of hope. I see the joy and love that I have for life. It is hard for me to explain, but I am a happy person. I like my life. I wake up every day ready to face the day and excited to see how the day is going to play out. I am a smiler. Maybe people would see the sense of contentment and joie de vive. I see the smiles flitting across the surface and twining with the lines of sorrow.

Those twined lines show a life that is being lived. I will take those lines and I will embrace those lines because I know both sorrow and joy. I have lived a full life and I believe that there is a promise of a future filled with happiness. I will rise every morning with the hope and the spark of joy that says life is coming. It is happening. I know that Phil loved that enthusiasm in me. I like it in me. I may be old, but I am not dead yet! For the record, I can outrun most people thirty years younger than I am. Wink!

The Shift in my Paradigm

Many have read my blogs since 27 and have heard me quote a song that I started to relate to in June. Skillet, A Christian hard rock band sings a song, "Awake and Alive" that speaks of where my heart is. I wanted to die with Phil if we couldn't have old age together, but I am seeing the person that God is calling me to be through my loss—the hardest loss a person can have. At times, grief hurt physically so much that I literally wondered what was wrong with my body. I lived in a fog of terror that is still evident on some levels even now. I second guess all of my major decisions and replay my errors ad nauseum, however, I am finding a sense of purpose and a sense of a new dawn coming. I am not quite sure what to do with myself.

First, I decided to embrace a strong alter ego. Sasha Fierce here loves pink, purple, polka dots, the flowers the adorn her car, and a rollicking fun pink flowered cruiser bicycle. Things may hurt, but those hidden polka dots rise up and pop leaving a small scent of promise. I can't see or understand the promise, but for every happy thought I have, I see my passion and personality returning. I embrace those polka dots and the inner girl because I have never done that before. I embrace them now because I am discovering how strong, resilient I am when I stand firm on my faith. Make no mistake, if I did not have faith, I would falter. There would be no reason to get up in the morning. I did not ever see this future and it makes me ache when I see a future without my Phil, but I know that God is working through the ashes to perfect the work he began in me.

Having said that, something happened this weekend that caused me to take a deep breath and step back unsure. Many of you remember my blog as to why I joined Catholic Match. I had just arrived in Europe. I was terrified and very alone. I needed support, but I was not comfortable talking eyeball to eyeball with anyone. I noticed the grief room. I hovered there for awhile before I began to look at the forums. I have made so many friends and I have learned so much about how we are all very similar in our insecurities and desires, yet I really was not on this site for companionship. I was and am aware that by living in Germany, I am safe. Long distance relationships are never the ideal, but I figured I could practice my friendship skills with men and that I could make good friends along the way. That is happening, however something shifted this week and I am not sure what to do.

The negative first. I hurt somebody's feelings for the first time in 30 years in the dating realm. I do not date just to date and my moral compass has not shifted. This person will be a good friend to have, but there is absolutely no future because he wants children and I do not because I have five wonderful grown up children. Compromising on this issue is a death knell at some point. Pleading and mega-e-mails will only strengthen my resolve. Is it more humane to give false hope or nip it in the bud from the start? I was nice about it and I explained myself well, but still it hurt someone.

More than the above, here is where I need help. Seriously. My paradigm has shifted. I do have a friend on the site who he and I communicate a few times a day. He is new to the site also. Those messages have just been hysterically funny. Many of you know how I have a wicked sense of humor and many of you have discovered how much I value that in my friends. The messages are surface, but something slightly shifted this weekend. The messages are a little longer and a little more, oh, I don't know...they have more of a personal stamp, if that makes sense. The scary thing is that I actually caught it and then my glasses shifted. The light is skewed. It is daunting because I have no idea how to be single let alone how to do it online. I am in no hurry, but the shift caused me to think seriously about dating again. ..Not just voicing it.

I am comfortable with the written words because I wrap them around me and warm myself. I am very, very foreign to dating and verbal words. In high school, I was a stalker girl. I don't like her and I haven't been her in years. In college, I was a celibate serial dater who dated just to date to prove that the boys in high school were stupid (sorry Bishop Kelly High School boys...I wouldn't have dated me either). It would be too easy to get in too fast, so I find myself withdrawing. This isn't quite fair because I actually enjoy his company, but is there really any future in an online relationship? Is there hope for the face to face relationship if the relationship is established online? At what point does a person give any personal information? For the record, people find me easily enough because of the writing, running, and Phil. Why do I feel like I am back in 7th grade figuring things out?

In seventh grade, I was truly an ugly duckling. I was overlooked and called Linda Leper. I sat in the back of my class with another boy who was also the brunt of some nasty taunts. For years, it has haunted me that I might have been part of his pain then. We were both so insecure and we were eaten by the piranhas of middle school. We were the late bloomers. We rock life now, but as a single person I am thrown right back to the 7th grade lonesome loser. I don't know how to navigate the unknown waters and I want to keep the friendship. I am not even sure what is normal. Besides taking any relationship SLOW (and no need to worry about that), what advice would my friends give me? I mean it. I stink at being single. I don't date to date, I don't hug to hug, and I don't sleep with people to sleep with people. What is the normal progression of online dating? Dating? Humorously, I know that I will giggle like a little girl when someone touches me for the first time. I will be scared and running to hide under the covers. I will peer out with those wide eyes and cower for just awhile. I just don't see it happening for awhile, but it the day is coming. The shift in my paradigm happened unbidden.

I Think I Got a Compliment Today

I think I got a compliment today. I must laugh however because it involves Kevin Costner. I noticed that Kevin is coming to Ansbach and giving a concert. I know. Who knew he could sing. Right? I went to pick up a free ticket today. There were 4 left.

The man working the desk said, "Only one?" When I confirmed I only wanted one ticket, he told me that I couldn't go to the concert by myself. Surely I had a lot of people I could ask. I laughed so then he says, "You just got here. I am divorced, too." Uh. . .no, I am widowed. He proceeds with, "You are going to get found really soon! I can't believe you haven't already found somebody!" What do I do with that?

Dating 101 Flunkee

Many years ago, I was a flunkee at Dating 101. I am older, but certainly not wiser in terms of stepping into an unnatural and unwelcome realm. I stand rooted in paralysis unsure of when and if I will be ready to start anew. I have made steps in this direction, but I am not a date to date kind of girl. I am old fashioned, but I tend to eclipse many men my age with the events of my life and the athleticism. I don't know how to navigate the churning waves, nor do I know how to start the plunge into the roiling waters.

When I began to actively date in college, I quickly grew weary of dating people just to have a social life. It wasn't/isn't fair to the other person. I discovered that I would rather sit at home on a Friday night versus hurting someone. This does not mean that I did that. I had many male friends due to my athleticism. It was nice to do things together, but I paid my way and they paid their way. We had fun matching each other up and supporting one another as we navigated the unchartered dating waters.

Being 50 and single is scary. Many women my age are barracudas—hurt by past relationships. Phil was hit on many times in his PhD program. He always told me about it and then I would make it my mission to friend the woman. It worked every time. I do not want to be one of those women who takes somebody else's mate. I do not want to be the woman that men think that they need to rescue. I may have been dealt some pretty crappy cards this year, but guess what? I am not cowering in the corner. I am not so insecure that I am looking to be rescued. I will tread water until I can navigate that whirlpool that threatens to suck me under into an indecisive insecure clutching mode.

I have a strong moral compass which is another issue in dating. I don't know men my age that ARE SINGLE that would want to give me time and space in this area. I think that saying no was easier in my 20's. Men expected it and they respected it. Not so much at this point. What happened to time in relationships and respect in this area?

Plus, is it normal to feel this insecure and doubtful of others? I know that I am capable of the fairy tale again. I know that I can fully love another person, but I will always love Phil. It will be a different kind of love. I see that, I feel that, I know that, however it isn't a competition. It is going to take time. Phil and I had over 23 years to develop the connection we had. We knew each other well. It is going to take some patience in this area. I am loyal and true and I do not need to have more than one person in my life at a time, however, I need the same commitment. Is that so rare today?

Advice Needed for the Flunkee

I am at that point where I am starting to look at dating again. I haven't jumped into it yet, but I am starting to let people in. Here is my problem. I don't know if I should talk about Phil or not. It feels disloyal to not bring up the elephant in the room. Plus, part of my journey this year is going to have some hard times. One such time is smacking me in the face now.

I should be very, very excited to be seeing Phil in Venice on Thursday. He has been gone since 11 January. This is the trip with just the two of us—the one we never took because I had three children when Phil married me. It wasn't until he went to Afghanistan that he wanted this "just the two of us" trip. If Phil hadn't been killed, I would be talking about this trip nonstop. I would be dancing around, packing my nicest clothes and just being happy. I feel an oppressive weight as I get closer to Thursday. Phil should have had his happy reunion and his fun midtour time with me. Normally, I would talk this through with the people who are close to me, but is it fair to another man to talk about missing a spouse?

See, I am not sure how much is okay to talk about Phil and with whom. So many of our before Phil's death friends couldn't handle Phil's death. I didn't see them or hear from them (or maybe once) since the funeral. If I talk about that terrible briefing to come on 7 November, or my anniversary, or anything about Phil, am I selling Phil short and am I being fair to someone who is falling into my life in a different way.

Because of this doubt and insecurity, I tend to take two steps forwards, one step back. It isn't like there is a manual for dating again after 23 years of being with somebody else. It isn't like most people have walked through the loss of a spouse. I constantly second guess myself. I want to step forward, but do I have to give up Phil in the process? I have said it before; I know that I am capable of loving again in another way than I loved Phil. I believe and I have faith that all the best days of my life are not behind me. I believe that there is room for me to love freely and to be loved freely. I want the fairy tale, but I don't want to give up Phil in the process, so can I talk about him with dates? I don't know. I stand rooted in my spot...scared and unsure.

The Dating Game and this Dating Flunkee

I was reading on a website that I belong to about men being happy when women ask them out. When did the rules change and why am I so helplessly out of date? As a teenager, I wasn't afraid to ask men out, but I quickly learned that it was like a death sentence. Even if there was a hint of something else, the potential withered once I overstepped the normal dating boundaries. Add to that, the normal confusion of navigating waters that I have not forged in nearly a quarter of a century. It is pretty darn scary.

In my teen years, I was such a late bloomer that when I finally did bloom, I did not know what to do with the attention. I withdrew from dating for almost a year. I find myself in a similar situation. While I am very flawed, I am doing okay. I am spunky and relatively not ugly for my age. Having said that, I am broken. I am naïve and unsure. I don't even know how to read the cues. I joined a Christian dating site primarily for the grief support forums. Recently, I have garnered a lot of attention from gentlemen. It is very flattering and intriguing, but the whole online dating process is terrifying in large part because it feels as if I am the option versus the choice. People can be anybody through the use of words, distance, and, space.

I find myself withdrawing and holding my heart closer. I am not sure where I am with the dating process. If someone I saw as having potential asked me out, then I would probably go, but here is my battle. I am at war with myself over the mores that I believe that should be in place...the old fashioned courtship, yet I am far away from my home, my country. I know that it is a lot to expect a man to want to take a chance on me when he knows that Phil will always be a part of my heart. While I can see the big picture and the capacity I have to love someone in a new manner, I think that it is going to be hard for a man to deal with that. I also don't want another Phil. My needs and wants are different because I am a different person. Without going into detail because I do not want to have some "try" to be what I want, the one nonnegotiable is faith.

Faith is a promise of things unseen. My faith stands solid on my belief in the Lord, but beyond that, I have faith that through patience and perseverance, God will provide someone with whom I can find love, companionship, and friendship again. I believe that there is more to my life than the life I had prior to April. I don't believe that the best days of my life are over now, but I believe that it is going to take somebody some work in terms of being a friend, making the first move, and navigating the waters, but I do believe that I have the capacity to love someone fully and well again. If I am wrong, then God will provide hope and faith in a different way. That is okay, also.

Sometimes I think that people get too caught up in defining themselves by who they are dating. Relationships consume a person's thoughts and heart. I am not saying that I do not fall there (it is part of the excitement and tantalizing lure of the new relationship), but I have discovered that I do need some time alone every day. I need to run and to write. I don't need constant reassurance or tokens to prove a commitment. I don't want or need grand gestures; I just need the first gesture to come the old fashioned way. This old fashioned traditional girl has a lot to give. I learned in high school not to chase down the boys I like, so I will be patient and wait. I will wait for God to fulfill the desires of my heart. He is working, I know he is.

Running at the Speed of Light

In a long term marriage, it isn't unusual to have periods of silence no matter how much a person loves another person. As I have blogged before, Phil withdrew before his deployments; sometimes this withdrawal would happen months out. Before he deployed to Afghanistan, Phil withdrew a little more than seven months out. He became more introspective and remote. It hurt me, but I understood. Phil had to withdraw to make it through the distance and through not having me in his day to day life. In a new relationship, however, people cannot get enough of one another. Both people meander sleep deprived in a fog of wonder.

Walking through the initial stages of discovering a person is very exciting and a little scary. I knew Phil as well as I knew myself, or so it seemed. I was comfortable with him and I loved the companionship we shared. I didn't doubt our love would last a lifetime, and it will, but I never considered that I would be in the position of letting someone else into my life...sharing secrets, hopes, dreams, and the disappointments that at times rock all of us. For me, the hardest part of this phase is that I have forgotten the social cues, the normal way of proceeding, and the all encompassing emotional trance.

I am not running away from my fear, but I am boldly stepping up to the plate. My knees are knocking together, my hands are shaking to bad that the bat slips, and my hat is in my eyes. I do not know where my adventure is going, but there are new discoveries and a sense of excitement as my life unfolds. I am certainly not abandoning my love for Phil. How could I? He is as much of me as I am to myself. He is carried in all that I am and he will forever be loved by me. If not for the ceasing of his life, I would be with him still, yet I know that he would want me to be happy and to move on.

I desire to live my life worthy of being a woman of God, but I often fall. I am unsure often, but I see the hand of God working. I do not always understand, and I may never understand the events of April 27th, but I am running towards the light I see at the end of this dark tunnel. Even when I will fall, I will I drop my sword and hide for awhile, but I will get up and I will press on because I see the promises and the light. I will go no matter where the light leads.

I may not always have a safe harbor to fall back on, but even in the roiling turbulent waters of indecision and not knowing, I know that eventually the seas will calm and all will be well. In the turbulence, I will enjoy the sense of excitement and newness. I will continue to journey on.

The Healing in Venice

Going to Venice on what was to be Phil's and my dream trip together brought me to my knees shortly before I left, however, I innately knew that if I could press on that I would emerge stronger, happier, and more settled. The day before I left, I still hadn't packed. I had a swimming suit and my running shoes in the suitcase. I threw in clothes helter skelter that last night. I forgot many things. I didn't have a warm jacket, one of my medications, or layers for running. I survived not having the items I should have had, but more than that, I survived this trip.

More than that, I merged from the cloud I have been living under for so long. I feel good...happy even. I know that the dark clouds still loom on the horizon, but right now those clouds look far off and less ominous than they did in September. I feel a sense of life beginning anew. While this isn't the life I planned for myself, nor would I have ever wanted, I am where I am supposed to be right here right now given life events. I suppose there will always be that sense of before when I was married to Phil and after as in after Phil was killed, but taking that first trip was monumental in moving on.

I forced myself to take risks in terms of navigating the city. By the time my trip was over, I knew how to use the water buses, regular buses, the train, and I could pretty much figure out where I was over the touristy part of Venice. People that know me well know that I am extremely directionally challenged and that I am not comfortable even driving where I do not know an area well. I ate alone in a restaurant. While eating alone will never be comfortable or enjoyable, I did it. I ran a race in a country where the race directors did not speak English and I survived. I also said yes to moving on in another way.

While I never even considered being single at 50, I am. I am lonely. I want the fairy tale again if it is feasible. I know (and we did talk about it) that Phil would want me to be happy again because that is what I would have wanted for him. I said yes to a date in DC this weekend. I am meeting somebody that I have been e-mailing for two months. I am scared and a little in awe of the fact that I am actually in a place that is good enough for me to even consider this step.

I know that there will be feelings that I will have to consider and get through, but I also know that there is a sense of renewed hope in the whole dating process. I am helplessly outdated and out of practice, and it may even be a little too early, but I am choosing to step forward in this area, also. I choose also to continue my journey to be the woman God is calling me to be. I see a quiet strength that I never possessed before. I see a resilience that has come from walking through the most awful flames a person can traverse through. I see hope and promise in a future that does not include my Phil. While that is unthinkable on some levels, I step forward.

I Have Changed and a Challenge

I have changed since the death of Phil. These changes are barely perceptible, yet I see them. I sense them, and I recognize that the feelings that I have are deeper and are felt more. I am not sure how it happened. I have been a girl content to hide behind a quiet façade of efficiency, organization, and insulation. It isn't that I sought to close people out, but in my shyness and business, I kept myself distant from people who surely were reaching out to me. In my brokenness, and in my need, I began to open my heart for the first time. I allowed people to be my friend and to help me. I even asked for help thereby admitting that I was not perfect and that I did have needs and wants.

I am a better friend because I have learned from the many ways people have touched me. I know the value of human touch and communication. I know loneliness so deep and so encompassing that a simple e-mail, coffee, a card, polka dots, pink pens, and I could go on and on meant the world to me. It gave me back a connection to the world. My heart is healing. The pieces and tatters are being woven by kindnesses. If I tried to count the many blessings in my life, I would have to look to the stars because I can't even begin. I learned that by simply reaching out, a person can find hope, and in that hope happiness and joy.

I have never been one to take risks. I am the play by the rules type of girl. I linger in the shadows and I do not venture beyond my safe bubble. Since April, I have had to stand on my own two feet. I have had to make career choices, family choices, investments, driving, traveling, and even the choice to step forward in friendships and a relationship. Normally, I would hide. I would wait until the decisions were made for me. I have become more confident in my own self's ability to making worthwhile decisions and I step forward. I no longer make excuses or apologize for the choices and decisions I make. This is a first for me.

I am a better friend because I see need and pain all around me. I see it and I feel it because I hid for so long. I reach out because I have found that small acts mean all. Kindnesses that carried me in my darkest days, and still carry me day to day, literally bring me to my knees. Many of my old students here on Facebook know my secret challenge every October/November. I challenge my students to pay it forward and to do random acts of kindness. I have done this for over ten years, but I have never realized the life changing impact that these events can have on another. Since April, I literally stand humbled and bowed. I cannot repay the random acts of kindness or the love shown to me and my family. Ever.

In September and October, I would give my students a small token and random acts of kindness certificate. I would explain the concept of trying to do something anonymously (or at least with altruistic motives) and leaving the certificate with a note. The idea is that the world can be changed one simple act at a time. I speak up now because I know where I would be if I had not been the recipient of these acts of generosity. I speak up now because I realize that with kindness comes power. Power in joy and in belonging. I belong to you. You belong to me. I have your back as you carry me.

I challenge you this holiday season (like I challenge myself) to reach out beyond your normal circle. Speak to someone new. Do a simple act of kindness just because. Just because a person looks put together and happy, does not mean that they are. I can fake it well. I did for a long time, but your intentional actions have made me a stronger person in my weakness. I thank you.

The New Linda

Sometimes I feel so unworthy of the attention and favors people have done for me. What have I done to merit or encourage continued blessings? I am not the person, the friend, the woman I want to be yet. I am deeply, deeply humbled by the many people who walk with me still. The people who love me in spite of myself on my dark days have shown me what true grace is. Grace is a gift that we have not earned, but that is freely given. Many people have shown grace to me. I have learned from their displays of unconditional love. While I strive to display those same assets in my life, I so often fall short.

I want to be a friend to the hurting, to the oppressed, to the people who are reaching. I want to be the woman God is calling me to be. I want to keep continuing on my path of healing. This path leads me to mountain tops and dark chasms. No matter where the rocky trail leads me, however, I have found that God's provisions in the way of reaching people have helped more than anything. I am weak. In my weaknesses, I have allowed people to see the side of me that I kept hidden away. I am good at looking strong and self-sufficient. I am not good at showing any type of need or want. I hide a little too well.

In my broken state, people saw my pain and my need. I couldn't ask for help, but too many people stepped up to reach that I couldn't even begin to acknowledge the grasping hands that gave me hope when I felt that all I wanted to do was to lie down and never get up again. I felt that my life was over….that I had nothing to give. I have discovered, however, a new path. This path is not of my choosing, but all change is not all bad. I am stronger and more resilient than I ever thought. I have discovered joy in my life that meshes with sorrow and it brings me to a much deeper understanding of my faith, other people, and even myself. I am human. I have needs. I have wants. I may not be able to ask for what I want or need, but people see me. They really see me now.

I am not the same Linda I was in April. I like the woman I am becoming because I see my faith growing. I see my friendships strengthening, and I see my own abilities abounding in my weaknesses. I step forward. I may step unwillingly, but I see the sun shining. I see the rays of hope shining into my life. While the clouds come and go, I reach for what I can see and what I intrinsically feel.

The Magical Season is Touching me

There is something so magical about the simple lead in to the Christmas holiday here in Europe. As much as I want to eschew the traditions and trappings of the season, I find myself slipping into the excitement and joy of the preparations for Jesus' birthday. The 25th of December is going to happen even if I hide in a dark room weeping and with that day, comes new hope, new life, and new joy. In the acknowledging of the friends and family in my life through the traditions of my holiday, I am acknowledging and affirming the place and importance these people have in my life.

While the gifts are the least important part of the holiday, I do enjoy shopping for my loved ones because I truly enjoy considering small things that will make my loved ones smile. I am not doing that so well this year, but I will again. Separate from the gifts, I love the lights. Lights blaze the skies and twinkle in the frigid darkness. Those lights beckon lost souls home. They are like beacons that call a lost mariner home. I am called to my childhood home and to those that love me best when I glimpse the flickering lights. This year, my heart runs home. Even if only in my dreams, I am already home with those that carried me in my darkest hours this year. Blaze the skies...light the way....I am running to the place I call home.

With each Christmas greeting and cookie baked or eaten, I find the joy of the season seeping into my heart. That joy is seeping like molten solder into the cracks from a so recently broken heart. I am not sure what family traditions will live on, but I do know this. While Christmas has changed, or is I who has changed, I cannot run from the holiday. As surely as I wake up in the morning, Christmas is coming. I am starting to wake up and I am starting to feel the joy and anticipation of a day that celebrates my Lord's birth and it celebrates my family, friendships, and new beginnings. I slowly embrace the simplicity and ease of the holiday here in Germany. I am slowly finding my way back to the girl I once was, but my appreciation, love, and joy for the people in my life brings me a new understanding and a new hope of the celebration of Christmas. I move forward. I reach for the star blazing the ebony sky and announcing the birth of my Savior this holiday season. I celebrate my own life and the people in my life with each greeting and thought. I am home in my heart.

I Choose to Find Happiness Somewhere This Holiday Season

I am going to find happiness in a season where I want to crawl into a dark hole and not emerge. The closer the time gets to 22 December, Phil's scheduled departure date, and thus is scheduled return by date, the more I reel. Part of it is the dark days of December. It is cold and the sun barely shines through the gloomy sky. The biggest part is feeling so disconnected from the happiness all around me. I want to feel the happiness and hope, but I am the wall flower lurking in the shadows. I see glimmers of the rays shining through, but I am still assaulted with trying to forge a new life without Phil. I am still discovering who I am as a person independent of every one for the first time ever. This transition is not easy.

I don't find it easy to make decisions and to believe in myself. I make the decisions, but I second guess myself. People see my strength; I see the doubt. I am good at being a wing man. I am good at being a behind the scenes kind of girl, but I am not good at standing alone. I kind of like that I am discovering the strength and resilience about myself, but as I face the jubilant times of sharing the holidays, I find myself at odds. Every tradition, every memory, every future hope was based on the shared times as a family. Most of those times were during the holidays where we took the time to enjoy and celebrate the people in our family. We were family and we were a tight family.

Our family looks different now. The holidays do not feel the same. I do not feel the excitement or event the motivation to press ahead. I am stuck in a painful inertia of waiting for someone who is never coming home. As I watch the many holiday reunions, it reminds me of how much I have lost. How many turbulent waters I must navigate. I am lost and adrift. I don't know how to find my spirit of Christmas hope without the network I once shared the holidays with. I don't know how to find Christmas without the entire family I established the traditions and memories with. My heart bleeds during the holidays most of all. While I have found the Linda that can navigate day to day and even be happy, I don't know where my compass is for these unchartered waters. I want my Christmas hope. . .my Christmas star. . .my Christmas Messiah.

I Run to Greet 2012 with Wide Open Arms

It is only fitting that I run into 2012 by running a midnight marathon to usher in a new dawning day. I am more the ready to leave the hard times of 2011 and to embrace the hope of 2012, with a known confidence; I believe that 2012 will bring joy and new beginnings. The sorrow and loss of 2011 is a part of me, but the victory is in stepping forward out of the dark shadows.

I am forever changed by the events of 27 April. Not all of the changes are bad changes. I am stronger and I am stronger and more resilient than I even gave myself credit for. I have taken risks and chances to include moving to Europe, buying a car alone, traveling in many different manners throughout Europe, and most of all, learning to live alone without my Phil. The future is not as scary as it once loomed.

While this isn't the life I thought I would have or in my worst nightmares envisioned, it is the life God gave to me and he is blessing me at every turn as I often cower in fear. The fear is less than it was and I embrace the joy and hope I have found in my life. I continue to grow into the woman God is calling me to be, and I continue to fall to my knees when I need direction which is daily and which is often.

I find it strange to be looking at a whole year where I have not seen or spoken to my Phil. I still find it strange that I do not have his steady presence in my life, but as I step forward in every sense of the word, I know that I am honoring the love he had for me that made me in large part the woman I am now. I know that Phil would be happy to see the new dawn rising and me running into it. Phil would be shaking his head and cheering me on as I leap into the "fearless Sasha" mode. He would be encouraging me to move on. All of those facets bring me peace and confidence as I sprint into 2012.

I.AM.SASHA and I Believe in ME

I have never been a very independent girl. While I have taken risks such as joining a renegade bunch of girls that crashed an all-boy cross country team at a school that was slow to embrace progressivity for women's sports in the 70's, I have generally been content to follow and support my family both growing up and in my adult life as a spouse. I have never really made a decision about where to live, vacation, how to spend money, etc. all on my own since I chose where I wanted to go to college at the age of 18 and that decision was made by finances and a scholarship. One of the hardest aspects of moving on from Phil's death is learning to trust myself and the decisions and choices that I make or don't make which in and of itself is a decision.

I chose to move to Germany to teach. It has been the best decision I could have made in terms of stepping forward, but still, when then loneliness hits and I am far from those that love me, I know that it is my own fault that I do not have a live body to spend time with. At times, I grapple with wondering how I could leave a job that I loved and a school that I adored to come here where I am still trying to impact families and children. I miss Colorado Springs because people knew and respected me. People liked me and I had a niche. I don't have that here yet, but I know that sense of belonging will come with time. What is more difficult is the sense of home. Will I ever feel that sense of home again?

For me, part of the decision to come to Germany was the loss of home in my heart because home for me is where my family is. My family lives all over the world because my children are grown and Phil is gone. Will I ever feel at home in my own skin? Only time will tell. I think I will because I am starting to take more risks like taking the train here in Europe and driving to new villages, but I am such a scaredy girl. I only waited 50 years to grow up and embrace my inner Sasha Fierce confidence. I am not even sure of what I am afraid of. As Pogo says, I think that I am my own worst enemy in that I am the one limiting and distrusting myself. Everyone else believes and sees the uber confident woman in front of them. Only I know the difference, but I see that I can be that girl.

I look in the mirror and I wonder who it is that stares back. Would Phil recognize the woman in the mirror. He always trusted me to keep the home fires going while he worked to provide for us, but we were very traditional in our roles. I found a lot of comfort in being the strong mom and the wife that stood behind her husband, but it isn't as if I really have any choices because I am not crawling into a corner to cower. The decisions I make and the repercussions of my decisions are mine alone. I kind of like the freedom that comes with having to rely on my faith to step forward with the confidence that should have always been there. I. AM. SASHA. I believe in me.

I Have a Dream

Martin Luther King had a dream. I had a dream that I would grow old with Phil. I used to tease him about getting old and reverting to his first two languages which I couldn't speak. I teased him about being the dirty old man chasing the nurse around the room. Beneath the teasing, we talked about being grandparents together and building our dream house in Washington State. Easter weekend, four days before his assassination, he sent me the web site for about 20,000 floor plans. While retirement was still quite far away, that was his promise to me—that I could pick the house and where we lived since I spent my entire adult life following him wherever the military took him.

When the dream of living out a fifty year marriage ended in April, I truly believed that my life was over, but at my fiftieth birthday celebration one lady, Kim, encouraged e to rewrite my bucket list. I couldn't even see a future without my Phil, but my friend Kim embraces life and challenges such as zip lining even though she is blind. If she can live with zeal and chutzpah, then I took her challenge to think about what dreams I might still have. My bucket list was quite simple in July:

1. To become a grandmother (happening in May)
2. To finish a marathon in all 50 states (getting closer)
3. To run the Great Wall of China Marathon (in 4 years)
4. To travel in Europe again (happening now)
5. To live the fairy tale again (taking steps in this direction)

I have begun to have more dreams. I would like to have my blogs published. I would like to give back in terms of the Gold Star Wives/TAPS and to mentor and be the soft place to fall for other wives/spouses walking this terrible journey of insecurity, loss, and despair. I don't need things, but I need a purpose and I need people to share my life with. I do have a dream and I take steps to making my dreams a reality. I step into the light of day and even if the clouds obscure the rays of light at times, I walk in faith and the belief that one day I will be so much more than my loss. I have a dream that my life's work is just beginning and that I have the fairy tale in my future again. I believe and in believing, I take the first steps.

I am a Different Linda Today

I am not the same girl I was a year ago. One year ago, I was quietly going about my daily life waiting for Phil to come home. I was content to go to work, run, and race. Throw in church and a monthly game of Bunco and I was content. I liked being a homebody and I didn't mind waiting. I was the girl in the shadows of my family. My husband and children are all quite successful. I was the mom who supported every one and who read a lot to my children. I didn't need accolades or an exciting life. I truly was content. On April 27th, I changed forever.

This change was borne out of necessity. It is one thing to be content to be waiting; it is a whole other realm to face a future when the person one loves never comes home. The four walls become quite oppressive. The nicest gifts I got were the people who gave me the gift of time online or in person. I couldn't ask for that touch. I didn't even know I needed it, yet people that I least expected came forward and have become that warm blanket that covers me. People who I thought I was close to, or even family, couldn't deal with the loss, so I have been incredibly grateful for the family that I was not born into, the friends that have become so tightly woven into my heart, that I will forever consider them to be my brothers or sisters. They have pushed me out of the darkness and when I doubt myself, they have been the cheerleaders who propel me forward. It

227

is deeply humbling to be able to share the deepest secrets of my heart and know that I am loved any way.

I was ripped apart by an erroneous Fox News story this week. I needed to vent. I used words and terms that would surprise many of the people who think they knew the Linda of the past. I wrote the words and then felt terrible, yet my closest friends laughed and said that the reporter deserved it. They stood behind me and tried or did sent ugly-grams to Fox News about the shoddy reporting. That laughter, camaraderie, and lack of judgment yanked me out of the roiling waters.

At the same time, my sister friends--the ladies who lost spouses or sons at the same time--sent a flurry of e-mails this week. When one of us is weak, the others surround her and carry her. When we are all weak, there is strength in our group brokenness. We stand together and we understand as few do the raw pain that compels us to step forward. Along with my sister friends, are military men and women who lived that awful reality of that unthinkable day. No matter where we are, who we are with, we understand and immediately respond to the needs of each other.

Having said this, I have lost a lot of the confidence I once had. This confidence was born from having been loved for 23 years. My marriage was a comfortable one in which I thought I would grow old and die in. Phil knew me as well as I knew myself. That girl no longer exists. I am lonely and often am afraid. I am insecure about stepping forward, but I am stepping forward.

I have begun to date again and I look in the mirror. I know that this is what Phil wanted--he even told me so less than two hours before he deployed. It is strange, though. I am not the confident Linda I once was. It is like I am thrown back to being 19 and worrying about being left. . .mostly worrying that I am too broken or not good enough for the man who is walking this with me. I am not ready to move at the speed of light. I am not even ready for the physical components of a relationship, but I know that if I do not step forward now, I will never be able to move on. It is frightening to be 50 and entering a world that I was terrible at the first time. It is awful to doubt myself.

As awful as the self doubt is, there is a sense of wonder. I stand in awe of the manner God is pushing this man into my life. There is a story so powerful and so great that starts in April before Phil left and then goes to that June day at my most broken state. The journey continues on to moving to Germany and getting involved in an online grief support group. There is a whole lot more to the story and it will be written after my friend knows the rest in April. He is not Phil. I don't want him to be. I will always love Phil and there will always be gaping holes in my heart, but I have changed in another way, also. I had unmet needs, wants, and love that I never knew were there until those needs, wants, and love were met by DC. It is still fairly early, but I have known from the start that if I didn't step forward and give him a chance, that I would miss out. I am blowing talking about this in my blog, but it is part of my journey--a very scary part of my journey.

The time line for people grieving is very different. I miss Phil and I would give anything if Phil had come home. I would be forever married to him if he was alive, but he gave me a gift that I am deeply awed and humbled by. He gave me the gift of freedom to move on by telling me that he wanted me to be happy and he wanted me to find love again if something happened to him. He told me this two hours before he left while I made jokes about it. He asked me one question that stopped me in my tracks, "Would you want me to be happy again if you die first?" Emphatically, the answer was yes. Phil knew me better than I knew myself. He knew I needed this blessing should something happen. I can only stand in wonder and look at my life. It isn't the life I wanted, foresaw, or even could have conjured up in my wildest dreams, but this Linda steps forward in her Sasha Fierceness and though insecure and broken, she is stepping into the light of day with renewed confidence in areas she could never have imagined having strength in.

I Need the Human Touch

The tiny white threads of surrender fall on me today. I am broken in a way that is hard to define without sounding like a slutty girl Linda. I miss the human touch. I miss all that comes with the human touch. A person that wants to be with you so much that nothing else matters. For many, the act of making love is something that is easily given. For this girl, I am old fashioned and committed to honoring the faith I profess, but I long for any touch.

I didn't grow up in a real touchy feely home. I never felt like I needed to be touched, but I derived great pleasure in holding my baby brother, babysitting, and by being rocked by my grandmother. In high school, I fell to running. The more I ran, the fatigue muted the pain I felt inside and the wanting of feeling like I mattered to someone. While running became about so much more, I would be lying if I said that today the two and a half hour run wasn't a reflection of that same teen sentiment.

In my adulthood, I began to realize the power of touch when my oldest son, Patrick, was born. I was a collegiate scholarship athlete who was in a bad marriage. I was on the pill when I got pregnant. I had very mixed feelings about my pregnancy, but that paradigm shifted when Patrick was placed into my arms. I never felt such a powerful love and sense of rightness as I did in that moment. I couldn't stop holding him, touching him, and kissing his little bald head. I felt that same pull with Josh, Emily, Alex, and Tiger. Nothing in my life was more important or worth fighting for as much as those five wonderful human beings that I was trusted with. It was natural to rain down love and affection on them because the pull was so deep. As they grew and I returned to work, I would run to the baby room at the child development center every day. I would rock or hold the screaming babies and talk gibberish and sing terribly to them. The touch calmed them as much as it allayed my fear, apprehension, and workaholic tendencies. All people, newborns through the dying elderly person need to be touched.

With the children grown, and my job involving older children, I feel more alone than I would like to admit. I crave any touch-the newborn baby or a masseuse killing my aching running muscles. While I would like to have the touch of love again, I do not mistake the act for love. I am not willing to cheapen something I hold so dear. My heart may give out the first time I am touched with agape love, but then I would die happy, would I not? I miss what comes with the love shared with a man. I miss the knowing looks, the inside jokes, the desire to want to spend time with someone, and the familiarity of another's body. I am scared to even contemplate this aspect of a relationship. As much as I want and desire touch, when it comes to physical loving in a relationship, that will wait until the emotional and spiritual needs are met. When those sparks ignite and blaze, maybe then. Until then, I may have to run more, get a dog (if only I were not traveling so much this summer), look forward to loving and kissing on my precious baby grandson due in May, and, I think I need to learn to talk to myself. If only I could get used to the quietness of the four walls and the sense of being all alone, I would be fine. God can remove that need, can he not?

With Valentine's Day looming, I retreat. I am lonely and unsure. I am second guessing myself at every corner. I threw up the white flag of retreat and I will sit and watch the tiny shreds of gossamer fall upon the pieces of my heart. I will close my eyes and hide for awhile because while this feeling is so crushing, this too will be compartmentalized and overcome with faith. I do believe. I do trust. I do want.

The Physical Need

Sex. I need it. I want it. I miss it. I am at an age where I felt my parents were ancient and I would have thrown up a little bit if they had talked about it or even acted like they did it. I don't feel so old to never want that closeness with another person again, but here is the thing about me that sets me apart from many people. I am not looking to just take care of a physical yearning. I am looking for the natural gift that comes from loving another person well. If I spend the rest of my life without making love with someone, I would miss sex, but I am not compromising on a fire that burns brightly-that fire drives me in my decisions and actions (most of the time). I want to be worthy of the faith I claim.

Yes, I am taking small steps forward. I am a little shocked at the number of people who ask me if I am attracted to this person. Phil was younger than I was. He aged well. He loved me better. . .As I step forward, I am looking for the fairy tale again. The person can't be Phil. They can't look like or even act like my Phil. I need someone who loves me well before he touches me. I need a lifetime friendship.

The shift in paradigms is that I need someone whose company I enjoy so much that I can see hours and hours together. I want the compatibility in the activities, conversation, faith, and then the physical. I am entering that phase of my life when I can see beyond working every day all day. I can see beyond daily needs of children. I see opportunity and I see where another person can fill a void that Phil never got to even attempt to fill. Phil had my youth and middle age. We raised a family and we loved each other well, but even he knew that the need for companionship, love, and a physical connection would soon arise if one of us were to die early.

Maybe if I was older, or even stronger, I wouldn't want the fairy tale again. I wouldn't feel the gaping holes of loneliness. Here is the scoop, however. I am getting stronger. I am starting to enjoy where I am and I am developing confidence in traveling and being alone. I don't need to have a person to rescue me; I want to meet a person half way and walk together. If I have to compromise the values I carry, then I would rather stay celibate to the end even if it is 40 years from now. Many people confuse good sex with love. For me, I need to be loved well and for the promise of the lifetime together to be there before I give the one gift I have to give.

Myself. Until I know that I have met the person I intend to spend the rest of my life with, I choose to be celibate. It does not matter if I am or if I am not attracted to someone. I worry about that aspect of a relationship least of all because I am a hot-blooded girl after all.

Being Single

It has been so many years since I was single. I was married to Phil longer than I was single ever. I do not know how to be single in that I don't read the cues well, I don't play the games at all—I am an open book --, and I don't trust myself and my reactions to anyone right now. I am a fleer by nature, so it is easy for me to sabotage relationships and to withdraw at the first sign of trouble. In college, I was a three date girl. I dumped and hurt men on the third date because I couldn't see myself settling down. I didn't want to be "owned" by anyone, yet I craved the comfortable companionship and the thought of a long term marriage like my grandparents. Right now, I do not see myself married again. I like the idea of falling in love again and the comfortable companionship with someone else, but is it so terrible that I don't want to change, that I am afraid of starting over?

I know logically I said the same things when I was single at 27. I met Phil and four months later we eloped. That is not happening again. I am so much warier. I should have been scared when I ran off with Phil, but I was younger. I just knew that we were better together and that he made me incredibly happy. Was it enough? Yes. We rarely fought. I hate conflict, but Phil recognized when he hurt me and he would use humor, nice notes, and he would chase me down at times to resolve whatever the issue was. He was like that from the night early in our marriage when he made me promise that we would not go to bed angry—that we would work through any problems for as long as it took. We did that even when the issues loomed large. We never fought over money, moves, behaviors, but the handful of fights I do remember were over the kids—stupid things, but we came to an agreement without killing each other or belittling the other.

I want the comfortable companionship of the 23 years I had with Phil. The companionship that knows when another person needs space, reassurance, a kindness, and a companionship that is comfortable in the silences. I never wanted new and exciting. I still don't. While I am taking slow steps into a relationship, I am terrified. I can see a future with someone else, but I struggle with the whole concept of being married—meshing my life with someone else. Trust of myself mostly. Maybe I am too broken and maybe I will be alone forever. I do not know, but it is a paralyzing proposition to go through all of the firsts again. I am not there yet, but as I inch closer, I wish that I had a crystal ball, that I trusted myself and my ability to make the right choice, and I wish for the fairy tale again. Maybe it is not possible, but how will I know unless I take a faltering step forward?

I Cannot Go Back to the Girl I Once Was

Someone deeply wounded me today and they probably don't even realize the extent of the destruction to my confidence or verve of life to me. Before Phil was killed, I was quite content to sit in the shadows and be a wife to Phil and a mother to my five children. All of their stars shone so brightly that at times, I felt insignificant. I felt left behind as all of them amassed many awards and recognition, but I was more than comfortable as the behind the scenes type of girl. I had a few people with whom I considered my friends, but I only let people see the perfection. I never let them see my frailties or need. I never asked for help, nor did I show weakness. I was the strong one even when I was dying inside.

When Phil died, the people I considered my closest friends couldn't handle my pain or they didn't know what to say, so they said and did nothing. My own family didn't know what to do because the order of life had been dramatically changed and the one vibrant healthy person gone forever in an unspeakable act of betrayal and violence. There are no words. Nobody understood except for the people that were there when there nine comrades were assassinated or the people closest to the nine lives taken far too soon. Innocence was forever destroyed. I no longer look at my word with rose colored glasses.

I chose to talk and to write when Phil was killed. Even as I was hearing the news, the media stood outside of my school. Even as I flew to Dover, the media was staked out at the airport. Even as we greeted Phil's body, there was the media. I chose to talk. Phil's life was largely hidden until his death. He always felt like he had to hide that he was an immigrant with English skills as a third language. He was a work horse/robot because he was deathly afraid of losing all he had achieved. He hid his pain, fatigue, cold, hunger, and his emotions because he always thought that the military would think he was second best. He took pride in looking young because he was afraid his age was going to limit his chances at success. While Phil was incredibly humble, he did care about the awards because they provided a modicum of job security.

What people didn't see was that Phil was a man of faith. He was a wonderful husband and father. Granted, he was not perfect, but neither am I. He was incredibly funny, but more than that, he was loyal, committed, and fiercely proud of our five children. He and my father were obnoxious when they got together. Never was a man prouder of the life he created. Because the world did not know Phil, the man, I spoke. He was so much more than the sum of his military career. He was loyal to his adopted country, to his job, to his faith, and to his family. It never mattered where we were, he extolled the virtues of the military, our country, and our family. Additionally, Phil had a heart for those people working what I call the invisible jobs. He noticed the maintenance workers and the housekeepers. He got to know their names and their snack and soda preferences. He talked to them and treated them the way he wished he had been treated when he first came to the USA.

Today, somebody that I trusted really hurt me. They picked an area that I am the least comfortable with in my life--the limelight. I have a son who does not understand my need to write and speak of his father's life. He does not understand that by honoring Phil, I am putting a face to the military losses that mount every day. He does not understand that in writing, I am healing and that other's may read and find faith. He does not understand that I feel that the Holy Spirit is leading me to do this through the 27th of April. It was not this son, however, that deeply hurt me. It was someone that I had let into my life and who knew how insecure I felt about the shifting paradigms of my life. I cannot apologize for the number of friends I have and I cannot take back the number of Google entries I have. I am forever linked to Phil, the deaths of nine wonderful soldiers gone far too soon, and to others who are the walking wounded. I will never be the girl I once was. I have a brightly burning fire that blazes for our military families everywhere. This fire is consumes me and compels me to step up and to live beyond myself. I cannot be the girl who boxes her emotions or hides in a dark corner any more. Wounded or not, I step forward.

Happiness Is a Choice

Choosing happiness seems to be an antithesis to what people expect to see when a person is walking through the most difficult event a person can go through—a loss so profound that it leaves huge gaping holes. There are simply no words let alone any understanding, as to why a person is snatched from the surly bonds of earth far too soon. Nothing can fix or replace the person, yet time creeps by one second, one minute, one hour, and one day at a time. Time that stretches on into a vast chasm of endless hopeless day, yet hope does float like tiny rills that burst through the roiling waters.

Granted, this is not the life I embraced or wanted. From a time even before I agreed to go out with Phil, I imagined us in rocking chairs 'with grandchildren galore. I never expected or feared a death from an unthinkable violence at the hand of a madman hell bent on robbing the world of nine wonderful intelligent people in the prime of their lives. I never once imagined that Phil would die before me, yet in Phil's senseless death, I have become a better version of my old self in some ways.

My faith has never been stronger. My testimony has never shone so brightly. People do not realize that when all is gone that a person invests in, there are two choices—to fall into faith, or to fall out of faith. I chose to fall into my faith and it has made all of the difference. I am still broken and I still wonder if anyone will ever see me as more than the sum of my losses, but I have never experienced the mercies and joy of friendships that I have experience from people all over the world. My closest friends at the time of Phil's death could not handle the loss. Many of these people have chosen me-carried me-Loved me even during the darkest hours. That love has given me a lifeline that sustains me on those days when I want to cower in a dark corner.

I have become more vocal and demonstrative. I no longer hide behind the mask of indifference or perfection. People see my brokenness. They see my want and need. It is written all over me and it is etched into the planes of my face. I write about things I could never vocalize. I write because a fire is blazing to get those words out. I cannot explain it, but I know it has been a part of my healing journey. I am not a girl who is comfortable in the lime light, but by the numerous people who have written to me about my words, I am humbled and I trust the Holy Spirit blazing the trail. I may not know the whys, but I reach and take the leap of faith.

In my times of deep profound loneliness, I am so appreciative of Phil's foresight to look ahead to the unthinkable. He left no stone unturned. He took out an extra life insurance policy, he saw his children all become successful adults, and he had the what if talk with me in which he gave me the freedom to move on. I didn't want any of the things he did, but I am stunned and I kneel with gratitude that he loved me in spite of myself. He loved me enough to look ahead to the possibility of his demise. He loved me enough to know that I couldn't possibly date or let another person in without his blessing.

I do choose happiness in a time when many cannot understand how I could possibly feel joy. Do I feel it every day? Gosh, no! I break, I bend, and I break some more, but I always can see beyond the all encompassing blackness. I can always see that a new day dawning might bring pink polka dots and hope that floats like tiny bubbles to break the iridescent water. I embrace my Sasha Fierce persona on the days when I feel the most uncertain and the most scared. I fall to my knees when I hurt the most, and it is there where I see that all will be well yet again. I choose today and tomorrow to be happy.

Dating Rules

As I begin to take some small steps into the dating realm, I am finding that I am terribly and hopelessly outdated in my expectations, yet I am unwilling to bend or to compromise the feeling that unless I find the fairy tale again, I would rather live a chaste lonely life. It would be far too easy to settle for what is available instead of waiting for the passion and the commitment. For me, those two things go hand in hand after establishing an unsinkable friendship rooted in faith, laughter, commitment, and time together. Is it so wrong to think that I might be enough for one person?

When Phil and I went on our first date, he told me that he could only date one person at a time. While we were no sure where we were going as a couple and there were many reasons we shouldn't have worked, he asked for me to date only him until we knew where we were going. I am old fashioned enough that I can't be with someone if I am thinking about someone else. I work really hard not to put myself in a situation where mixed signals are given or received and I extricate myself with dignity when a situation shifts and lines start blurring. I do this because it is too easy to settle or give into human nature. We all like to be touched and to be loved, but I just can't compete with another person in terms of proving myself.

I am the girl next door. I am nothing special. I am the most comfortable in running shoes outside. My feet hurt in heels. I am the girl that everyone is comfortable with, but nobody sees like a girl. I don't sparkle and I don't shine. I never learned to do makeup or hair. Heels hurt my feet; besides, I walk like a studette. I am comfortable being the homebody and I don't need to be rubbing arms with superstars. Yes, men like that I am athletic, but it seems that they are always looking at the Veronica's of the world (Archie comics). I am not so special. I am not so sparkly that I am enough for most people, but I will be the lonely and chaste girl until I find the one person whose world I rock and with who is as gaga over me as I am for him. When I find that, I will know that I have found the fairy tale again. If that never happens, I will be content with having had it once, but I do believe that it is a possibility, thus I step forward into yet another terrifying realm in which I am lost and confused at the shifting rules of play and strategy.

I am astute enough to realize that the problem is probably me. With Phil being assassinated by someone he trusted, it is as if my trust for myself, my confidence, my ability to read people is skewed. I struggle with self-doubt and worth. It has been so many years since I have felt like I was invisible or so needy. I hate that I am that girl. I do not need a relationship to prove my worth, but the wrong one can crush what little is left of how I feel good about myself.

Isn't it enough to worry about being with someone besides Phil? I don't know my boundaries or what my reactions will be. Add to this the normal expectation of physical intimacy quickly. That is not my style. It was never my style. I don't keep options open when I am in a relationship, but why is it that I feel that this is normal? Why do I feel so helplessly old fashioned? While I could learn to be more of a girl in terms of outward appearance and possibly behavior, I like who I am--I like being Sasha Fierce the Studette. I like being strong and in shape. I like being able to play without worrying about makeup running or my feet hurting in high heels. I may wear dresses, but even in a dress, I exude Sasha, the athlete. I don't quite walk right, sit right, or behave right, yet my heart is that of a girl that probably should have been a single girl long, long ago. I may be a single girl for a very long time, maybe even forever, but if and when I find the fairy tale, hopefully my prince will see that this girl is worth waiting for.

But then Comes the Morning Sun

Spring used to be my favorite season until we lived in Colorado when fall moved into the number one spot in my heart. Spring was never far behind. Through the gray and cold of winter, spring creeps in. Warmth comes back in small increments with many winter like days, and then one day the tulips are up and the lilacs wave wildly in the May promise. It is like that now.

I lost so much last April. I lost the man I had every dream, hope, and longing for. I lost the vision of the two of us sitting on the porch in Washington State enjoying a whole gaggle of grandchildren. The joke always was that one of them was going to have a little girl with dark pig tails saying, "Oh, Grandpapa, I am hungry. I need ice cream." He would have caved in a nanosecond even if lunch was minutes away. Phil looked forward to being a grandpa. He is about to be one, but sadly, his grandchild will never know of the man who painted one son's toes purple after a scout camp out to scare me about frostbite. Sadly, this namesake grandchild will never know the joy, the patience, the faith, and the fun his grandpapa would have brought to his life.

I lost someone to talk with about all of the adult history with. A man who knew me when I was still young and a man with whom I shared so many secrets, memories, disappointments, happiness, and just life. We eloped after four months which was huge for two super responsible adults who were deathly afraid of getting it wrong. I am so glad I did….never regretted eloping, not once. I never thought that Phil would meet Jesus first because I am older and my health is more fragile. I wanted to die first, but God knew the number of days Phil had. His death plunged me into the dark cold night of winter. A night so cold that no hope, no joy, no warmth could be seen, yet beneath the frozen ground, the tulip and crocus bulbs wait for a ray of warmth.

Like the seemingly withered tulip bulb bushes through the frozen ground to the warmth above, I, too, am pushing towards the light of day. I can stop time, and I cannot stop the future from happening, but I can grow towards the light. Winter moment still pierce the early spring days, but there will one day soon be the tulip and lilac garden in full bloom. I may not understand why him and why not me, but I do know that something beautiful is arising from the ashes and from the piercing cold of winter. I may not see spring all of the time, but, oh, how I feel it and reach for it.

Moving On

I cannot keep descending to the bowels of hell in terms of falling into the deep dark morass of hopelessness and defeatism. I can no longer live paralyzed by fear. I lost so much in April of 2011. I will never understand why, nor will the holes in my heart close the gaping weeping wounds, however, if I live in this state, then the gunman has effectively killed both Phil and I. I have two choices--to move beyond the fires of despair that have consumed me, and lose the promise of life I have been given, or step out in faith. It is easier to stay mired in the tether of sadness and darkness, but that is not going to happen. I am going to step forward and choose happiness. I may not feel that I will be able to go on, but I see that I have.

Moving on does not mean that I loved Phil any less. In fact, because he loved me well and believed in me, I believe in myself and I honor his one last request before he left for Afghanistan--to find happiness again should something happen to him. Sounds easy, but in reality, I sabotage my own happiness usually. I get stuck in a rut of defining my life by loss, but my life is so much bigger. Faith gives me a reprieve from feeling that Phil's life is forever over. Faith also gives me hope in things unseen in terms of the life song and lifeline I have. This isn't the life I chose, wanted, and it is the life I would have begged for death over, but it is mine. I am choosing to honor Phil's life, the life we shared, and our faith by stepping up and choosing to look forward.

I do not know what my future will hold. Yes, I hope for companionship and to find the fairy tale again, but even if. . .even if. . .it doesn't happen, I will find contentment and joy in the life I have been given. I do not know the days of my life, but I appreciate even more the days I do have. I am not going to put off the vacations, the time spent with people, the joy in small things, or wait for the appropriate time for things. I am going to lean on my faith and I am going to step forward to the shafts of light piercing the darkness because some where happiness and contentment in entirety is a reality. I am not a brave person or a strong girl, but Phil's assassin is not getting more than he already took from me. Phil's assassin won a big battle, but he is not winning the war. He is not taking me or my soul. I choose happiness and I choose to dream. I choose to remember, but I choose to look to tomorrow. There is hope.

Isn't 50 Too Old For This?

Sometimes I wonder if only another person who has lost a spouse to unexpected death is the only person who could truly understand and love me as I am. I had recently begun to take small, very small, steps forward with a person. This person deeply wounded me the day before Phil's birthday. His sense of timing was impeccable and I immediately shut completely down. During a month when I need to be able to talk about my feelings and have support from someone who claims to care about me, that person flees. At some point, when he realizes, it will be much too late, for how does one fix an egregious misstep? It is possible that in another month, I could laugh it off and move on, but now? Really?

I already have trust issues--trust issues primarily with myself. I second guess myself at every turn. This started when Phil died. I was moving at a snail's pace forward in the area of letting someone in all the way. I still can't fathom another person touching me without complete trust, thus when a person hides behind not being a good communicator or a healer of broken hearts, then what is there left to say? Is it so wrong that I might need some empathy and compassion this month--especially this year? All I know is that trust is totally destroyed and I am further than ever from letting someone else in. Full retreat is easy, but trust and faith is a whole other issue.

I do believe that I will find the fairy tale again. I believe that because of the talk that Phil and I had on 11 January mere hours before he deployed. I believe it and know it based on what happened that day in June. That singular event that occurred as I lay broken and weeping under the covers of my bed was the biggest sign that it will one day happen. I am not in a hurry, but I am not interested in trying again with anyone. I don't think that nonmilitary people get it and I don't think that others that haven't lost get it in terms of a normal dating relationship. Maybe I am wrong, but at fifty, I don't know the games, the rules, and the options that some people want. I am still an old fashioned girl that believes in marriage, fidelity, and loyalty of thoughts and actions. I believe that two are better than one, but relationships take time and work on both people's part. I mourn for the loss of the relationship I had with Phil--the relationship that took 23 years to cultivate. I knew Phil almost as well as I knew myself. He knew me the same way. It was a comfortable shroud that brings me peace still. I could look at Phil and I knew what he needed. I knew just how to touch him, and I knew just what to do. I miss the comfortable place to land when I was happy, sad, bored, or just in need of a friend. I miss the laughter most of all. In my lifetime, I may be lonely and afraid, but I am not going to cower in a corner or accept a relationship in which another person cannot understand that Phil is a part of me. I don't need to talk about it all of the time, but I do need a person to show up on certain days or hours. All in or all out. All out is an area I drop to very quickly. I am there.

What Next?

As my life imploded again this April, I sat weeping in the dark of night wondering just where the loving God I knew was. I begged him to come and take me then. In my brokenness, I had a severe crisis of faith, yet I knew that I needed to find my way back to the faith that has sustained me for so long because in that faith comes confidence and hope. My life may not be the life I envisioned or wanted, but it is the life God is giving me. In my human frailty, I see only the darkness, but there is so much more to my life than what is defined here on earth. I began to reread the book of Job.

Job had everything taken from him. His family. His wealth. His status. At one point, he railed against God, but eventually he asked the question of what next. What next God? What is it that you want me to do? What lessons do I need to learn? I may be alone and lonely for many years, but somewhere in that roiling pit of despair, God's grace is sufficient and mercies are given. I am seriously contemplating my future. I have a two year contract here, but what next? I have another 9 months until I need to figure it out, but it is scary trying to decide where to live, what to do, and to think about what I want when I have no idea where to live or what to do. I am scared and unsure. I have a dream, but I am paralyzed in the actually execution of it. I want to get another master's degree in family studies and health and wellness. I want to combine the two programs with an emphasis on reblended families and grief management and then one day work in family support or even family advocacy. I love my job, but I am looking at where I am being pulled to go and I know that this is it.

What next? I feel inadequate to even make these decisions. I am 50 years old and on the downhill slide into 51. I can't make a simple decision and it drives me nuts. I could go to school full time and not work, but that is scary. I would be older than my peers and I would be further isolated. Once I make a decision about where to move after this, that is my one military move that I am allotted. What if I get it wrong? I stand here among the ashes of my life and I find that I am incapable of making a decision and I am sabotaging myself I sabotage out of fear, but I am standing covered in the shadow of my faith in God. What next? Show me and give me a willing heart no matter what direction you want me to go. I will step in faith and I will trust that even if I am alone and afraid that the mercies of my faith will sustain me until the end.

The End of my Journey

I started writing when I lost my Phil because I couldn't talk about my feelings or the pain that rain so deep that it physically hurt my body. I stepped in faith and confidence because I knew that the Holy Spirit was nudging me and compelling me forward because the words did not come from me, but rather, they evolved after running with the whispered prayers of my feet. I always knew that there would be an end date and that I would know when that day was. I really thought that day would be the 27th—the one year mark--, but I know with certainty today that today is it. I need to be done. People have started to use my words to inflict deep wounds on me. My words have impacted a relationship and my job in terms of people using my words for their own agendas. While the relationship ending deeply hurt me and there will always be the residual impact of trust and not letting anyone in that close again, it is the job that worries me the most. The false impression that I am somehow obsessed or depressed is skewing the way people look at me, thus it is time to retreat and not so much move on, but step forward into the life that was created when Phil was assassinated.

I am a different woman since Phil was ripped from my life. I never wanted to know that I was this resilient or strong. I was content to sit in his shadow and the shadows of my five children. All shine so brightly that I got lost. It was an easy role for me. When Phil left, I was content to be waiting. I worked, coached, and ran. I was lonely, but I was waiting for the day Phil came home. I wouldn't have let anyone in, but I ran into a mother of a student of mine in the Petersen AFB BX the weekend Phil left. She asked me to a Bunco night. I never did this kind of thing. I almost backed out. I was terribly overwhelmed the first night when I sat in a full house of laughter and fun. I said yes because my student was standing there and she was so happy that her teacher was coming to her house. I went to church with this woman and daughter on Easter Sunday. These women are among my closest friends now. They walked this terrible year with me and they walk with me still.

I was quiet and reticent. It is a role that I embrace and fall to naturally, but on 27 April 2011, my life was forever altered. Even as I heard those awful words, the media lurked just outside of the doors of my school. Everywhere I turned the media lurked. I made a choice to speak initially to tell Phil's story of an immigrant boy who died for his adopted country, but then I spoke because I became a face for Air Force loss. Nobody thinks that if they are in the Air Force that they are in danger. Even among the branches of the military, the AF is considered the country club branch. Phil and I even encouraged our children to join this branch of service because the deployments are shorter, safer, and less frequent. We were guilty of that false sense of safety. I continued speaking out because every one of those names that flash across the television is a person—a person who was loved and waited for. A person who wanted to go home. A person who was about more than his military job or the manner in which he was taken far too soon. Each of these people is gone and the families left behind are struggling and walking this same awful walk of darkness that few can comprehend or understand. Our families do not understand let alone the general population that often wants to exploit our loved ones deaths for political reasons.

I have changed so much this year that even my family does not understand. I do not understand. I feel like a freak of nature. Trust is a problem. It was never before. Phil's assassination at the hands of someone he should have been able to trust (and he had a very friendly relationship with) shattered my own confidence in my ability to trust myself and my own perceptions. I am no further along with trust right now. In fact two events have pushed me to the edge of retreat. I had begun to trust one person implicitly and I had begun to take small steps forward. When I was totally blindsided, I went into full retreat. I do not think that this person knows how much he caused me to second guess myself or how much he caused me to shut down. It doesn't matter. Maybe the best of my life ended with Phil and the fun girl that I am is forever gone (and, yeah, there is a wicked sense of humor that lurks just below the surface that is totally gone). Just after the one person I let in sent me reeling, I went to talk to someone I considered to be a friend. She is in a profession that should have guarded my secrets unless there was worry about self-harm. She shared things I did not share on Facebook (I know, surprised, aren't you—laugh). She shared them with my boss which is now impacting my job. I may lose my job because it is coupling with a few normal teacher things of one parent complaining (one parent complains, but nobody ever tells the good things—laugh), an observation in which my timing was probably off (first observation in which this is the case), and softball.

I feel like there is no light. Phil's loss may have created this sense of isolationism forever. I am scared for my job, my family, and that I will live the rest of my days too afraid to trust fully. I am afraid that I am a broken woman that nobody wants. I feel like a freak of nature. I am too young to be alone, but too old to be entering the dating games again. My family has shifted. Even many of my children want me to deal with the loss of their dad the way they want me to deal with it. We are no longer close because it is like I am an oddity or a pariah. Why is it that I am letting everyone down because for the first time ever I am being a person that nobody else wants me to be. I am stronger and more resilient than I thought, but in that strength and resilience, the people who liked me in the shadows want me to go back to that area of hidden presence. I am not sure that I can do that. While the media interest and my blogs are over this month, I will probably forever be involved in organizations that support military loss. Maybe it is time for a career shift, to return to school, and to cut my losses with the people who cannot support me, but to do so I will be giving up more things that matter so much to me. I just keep thinking that it is possible for both the new life I have and the Linda I once was, to create a girl that can be liked and respected even by the people who rather I would be the girl in the corner waiting for a man that will never come home again.

My faith has deepened. I would have given up my life if not for the faith I fell into. I had two choices that awful day—fall into my faith or out of my faith. I chose to fall into the arms of Jesus and it has made all of the difference. Even as I heard the awful words as they were read, I chose to reach out to Phil's parents. I didn't have to, but I did. I chose to do forgive the silence and distance they wanted after Phil and I eloped 23 years prior. I wanted to share Phil the husband and father with them. Though they ultimately decided not to be a part of my life, the funeral, the children, it didn't matter. I stepped in faith. That first step was conscious, but the steps I have taken since have often been just reaching a broken finger up and using only the language of tears. God has provided at every turn. He has worked through the many reaching hands of people who have come into my life since 27 April. He has blessed my life and given me hope. Right now today, I am struggling because of recent events, but I am trusting that God will provide. This is not the life I wanted or ever saw, but I am so thankful for the 23 years I shared in Phil's shadow.

Yes, we had a good marriage because we loved and respected each other. We were rooted in faith and we were good friends. He made me laugh. When he would be a cad and hurt my feelings, he would wave a white hanky/rag. He would send e-mails with white flags. He would put on his chollolo accent and kiss all over my ticklish neck in a very obnoxious way. He made me laugh so hard. Were we perfect? Am I perfect? No, but he set the bar really high. I do not want another Phil. I have discovered that I can love between the holes of my heart, but I am not sure anyone is strong enough to live in that legacy. I just know that friendship rooted in faith is a nonnegotiable and that the marriage I shared with Phil had enduring power because of that friendship rooted in faith.

As I contemplate moving on past the one year mark, a possible career change, and shifting relationships, I stand confident in my faith. I am a better friend than I once was because I do see the walking wounded and I do let my heart bleed. I talk about need and want now and I show my weaknesses. I hope that I show my strength and confidence, but if not, it will come. I am not the girl I once was. I never can be her again, but I have to believe that God is working in the ashes to create something beautiful. While I continue on my journey, the journey is going to become more introspective and private. I always said that if I followed the nudging of the Holy Spirit, I would know when the day came to end. That day is now. For those of you that have followed my story, thank you for your support. Chapter two starts today.

Humor is something that has been missing from my life since last April. While I have had moments of laughter and joy, most notably at my fiftieth birthday party, I felt sucked into a deep vacuum of darkness and despair. This April, I caterwauled through this chasm of fear and helplessness, but I found my funny bone and hope somewhere in KY. I had caught glimpses of humor even in the dark days of Dover and the funeral at USAFA, but I just could not move beyond the quagmire of seriousness I stood in. While others are content and growing there, I could not move beyond my inertia until I began to seriously laugh with my heart.

Does it mean that I have forgotten or that I loved any less because I can laugh? For me, laughter is normal and cleansing. For me, laughter brings healing. When things are too big for me to get my arms around, if I can find a way to laugh, then I know that somewhere, somehow I will be happy again. For the many years of my youth, I was serious. Too serious. I took everything too personally and I beat myself up all the time. In college, that quiet unexpected sense of humor took over. While people still see the quiet and shy Linda, those that know me well, know that underneath it all, I have a wicked sense of humor lurking.

I have humor-a humor that defines me and gives joy and resilience to my life. I have a sense of humor that says bring it on. Even if things get worse, there is going to be a pivotal moment when things shift and begin to change for the better. April was terrible. So what? May is here. The big blue bus did not come to get me. My life has been the things that drama filled shows are made of. I am ready for the fun to end, but really? People get paid a lot of money for reality TV that is contrived. Nothing contrived about my life, but the shift is starting.

No matter what happens at work and no matter how unfair things seem, I am going to see joy again. I know it. As someone announced to a whole bunch of eye doctors this weekend, "doesn't she look wonderful. Don't you wish you could take her out?" I found laughter in the many ogling eyes in the elevator. I laughed as I practiced being a woman for the first time in years even as I shot them down, but I found the girl that has been there all along. I found the girl who once convinced her supervisor of a blue flu employee outage. I found the girl that laughed on the way to bury her husband as she looked at the naked burrito picture. I found the girl who once snuck into a boy's room at college to tie all of his shoes together to hang it from the eighth floor. I found the girl I like. The one that I am comfortable with. I like her. I think I will keep her as I laugh my way through whatever comes my way. I choose pink polka dots and bubbles as I fall I to the faith that sustains me always.

Very few people truly understand or get why I run. I have run for 35 years and I have learned so much with each step and with each race. Running, like life, is totally unpredictable, but that is what I love about marathon running. There is never a race that I have started feeling fully confident in finishing. 26.2 miles is a long ways to run. The older I get, the harder it is sometimes, but I am more patient than I was at 16 when I ran my first marathon. I am no longer speedy, but for me, my marathon journey is the story of my life. A story written and defined by worn out running shoes and tee shirts.

When my life imploded on 27 April 2011, I ran. I ran even though it hurt to step and to breathe. I ran because I could process and deal with the loss of control of my life and the loss of a man who loved me well for 23 years. A reporter asked me yesterday a question that caused me to take pause. He asked me if I knew the outcome of Phil's military service, would we do it again. Yes, yes, and I know that Phil would do it again for you see;

he never lost sight of the freedoms and opportunities that citizenship in our country offered. He was proud of what he did. Running is like that for me. I am proud that my body can withstand test after test athletically. I am no longer fast due to a major medical issue, but I am committed and deeply passionate about running because it is as much of whom I am as anything. The military defined my Phil. He loved our country and taught me to love her, also.

Runners often suffer from hitting a wall or injuries. Life is life that. Runners have to decide how to get through these setbacks and the pain. They often push on, but many do know when to take a step back. In a race, every runner considers quitting or taking the easy route, but somehow they dig deep and conquer yet another mile or hill. Yes, sometimes they walk and sometimes they rely on friends to help them get through those hard miles, but they press on. I press on in my life. I reach out for help when I need it and I take the hills one step at a time. Sometimes I walk. Sometimes I fall, but I keep my eyes on the finish and I press on. This April has been harder than last April for many reasons, but I am pressing on one step at a time. I am keeping my eyes on the finish and I am HOPING.

Runners rarely stop hoping in finishing a race or improving a time. Runners set goals and keep to the defined course until they emerge at the finish line. There is not an event or a person that will take my eyes off of the final prize of emerging happy and hopeful. There is not one set back that will cause me to sit on the side of the road waiting for the big blue bus. I may limp and I may cry. I may even hurt so bad I want to lie down, but I am going to stumble my way through because I know that one day there will be the sense of happiness, wellness, and completion. Runners often distance themselves from the snobby runners, the ones who are not positive, and the ones that encourage others to quit. I am doing that now. My life, a life I diode not choose, is going to honor the faith I carry and the perseverance I have learned with running.

Runners look to their next race often just after the completion of a race. I am doing that now. I am looking at my life and I am looking for my next challenges. Where do I want to live? Do I want to date? Who do I trust? Can I forgive? Do I want to go to school? Who do I choose? Faith propels me forward. My life is changing like the race scenery. Every step propels me up a hill, down the street, though the mud, to the mountain top. I stand ready. I see the hope that the girl with the purple polka dotted balloon and flag received as the miles flew by. I see the hands of

God working through runners who found me on the course. I see the HOPE of a new day dawning. I run on. . ..`

One year. One year. It has been one year on the 27th since my life imploded. The trees were budding with promise, and the tulips, daffodils, and crocuses were popping up to usher in spring. It is as if the world stood still as I stood in numb disbelief. It felt like my life had ended when I got the news of my husband's assassination. The promise of spring was and is long gone. Miles and miles of frozen tundra stretch before me. I am rooted in inertia just below the surface as the rest of the world joyfully greets the dawning days of hope.

I was further along before April. I had begun to stretch through the frozen cracks in the soil and I had begun to feel the new life emerging from the frozen bulb hovering in darkness. As I sit on a plane flying towards my American soil, each time I close my eyes, all I see is the plane that landed in the dark of night at Dover AFB in Delaware. In the blackness of the ebony night, my heart and life ended as the flag covered box carrying my Phil was wheeled out and placed next to eight other flag covered boxes. In the darkness, Phil and eight others received a reunion nobody wanted. A reunion orchestrated in the dead of night. Happy reunions are public in nature and people want to see them. People, nobody really, wants to see nine families bent, bowed, and broken. The anguished sobs that filled the lonely night could not have been tamed or fixed by the many important people who stood with us.

Where is the joy and laughter? Where is it now? I have become a true patriot who stands with her military family. My heart is awake and alive to the very life that I lived for 26 years as a military spouse and mother. In those 26 years, however, I just didn't get it. I thought I did. Now, I feel it, I walk it, I live it. I recognize fear and a false sense of bravado. I see the pain in the rebellion and anger of my students. I finally understand the cost which is paid not only in death, but with the living who walk in fear, loss of brothers and sisters in the military family, and in the lengthy deployments. While I do not go about my life thinking that lightning is going to strike twice, I do know that it is possible. I will never be the same Pollyanna I once was. My tulip bulb has frozen and may be too damaged to blossom again.

I still feel like the broken girl who stood in numb disbelief as box seven was wheeled down the ramp. As the clacks and sounds filled the biting cold air, I heard only the broken sobs of one as her heart shattered into a million unfixable shards. One year has passed. Some say that I should move on and get over Phil. Others lament that I was lucky because few get what Phil and I had. It isn't as if I haven't had blessings this year. It isn't as if I am unhappy where I am. I haven't lost my faith, but this month, once my favorite, has reshattered the few shards of my heart that had come together.

Betrayal. That is a word I know too well. I am living in that hell of fire behind me, in front of me, and on either side of me. How does a person explain this to anyone? I live by the credo of the Air Force--Integrity first. I trusted Phil when he told me that he was going to be safe even as he prepared for the what ifs. I trusted Phil when he told me that he was practicing his language skills with a man that would one day look at the fear in my Phil's eyes and shoot him time and time again. I trusted a man and had begun to take small steps forward. He blindsided me. I trusted a counselor who I thought was a friend. This counselor told all of my private secrets that I had shared verbally and she took my blogs and wrongly judged them to be an obsession with Phil.

How do I defend myself? I am broken this month, but I truly believe in a life beyond this life. I have been carried by so many. While initially I wore a mask, I began to feel some of those frequent smiles and I had begun to feel like I could find a measure of happiness in my life. Perhaps that was an illusion, but time will tell.

I miss Phil. I am lonelier than I ever thought possible. I miss the family we were. I miss the inside jokes, laughter, and the naivety that death like Phil's could never happen to an Air Force language instructor. I miss living in Phil's shadow and I miss falling into his arms when people were less than kind. I am alone and as the mean people seek to control me with words that do not help or with words that betray confidences, I feel just as broken as the broken body of my husband--or is it the heart that is broken and beyond repair?

Again, it will never be the same, but I had begun to believe and see some green shoots popping up. I had begun to feel hope, happiness, and a purpose in my breathing moments, but I do not understand the people who tell me that writing equals obsessing or that I should move on because it has been a year. I do not understand people who use me for their own agendas or as an option. Surely, I am worth more than the Linda who is now back on the frozen tundra. While I am no longer lying inert waiting for the icy tentacles to take my life, I am on my knees trying to stand. I 'm trying to make sense of my life and I am trying to figure out who I can trust and believe in. I am trying, trying to find foothold and faith in myself and in my perceptions. I am so mired in the pain of betrayal that

I do wish I could share it in the warmth of Phil's arms, but I am falling to my faith. I write because all is well with my soul.

People have questioned why I chose to write about my journey. It has cost me in part a relationship that I thought was important to me and for a brief time, it distanced me from one of my children. Initially I wrote because I felt the nudgings of the Holy Spirit and I needed a way to express my pain. I have never been good at voicing my pain or need. By writing publicly, my life has been blessed by the many reaching hands of God. Friendships were moved beyond the realm of mask wearing into a genuine gift. I continued writing because hope and happiness sparked in the midst of my darkest hours.

I am a writer. While my public journey is over in large part, my writing is as important to me as my running. In both realms, I show my weakness, strength, and need. I let others in and I reach for others. I fall to my faith and I find hope floating like tiny rills of bubbles that burst through the most turbulent ocean waters. I am thankful that I did not fall to my normal mode of living--stoic silence. God answered my pleas with many reaching hands.

So, here I kneel. All I see is miles and miles of barren landscape. I am sucking in the frigid air that is searing my lungs. I can barely breathe. I miss Phil and I miss the life we shared. I would give anything to have that life back, but that is not going to happen. I was creating a life and moving on, but it is what has happened this month that totally broke me. I wonder if I will ever be normal or if people will ever see me as more than the sum of my loss--a loss hidden and shrouded in the deepest darkest hours of night. I wonder if I will ever be able to read people and trust completely again. I wonder if I will ever feel the green sprouts of hope again. I am on my knees hoping, ever hoping, for a world that sees my value and for a life that shines for Jesus even if I stand forever alone. I stand hopeful that I can learn to trust and believe in people again, but it is going to take me time and strength. I need more of that than I needed a week ago, but I do believe that the tulip will bloom blood red again and that my petals will wave with promise as the spring zephyrs compel me forward.

Goodbye for Now

One of the hardest aspects of the military is all of the goodbyes. Goodbyes are a way of life. We meet so many people and we bond very quickly over shared lifestyles and family members being gone. We live far from our given families and claimed hometowns. We bear each other's joys and sorrows because we cling to the normalcy of shifting faces and places. Nobody else understands--certainly not the people who grow up in the same city that they now reside in. After living like this for over 30 years, I have friends that are now family all over the world. Today, I say goodbye to a chaplain that got me through so much.

While the goodbyes are painful in the military, all goodbyes, I have been given the gift of lasting friendships that continue to sustain me even still. When Phil was a young airman basic in Mountain Home, we could not wait to get out of that place. We did not yet value the military family and friendships that we had forged there. When I personally was called to say goodbye to my Phil far too soon, I turned to my military family because I felt like the families living this walk got it. Yes, I have close friends that walk with me that are not military, but those few are precious. Somehow they get it. My military family from Mountain Home AFB found me. They have walked with me and supported me 24 years after we all lived in the same zip code. That is family for you. I haven't even heard from them in 24 years, yet when I needed them the most, they gave me the gift of my early memories with Phil.

Some of my military friendships are with people I have never met. We became brothers and sisters on that awful day in April 2011. When life becomes so crushing and unexplainable, who else but someone walking the broken road understands? As a military family, we always knew what the ultimate price could be. We never once thought it would be us. Phil and I have four military children and I can honestly say that I do not worry that the unthinkable will happen again. It comes down to faith and trust. Having said that, my children were carried by their military families. How can I explain the invisible threads that bind beating hearts that stand true and loyal not just to our country, but to each family?

I say goodbye until we meet again. That meeting might come after I take my last breath, but I will recognize the brothers and sisters who have carried me and walked with me. I stand humbled by my network that stretches the globe. After 30 years, I cannot call a city or place home. Home for me was where ever the military sent me and where my Phil was. I do not have a home, but I do have a military family that I run to when my life becomes too much. I stand with you, and I walk with you in your hard times. Goodbyes do not minimize or end my sense of community and connection to the people I meet along the way.

Would He Even Know Me?

Lately, I look at the girl in the mirror. I see a much more confident and I am more involved in the lives of the people around me. Phil knew me as someone who stood in the shadows. I was comfortable in my own little corner of the world. Home was Phil. I was the ecru crayon in the crayon box. What happened? Would Phil even like me this way?

I didn't have to make decisions about where I lived or rely even the jobs I held. I didn't socialize outside of running the occasional races. I am still not comfortable going out, but, damn, it is lonely when nobody is coming home. I feel compelled to advocate and be involved in military families through the TAPS program, Gold Star families, family support, or even my students. I don't understand. My heart and focus have shifted so much.

Phil was a quiet homebody. Okay, so he wasn't quiet at home. He was the king of his castle--truly. At times, it was like having a sixth child. He loved the noise and he loved the fun in our home. I would have to run to get quiet during the holidays, but how I wrapped those memories arund me like a warm prayer shawl. He liked me being the unemotional, stoic, and he liked that I didn't need a lot--that I was self-sufficient. I made the perfect military spouse in many ways. I am proud of that, but Phil was uncomfortable with tears, especially the tears that came from the heart. I am not a crier, or at least I wasn't.

I cry now. I have put myself out there. I am lonely. I am afraid. None of this is in my comfort zone. I often fall to my knees and think that I cannot carry on. My eyes tear as I even write this. I am scared of what I feel called to be. I wish that I could talk to the one person I trusted with every secret and dream I ever had. He would laugh at my predicament. Phil was young and vital. I lit up like a light bulb when he was around. Everyone else pales next to him. Phil could make me laugh so hard. I found humor with him. Laughter is the one thing I miss the very most in my daily life. I miss hiding in his arms and his accents as he joked around playing the chollolo boy or dirty Frenchman (and he did it just to make me laugh--no ulterior motives)

I see Phil in all five of our children. Who will I share that with? I have a beautiful newborn grandson. Who will ever want to share my life, my children, and my past? If only it were as easy as shutting down. I have changed so much. I realize now that he filled so many holes and that he made my life shine with potential. He loved me well, but I am so unprepared to walk it alone. It has been a year. I know what is missing. I have changed so much that even if Phil were here, I wonder if he would want this life.

I would give up the way I am and all that I have if only. . .if only's are fruitless, so I have to step out of the shadows. I wish that I could see his smile, feel his arms, and hear what he thinks. Yes, he would laugh about the pink polka dots and he would love Sasha Fierce, but he would probably not understand the fire that pushes me into involvement and advocacy. I wonder if I will be able to get used to the loneliness and the wanting--the wanting to share my vision, my pride in my children, my fears, my hopes. I wonder if there will ever be a soft place to land or arms to hide in. I wish for the laughter and the history that only the two of us knew. Tonight, I want the young vital Phil who could make me laugh like no other and who could look at me with his big blue eyes and tell me that he likes the Linda I have become.